BRITAIN'S FUTURE NAVY

Also by Nick Childs

The Age of Invincible: The Ship that defined the Modern Royal Navy (Pen & Sword Books, Barnsley, 2009)

BRITAIN'S FUTURE NAVY

NICK CHILDS

Pen & Sword
MARITIME

First published in Great Britain in 2012 by
Pen & Sword Maritime
An imprint of
Pen & Sword Books Ltd
47 Church Street
Barnsley
South Yorkshire
S70 2AS

ISBN 978 1 84884 291 5

Typeset in 11.5pt Bembo by Mac Style, Beverley, East Yorkshire
Printed and bound in the UK by CPI Group (UK) Ltd, Croydon, CRO 4YY

Pen & Sword Books Ltd incorporates the imprints of Pen & Sword Aviation,
Pen & Sword Maritime, Pen & Sword Military, Wharncliffe Local History,
Pen & Sword Select, Pen & Sword Military Classics, Leo Cooper,
Remember When, Seaforth Publishing and Frontline Publishing

For a complete list of Pen & Sword titles please contact
PEN & SWORD BOOKS LIMITED
47 Church Street, Barnsley, South Yorkshire, S70 2AS, England
E-mail: enquiries@pen-and-sword.co.uk
Website: www.pen-and-sword.co.uk

Contents

Plates

Acknowledgements

The Royal Navy is a unique institution. And it has held a unique fascination as far as I am concerned from an early age. I have never served in it. But I have followed its fortunes closely, and reported on it regularly for pretty much my entire journalistic career. So it was a great opportunity for me when my editor, Philip Sidnell, suggested a book on the Navy's future. I was tempted to joke at the time that, the way things are in defence at the moment, it could be quite a short book. Of course, the Royal Navy will endure. But that flippancy reflected the fact that these are particularly turbulent times, and I discovered that this would be a real challenge in terms of bringing this particular project to fruition, and trying to anticipate even the near-term future, let alone beyond. So my first acknowledgement must be to Philip's patience. I could also not have even attempted this project without the help of several senior serving members of the Senior Service. Again because of the climate, they would probably prefer that I not mention them by name. But you know who you are. I would, however, like to record my thanks for the support that I received from Commander Gerry Northwood, Royal Navy media and communications, and also thank the ship's company of HMS *Diamond*, who offered me a very tangible glimpse of the future. Thanks also to Commanders Tim Ash and Jonathan Worthington, successively heads of Royal Navy Defence Studies, and to their boss, the Director of the Naval Staff, Commodore Bob Tarrant. In terms of distinguished former naval persons, my thanks to former First Sea Lords Admirals Sir Jonathon Band, Lord West of Spithead, and Sir Jock Slater for their insights, and former Commander in Chief Fleet Admiral Sir James Burnell-Nugent, who was generous with his time and thoughts. Also, for their broad perspectives or particular expertise, my gratitude to Vice Admirals Sir Jeremy Blackham, John McAnally, Tim McClement, and Anthony Dymock. The always stimulating views of Rear Admiral Chris Parry were also a great help. Captain Peter Hore RN (Retd), a former head of Defence Studies for the Navy, was another who offered generous assistance to a fellow naval author. During the time of this book's gestation, I found the Royal United Services Institute for Defence and Security Studies an immensely valuable arena in which the full spectrum of issues relevant to my musings were aired, and my particular thanks go to the head of the maritime programme there, Dr Lee Willett. In various ways, Professors Eric Grove, Hew Strachan, Gwyn Prins, and Julian Lindley-French helped to shape my thoughts, particularly on some of the strategic themes with which I attempted to grapple. On more technical matters, senior members of the staff of BAE Systems were kind enough to share their perspectives, and I thank Kristina Crowe for facilitating that. My thanks also to fellow journalists Richard Scott and Iain Ballantyne, who helped to keep me up-to-date on the latest Royal Navy developments. And, once again, my gratitude to Philip and Pen and Sword for allowing me this opportunity to write on one of my favourite subjects, and to Richard Doherty for ploughing through my draft manuscript. And, of course, to my wife, Jill, for her patience and support.

Nick Childs

Foreword by Admiral Sir Jock Slater GCB LVO DL

First Sea Lord and Chief of the Naval Staff 1995–1998

Vice Chief of the Defence Staff 1992–1995

In 2009 Nick Childs published *The Age of Invincible*, a masterly analysis of a challenging period in the history of the Royal Navy, not least an important contribution to the long-running Aircraft Carrier debate. His deep and growing interest in maritime affairs continues and this book, drawing all the strands together, is a well researched and enlightened study into Britain's Future Navy.

For many it will make uncomfortable reading as some firmly-held views are challenged. Indeed the author is, in places, intentionally provocative and, in other places, perhaps a trifle cynical about conventional naval thinking. He would therefore not expect me to agree with all that is written here; but I applaud his commendable attempt to present all the arguments in a most readable way and his book gives us all food for thought and not a little cause for major concern.

In 1997–98 the incoming Labour Government conducted a most responsible root and branch Strategic Defence Review and, at the time, I had the lead for the Royal Navy. I believe that, after a year-long and constructive debate under George Robertson, the Defence Secretary, we charted a pragmatic way forward for our Armed Forces and their future role, not least the maritime contribution to that role. However, the Government then utterly failed to ensure that the way forward was adequately funded, resulting in over a decade of cuts to personnel, equipment, support and training, thus significantly hollowing out our military capability. As a result it was inevitable that, as the necessary funds were denied, the Chiefs of Staff were at loggerheads fighting their individual corners and the tri-service spirit that characterised the

1997-1998 Review was sadly eroded. I hope that the new generation of Chiefs will recognise the real value of a tri-service approach.

When the Coalition Government took office in 2010, a so-called Strategic Defence and Security Review was rushed through set against a desperate international financial crisis. Little serious attention was paid to the strategic aspects and a detailed analysis of Britain's place in the world and what military capability was needed to support it was sadly lacking. In effect this was a major cost-cutting exercise. Furthermore, it was right that the pressing demands of our operations in Afghanistan – where all elements of the Armed Forces have been acquitting themselves with great distinction – should initially take priority.

We successfully argued the case for carrier-borne aviation in 1997–98 as a key plank of the Government's Defence Review as we collectively firmly believed that a balance of adaptable forces – land, sea and air – was our most prudent insurance against the uncertainties and dangers that lay ahead in a turbulent world. Hindsight is a wonderful thing, but had I been told then that two aircraft carriers would eventually be built but with greatly reduced force levels of destroyers and frigates, nuclear submarines and supporting forces, a diminished amphibious capability and no fixed wing aircraft for the first ten years or so, I could not possibly have sustained the arguments, strong as they remain. Indeed it will be extremely difficult, but not impossible in the longer term given strong advocacy and the political will, to reverse the downward spiral.

So today, in 2011, the state of our Armed Forces is verging on precarious, not least the unbalanced and despairingly low force levels in the Royal Navy, and the risks that the Government is taking are frankly unacceptable. Moreover, optimistic noises about 'Future Force 2020' are viewed by many with considerable doubt as promises of 'jam tomorrow' in Defence terms seldom come to pass as planned.

This book is a most valuable contribution to the debate.

Jock Slater

Introduction

S ome years into the future from the time of writing, at sea somewhere in the Gulf of Aden:

'The commanding officer of the old Type 23 frigate HMS Kent leaned forward thoughtfully in her captain's chair as she stared out through the bridge windows into the gathering dusk. A few hundred metres ahead of her ship was the now rather ghostly grey outline of the Type 45 destroyer HMS Diamond, one of the big, blocky air defence ships that the Royal Navy had craved for so long, which had had such a troubled history, and which remained controversial to this day even though all six had been in service for some time.

But Kent and Diamond – plus the US Navy destroyer Halsey and the French Navy frigate Aquitaine, out of sight in the growing gloom near the horizon – were merely consorts to the great dark presence looming off the frigate's port bow in the dwindling half-light. The frigate's CO could still just make out the bustling activity around a couple of Merlin helicopters at the aft end of the vast flight deck of the aircraft carrier Prince of Wales.

Kent had hurried from the Persian Gulf to join the other ships which made up the Prince of Wales' task group, as they had all been ordered with despatch to the waters off Yemen, as the crisis in that country had escalated. The battling forces in that benighted state – the mix of political, tribal, and religious groupings – were threatening violence and disorder in and around the port of Aden. To safeguard both the local civilian population, and also the large international community of contractors and other workers who were engaged in the latest effort to modernize the port and turn Aden once again into the major shipping hub that it once was, the UN Security Council had declared it a protected area.

Prince of Wales and her reinforced group were there to show the UN's determination, if necessary, to support its words with action in a show of force. Another mixed task force, led by the Indian Navy carrier Vikramaditya, was also on its way. The two carriers had been exercising together in the Indian Ocean only a few weeks before.

Although HMS Kent had only joined the group a couple of days earlier, her ship's company was – like the other accompanying ships – already referring to the great carrier half resentfully, half reverentially as "the Death Star", after the menacing battle station from the old Star Wars movies. It has been the lot of the flagships of Royal Navy flotillas down the ages to earn double-edged nicknames such as this. Prince of Wales earned her unofficial title simply by her size, and what she represented in terms of capability, which was on a scale that the Royal Navy had not been able to wield for a very, very long time.

Indeed, for most of the crew aboard HMS Kent, this was the first time that they had set eyes on the carrier. She was still relatively new, and had spent most of her time up to now away from the Fleet on trials, often with the Americans. It had been a long, long introduction. The Royal Navy had had a lot to re-learn in terms of operating aircraft at sea from such a big ship. Many in the Navy thought it would never happen. Many outside it thought that it SHOULD never have happened.

In fact, Prince of Wales had been on her first operational deployment in the Arabian Sea. With the US Navy increasingly stretched itself in recent years, and more preoccupied with matters in the western Pacific, HMS Prince of Wales had been filling in the longstanding role of maintaining a Western carrier presence in the Arabian Sea.

As the ships prepared to begin enforcing the UN mandate, the battle staff aboard "the Death Star" had been receiving updated information on dispositions on the ground around Aden from a high-altitude, long-endurance US Navy version of the Global Hawk unmanned aerial vehicle (UAV), a large, loitering drone. The F-35 Lightning Joint Strike Fighters (JSFs) aboard Prince of Wales, with their own surveillance and intelligence-gathering capabilities, would soon be adding to the picture. And theirs would, of course, be armed reconnaissance missions, so they would be ready to intervene if necessary. As well as the weaponry on the ground that could threaten Aden, it was known that the various factions on land also had a mixture of anti-aircraft missiles, their own rudimentary armed drones, and anti-ship missiles which might threaten the task force itself or shipping generally in the area.

As for HMS Kent, she would be keeping a watch out particularly for potentially menacing shipping – from apparently innocent fishing boats to armed or explosive-packed speedboats. This remained one of the world's most dangerous waterways. Stability around the Arabian Peninsula generally was a concern. It was known that Iranian forces had been operating in the area. Tehran had been making angry noises about the build-up of forces in the region. Potentially, there was a long-range missile threat to consider, that might require a response.

Officially, the enforcement operation would begin at midnight local time. But there was already a high level of tension, and vigilance, on Kent's bridge, and around the accompanying ships...'

This may be a possible future for the Royal Navy. But is it a probable one? And, even if it is, is it the right kind of future for either the Navy or Britain?

From the perspective of 2011, a decade into the twenty-first century, the condition of the Royal Navy seems to be pregnant with powerful and painful paradoxes. On one hand, after what must seem like an almost endless wait, it appears finally to have within its reach some extraordinary new warships of unprecedented capability. The reaction of some observers with perhaps only a detached awareness of the Navy must surely be to marvel that the admirals have managed to protect these huge investments in the face of an economic firestorm in Britain and around the world, plus the relentless tyranny and anguish of the two grim and largely landlocked military campaigns of Iraq and Afghanistan that have so preoccupied the military's attention for a decade, cost many lives, and sucked in so many resources. To those less detached but more hostile to the naval case and the Navy's ambition, the new and impending acquisitions must equally be a source of maddening frustration, coupled with a curious puzzlement that these huge programmes continue to sail on.

And yet, on the other hand, from the vantage point of some of the Navy's most devoted followers, its horizons seem to be filled in almost every direction with gloom-laden skies. Proud ships, in what appears to be a sad procession, have been making premature final voyages home from distant stations as a result of the latest rounds of defence cuts. Physicists may not approve of the way the term has been bandied about, but the talk has been of the Navy being reduced to its 'critical mass', even that it has fallen dangerously below it. The sentiments of many of those with deep attachment to the service – including seeming cohorts of retired officers – are of foreboding and sorrow, dismay and disbelief, indignation and recrimination. The letters columns of newspapers and the naval blogs have been full of anguished commentaries.

Caught in the middle of all this have been those who have been charged with running the Navy in recent years. They could be forgiven for feeling a touch besieged. They have certainly been under attack on at least two fronts. Berated from one flank for supposedly clinging on to past glories at the expense of the country's current and future needs, they have been equally accused from the other of being outfought in the corridors of power and failing adequately to protect 'the Fleet', to make the Navy's case effectively, and, as a consequence, to safeguard the nation's true long-term strategic interests.

Privately, the Navy's leadership will have been muttering some complaints of its own. First, to those who see it stuck in the past, the refrain will surely be that it is those critics who have a blinkered view of the past, the present, and the future. Secondly, to the despairing naval loyalists, it will be that their cries of alarm ignore what has actually been achieved in the face of some daunting odds, and that they betray a naivety about the realities of power and decision-making in government, and the Navy's ability to set its own course in the modern world. There might be the added caution that idle talk of a navy heading towards irretrievable decline is both wrong and potentially dangerous. In fact, the Naval Staff would argue, it has done its best to preserve enough of the essential elements of the Fleet to give it a fighting chance – despite what will undoubtedly be a difficult period – of survival, perhaps of recovery, and even that some kind of renaissance might be possible.

Much will need to go right for the Navy for that to happen. For some of the sceptics even within the naval community, something significant will need to change for there to be the chance of a real revival. And other issues loom. Has the case really been established as to what the Navy can and should be in the future? How much does that hinge on its relationship with the other services? How much on what part military forces will play in the United Kingdom's view of itself in the future? And what are those essential elements of the Fleet that should be preserved? What is the Navy's vision of itself, and does it accord with the nation's needs? None of these issues seem to have definitive answers.

For better or worse, the Naval Staff has had a fairly set view for some time of what Britain's future navy should look like. It is of a high-end, fighting navy built around a core of strategic capabilities that set it apart from most other navies, and bestow on the United Kingdom membership of an elite club of nations. It is of a navy essentially of top-quality capital ships able if necessary to project real power in the most demanding of military scenarios, but with enough flexibility to fulfil those other routine tasks of trade and maritime protection that have been the day-to-day tasks of navies down the ages.

The Naval Staff argues that it is a vision dictated by the guidance of successive governments on what the armed forces should primarily be able to deliver. But it has been one that has, indisputably, been at the expense of numbers of hulls. And that has laid the Navy's leadership open to the charge – both from within the naval community and without – that, in pursuit of the holy grail of 'the balanced fleet', it has got the balance wrong.

The debate over quality versus quantity is an old one. It is one in which the Navy stands charged in modern times of always choosing 'gold-plating' over numbers and the benchmark of 'good enough'. And, as the balance has tilted ever more precariously away from quantity and towards quality, as the size of the Fleet has dwindled to previously undreamt-of small numbers, so the arguments have become more acute and heated. Here, the doubters have argued, whatever the strength or otherwise of the maritime case in concept, the Royal Navy itself – or those who have led it in the last decade or more – has lost its way, and forgotten what being a navy is really all about. It is about presence and policing, and the day-in, day-out job of being there on the oceans.

The perennial nature of the debate reflects the fact that the Navy has never been the staid monolith that it has so often been portrayed as being. But, somehow, at this stage in its recent history, the stakes have never seemed higher.

And, of course, all of this has only sharpened the controversies that have swirled around the shining new ships that are entering service or are about to do so. There are the new Type 45 destroyers, representing a step-change in technology and capability, but also an investment of more than six billion pounds. The new Astute-class nuclear-powered attack or hunter-killer submarines (SSNs) have also begun arriving, with similar price tags to those attached to the Type 45s, but also representing a similar leap in capabilities over what went before. Each, in their different ways, might lay claim to being among the best in the world in their respective roles.

Above all, of course, are those oh-so-controversial new Queen Elizabeth-class aircraft carriers, the biggest warships ever designed and built for the Royal Navy. Potentially, they will offer a level of capability that will not have operated under the White Ensign for more than a generation, if ever. But is it a capability that the country needs, and what will the ultimate cost – direct and indirect – be? One of the conundrums surrounding these vessels and what they represent is that still – after so many years of divisive debate – there are no clear-cut answers to those questions.

Amid all the arguments back and forth, there is a further sense of malaise – and of edginess – affecting the Navy and its supporters. It stems from a conviction that the Navy simply does not occupy the position in the British consciousness and sense of identity, the business of defending the realm, or the unfolding of events on the world stage that it either did in the past, or can and should do now and into the future. The Navy has been feeling unloved and overlooked in its own land. To compound the problem, it has as an institution given the impression that its reaction to this state of affairs has been to become paralyzed by a sense of vulnerability and gripped by unease about the future.

The Royal Navy has been one of the most strategically influential military forces of the last two centuries. It has certainly been the most influential of the United Kingdom's armed forces. And it is a boast regularly made for it by others that – in a real sense – it has played a huge part in shaping the modern world.

But is any of that a help, or is it more of a hindrance, in the Navy's attempts to find a place for itself in this modern world, given both its and the country's diminished standing? The fact is that, in the current climate, the Royal Navy's glorious past has seemed to be more baggage than benefit in the articulation of a maritime case. Whoever the incumbent First Sea Lord has been in recent times, he and his colleagues have often been lampooned – all too readily it sometimes seems – as wanting simply to turn the clock back to an age of battle fleets and Atlantic convoys. The very job title First Sea Lord, for the man in charge, almost seems to be part of the problem, because it sounds like so much of a throwback.

Modern British admirals in their turn regularly express frustration at what they describe as a 'sea blindness' that has infected the country, an inability to perceive the importance of the maritime environment – and particularly the safety and security of it – to Britain's prosperity and long-term interests. But is there really such a malady? Or is it a perceptive popular manifestation of the fact that this is now a 'post-naval era', in which the maritime domain may indeed be as critical a factor in maintaining global economic well-being as it has ever been, but in which such threats to the system as exist are of a different nature to those that have gone before, and in which the role of navies – at least as traditionally constituted – is far from clear? Has the classic age of sea power truly passed now, not just for the Royal Navy but for navies generally?

After all, when was the last major naval confrontation, apart from the 1982 Falklands War? And, in some minds, even that hardly counts. Is it also a world in which there is far from a self-evident role for a navy which – for all its unique tradition – belongs to what is now merely a medium-sized power which has an uncertain view of its place in the world, and which now has fewer than twenty major general-purpose warships with which to exercise maritime influence?

That the Navy does not any longer have a significant popular constituency is hardly in doubt. Of course, even at the height of its power and the country's imperial reach, there were those who would fume against the admirals' ambitions and the scale of what were then called 'the Naval estimates'. Members of this group could easily be found both in fact and in the fiction of the time. But then such voices were easily dismissed to the margins as 'little Englanders' by a vigorous and numerous pro-Navy lobby, which drowned out their protestations with cries like 'we want eight and we won't wait' in the row over dreadnought numbers in the naval scare of 1909.

There were expressions of public surprise and criticism when the 'Fleet flagship', HMS *Ark Royal*, was slated for early disposal as a major victim of the Strategic Defence and Security Review (SDSR) at the end of 2010. But the chances of galvanizing a popular 'bring back the *Ark*' campaign seemed rather remote from the outset, try as a few retired admirals and Fleet Air Arm (FAA) stalwarts did to make things awkward for the government in the aftermath of the announcement, and despite the surprise intervention of an unexpected crisis in North Africa that provided at least some extra ammunition for their arguments. For some time now, it has seemed as if it is the Navy's most ardent supporters who have been on the margins, and out of step with popular sentiment. Is that about to change?

At the time of writing, the only modern admiral to have come close to becoming anything like a household name has been John 'Sandy' Woodward, the commander of the Navy's Falklands task force. With the military traumas of the last decade, it has really been only generals and colonels who have been able consistently to grab the public's attention, and who have enjoyed any sort of public recognition and a broad public hearing. Rightly or wrongly, that has swayed the public discourse on defence and security in more ways than one.

Certainly, in what is an age of exceptional uncertainty and flux, with so much attention fixed on firefights in deserts and mountains in Iraq and

Afghanistan, many navies are suffering similar anguish, even as others belonging to nations on the rise appear set to prosper. But, for the Royal Navy, the grief has seemed somehow most acute, perhaps because its past has been so illustrious and so universally acknowledged. Its reputation has meant that its troubles have been widely noticed and remarked upon beyond Britain's shores.

The Royal Navy is still held in the highest regard by other navies around the world for its professionalism and prowess, and its current powers-that-be continue to parade these, plus its experience and rigorous operational ethos, as part of what still sets it apart from what would otherwise be its peers. Other navies still look to the Royal Navy to set professional standards and offer professional guidance. But, increasingly, the skills of its people have seemed like ways of making up for ever more obvious material shortfalls and gaps, as the Royal Navy has watched others appear to be leaping forward and overtaking it in key areas of technology and capability.

What is more, some within the Navy's own ranks and in the community of retired officers have questioned whether those standards and the Navy's famed 'fighting spirit' have themselves been eroded. Some of that they would put down to a lack of major action. Some of it they would also attribute to the corporate culture which the Navy now inhabits – within government and the Ministry of Defence (MoD), and between the services. In an era of more centralized political control, and of increased 'jointness' between the services, there may be operational benefits, but the Navy – like the other services – is less the master of its own fate than it used to be, with less room for manoeuvre.

In addition, a decade of hard pounding in Iraq and Afghanistan has certainly left its mark on British society and strategy. These have been campaigns that the British public have neither fully supported nor really understood. That has had implications for all the country's armed forces and what place and purpose they have in society, as well as for what the public view of what the nation's place on the world stage should be. After a succession of interventions in the 1990s which seemed to reinforce an image of British military prowess and influence, these latest 'wars of choice' have suddenly and unexpectedly raised doubts about the extent and purpose of the country's military capacity.

For the bulk of the British public, the wars that the country has been fighting have been at once remote in terms of personal involvement and yet vivid in terms of the images beamed onto the television screens in people's homes. Those images have tended to tell a tale of frantic fighting, often with inadequate resources, of real costs and losses, but uncertain benefits. There has been a public perception of British soldiers caught up in desperate combat being short-changed in terms of equipment and support. That has not only put politicians on the defensive, but also the Navy and the Royal Air Force (RAF). The admirals and air marshals have been accused of siphoning funds away from soldiers for exotic equipment programmes which have minimum relevance to the current operations, are hangovers from history, and have no justification except under the most fanciful notions of the future.

That there has been grotesque waste and mismanagement in the delivery of national defence over many years is also not now much challenged as a proposition. That has fuelled the arguments that the armed forces – and especially those reliant on the most elaborate equipment – have in large part been the agents of their own plight. The talk has been of a 'conspiracy of optimism' between the defence establishment and the defence industry over the estimated costs of new projects, which have inevitably then mushroomed out of control and all recognition. How did the Royal Navy really end up ordering the biggest warships ever in its history, the 65,000-ton Queen Elizabeth–class carriers, which will be half as big again as was originally estimated, and cost about twice as much? For the Navy, for the armed forces more generally, and for the MoD as a whole, there will need to be a dramatic change in the public perception, as they are widely regarded as inefficient, wasteful, and generally dysfunctional.

These myriad challenges complicate the search for the answers to the other questions which are asserting themselves. What is the role of conventional military power, as represented by the armed forces, in Britain's future? It is not just that the rather extraordinary procession of land-based campaigns, which began with the first Gulf War in 1991, then switched to the Balkans in the mid-to-late 'nineties, then moved both on to Afghanistan and back to Iraq, has largely obscured the maritime dimension of defence and security. There has also been an uncertain narrative about what the real risks to the country's security now are, and what role – if any – traditional armed forces have in defending against them.

There is, in other words, a continuing debate over how to define security in the modern world. If the risks are deemed now and for the future to be mainly terrorism, cyber assault, and a deficit in global governance, surely intelligence, policing, the courts, centres of information technology excellence, civil resilience, and soft power are the answers, rather than high-end military prowess. Britons probably feel the safest that they ever have from violent attack. So where is the strategic imperative for a heavy outlay on traditional defence in general, let alone on the Royal Navy?

Of course, the military still has a potential role even in home defence, even now. But are the armed forces properly equipped for that, or do they need to change direction dramatically? There is still the refrain that it remains a dangerous world· out there, in ways that will affect the national interest, whether broadly or narrowly defined. But have recent experiences only shown up the limits of military force in dealing with such challenges, let alone in being a suitable lever with which Britain can exercise whatever influence it chooses to wield in the world?

Much of the maritime case is that a sea of potential troubles beckons, and attention and action are needed first to try to avoid it, but if necessary to deal with it. How that line of argument unfolds, whether it takes hold of the public's imagination as attention moves beyond the wars of Iraq and

Afghanistan, will have a major impact on the Navy's future fortunes. So too will the extent to which it is ready to influence the debate, and respond to it.

At the beginning of the twentieth century, the Royal Navy was facing a crisis. Its absolute supremacy was under threat from what turned out to be irresistible global trends in economic and strategic power. Being unable to defend its position everywhere, the Royal Navy – under radical leadership – took revolutionary and controversial steps in organization, dispositions, and warship design to respond to the evolving strategic picture. It had to make difficult choices.

In the opening phases of the twenty-first century, it is the US Navy's position which is, of course, most comparable to that of the Royal Navy a century ago. It remains pre-eminent, indeed even more so by some measures than the Royal Navy was at its height. But its relative position is weakening. Washington will have to make choices about where to concentrate its attention and resources. And that will require decisions among other powers – allies and potential adversaries – on whether and how to fill the gaps that will inevitably open up.

At least, amid all the pressures of the early 1900s, the Royal Navy's prestige and the prominence of its position at the heart of defending Britain and the empire were hardly questioned, except at the margins. Of course, the rest of the twentieth century saw profound upheavals in the character of warfare generally and naval warfare in particular, and in the position of the Royal Navy in the world. So now, it has no such security.

In the light of this, does the Navy need to be bold to survive and prosper in the early years of the twenty-first century? And if so, how? What are the answers to the questions of what the Navy is really for in the decades ahead, and how it should design itself?

And these are questions which – at the moment at least – can span decades. Judgements made now on the future of the Royal Navy are fifty-year decisions at least, given the time currently taken to decide on, develop, and build modern warships and weapons systems, and the span of time that they are now being expected to remain in service.

The current workhorses of the Fleet, the Type 23 frigates, were conceived in the early 1980s. Some could still be serving in the 2030s. The Navy first started thinking seriously about new aircraft carriers to replace its existing Invincible-class ships in the early 1990s. Their much-delayed entries into service in the second half of the second decade of this century – assuming that still happens at all – will already make them a twenty-year project. Whether one or both of them are retained, notionally they could serve for fifty years. That may seem fanciful, but it is a planning assumption. So it could mean the second ship paying off in about 2070. If that does happen, there could be young crew members aboard for that ceremony who would be the great-great-grandchildren of the senior officers who helped first conceive the ships.

But taking on and breaking such a hideously long gestation period may itself be one of the crucial challenges for the future. At the very least, if adaptability and flexibility are to be the touchstones for the future, as apparently they are, tackling the current inefficiencies and bureaucratic inflexibilities of defence procurement and planning must be a priority.

Even so, does Britain – and therefore the Navy – have to face up to the inevitability of ever-smaller forces in the future, being supported by a shrinking and therefore less capable defence industry, funded by a dwindling real defence budget? Will real defence costs continue their seemingly inexorable rise? What are the choices to be then?

The Royal Navy is facing a very difficult decade, and also a critical one. Many of the building blocks of Britain's future navy are either already in existence or are taking shape. How exactly they will all fit together, what the whole will look like, and how it will be perceived, are in contrast much more uncertain matters. And is the Royal Navy as an institution ready for the future, and most particularly for the future that it has been striving so hard to achieve?

CHAPTER ONE

Troubled Waters

It turned out to be something of a long goodbye for HMS *Ark Royal*, the fifth ship of the Royal Navy to bear that 'illustrious' name. It was late in the evening of 18 October 2010 when news began to leak out of her shock early disposal as part of the new coalition government's defence and security review, the SDSR. The news was to be unveiled officially the following day. The manner of the leak certainly angered the top brass in the Navy. Neither the ship's commanding officer nor her crew had been warned that they were about to make news, or why.

A few weeks later, at the end of November, in the choppy, dark waters of the North Sea, under slate-grey skies filled with icy, driving rain, Harrier jets had leapt off *Ark Royal*'s flight deck for the very last time, kicking up great clouds of spray in the process. Indeed, it would, according to the SDSR plan, be the last time British Harriers would ever operate from any British carrier.

And a few days after that bit of history, on 3 December, *Ark Royal* would emerge from an obscuring, freezing mist to make her own last, sad entry into Portsmouth harbour. There would be further ceremonials to mark her passing. Her final, formal decommissioning on 11 March 2011 would take place almost unnoticed, as the world was gripped by international events elsewhere – the convulsions of a developing civil war in Libya, and the dawning horror of an unfolding combined natural disaster of earthquake and tsunami across the globe in Japan.

The committed navalists were quick to point out that an aircraft carrier might have come in handy amid all the talk at the time of no-fly zones and limited intervention in Libya. And in the Japanese disaster, of course, one of the first responses of the United States was to send an aircraft carrier as a floating base for relief operations.

Whatever the validity or otherwise of these observations, *Ark Royal*'s departure had a greater significance than just another big warship with a famous name falling victim to the latest in a long succession of post-Second-World-War defence reviews. Her withdrawal and that of the Harriers that she could operate removed a major pillar on which the Royal Navy had been building for the future. With that pillar taken away, can the core of the Navy's vision still be achieved?

The official line was that this was a temporary arrangement. Against the background of the new government's determination to cut the public deficit – its overriding strategic priority – the Navy would give up what was an admittedly by now limited current capability in return for a renewed commitment to a much greater capability in the future. Indeed, the big new replacement carriers that are under construction, and would continue their prolonged and painful journey towards final completion as a result of the SDSR, offer the prospect of a transforming capability.

But the gap in that capability between *Ark Royal*'s demise and the arrival of a new, fully-functioning carrier, would – under the SDSR plan – be a huge one. Potentially a yawning ten years. So what some defended as a rational trade-off others decried as foolhardy and an absurd gamble. It would, by common consent, be an enormous undertaking to resurrect such a complex and demanding set of skills and expertise after such a long time. It has not been attempted before. Maybe it cannot be done. Many were convinced that it will never happen.

With the arguable exception of the Royal Fleet Auxiliary (RFA) support ship *Fort George*, *Ark Royal* was physically the biggest casualty of the SDSR, while the Harriers were the most iconic, and their joint departures with no immediate replacements its most hotly-contested outcome. It hardly helped the government's presentation of the case for this set of decisions that they would result in the first of the huge new carriers – for which so many claims had been made about their potential – sailing for her first three years in service with no jets aboard. Indeed, she might never operate fixed-wing aircraft at all. Sceptical commentators and unhappy retired naval officers muttered about the latest British naval invention, the non-aircraft-carrying aircraft carrier. And only one of the giant new ships would be kept operational.

Ark Royal herself was the product of a previous upheaval in the Royal Navy's fortunes. At 20,500 tons, she was the youngest of the three revolutionary Invincible-class small aircraft carriers which entered service between 1980 and 1985. With a naval version of the even more revolutionary vertical/short take-off and landing (V/STOL) Harrier aircraft, the Sea Harrier, and another brilliantly simple British invention, the ski-jump ramp at the forward end of the ships' flight decks to aid rolling take-offs, they kept the art of fixed-wing flying at sea alive in the Royal Navy for more than a quarter of a century. Otherwise it would have died in 1978 with the retirement of the last of the Navy's traditional large Fleet carriers, the previous *Ark Royal*, at 50,786 tons a real heavyweight compared to her younger namesake.

Whatever one's view of the current condition of the Royal Navy, it has arrived at it via a rather tortuous course over the past few decades. In that time, it has had to reinvent itself more than once, and on some occasions more painfully than at others. Of course, it entered the Second World War as still the pre-eminent world navy. It emerged from it as very much the junior partner of the US Navy. But that difficult transition was overshadowed and greatly influenced by the nation's own diminished economic standing and overall struggle to find its new place in the world. On top of all that, the Navy had to contend with the advent of air power and the establishment from the early part of the twentieth century of a new and enduring British continental commitment of military power, something that the country had striven to avoid previously through careful diplomacy and the balancing of power in Europe. Both of these developments impinged on the Navy's position as the ultimate bastion of national defence, and inevitably drew away resources.

As if that were not enough, the inauguration of the Cold War would present another challenge. For much of it, the nightmare scenario was of short, sharp nuclear devastation. That raised questions about where the traditional and often slow-moving levers of sea power would fit into Western defence. The Navy was haunted by the judgement expressed most famously (or notoriously) in the 1957 defence review authored by Duncan Sandys, that 'the role of naval forces in total war is somewhat uncertain'.[1]

If there was a silver lining to that particular mushroom cloud, it was that the Royal Navy – and indeed navies generally – would prove themselves to be uniquely useful in a succession of limited conflicts or 'brushfires' that broke out during this period. There was also the particular British requirement to engineer as dignified a withdrawal as possible from its dwindling colonial commitments. Here again there was plenty for the Navy to do, at least for the time being, and especially as the number of British overseas bases declined. It helped that some of the Navy's most prized possessions, its aircraft carriers, would demonstrate their particular value in these different scenarios. Its carrier force played a significant part in the UN-backed campaign in Korea in the early 1950s. Even the 1956 Suez crisis, while politically so calamitous, underscored the military utility of the country's naval power, not least again its carrier aviation and amphibious forces. In 1961, the carrier HMS *Victorious* and other naval vessels rushed to the waters off Kuwait when that newly-independent nation was threatened by neighbouring Iraq.

All this helped to burnish the Navy's image, and perhaps even reassure the public that Britain remained a country of weight and influence. Reality, of course, belied that comforting image. In so many ways the country and the Navy were falling behind. Throughout this time, the Royal Navy remained indisputably the most significant Western navy after that of the United States, and still the third most powerful in the world. And yet it had fallen so far below the US Navy. Moreover, it was already being seriously overshadowed by its main potential adversary, the Soviet Navy.

In 1967, *Jane's Fighting Ships* listed the strength of the US Navy fleet at seventeen large aircraft carriers, including the first nuclear-powered one (the USS *Enterprise*), twenty other support and helicopter carriers, eighty ballistic missile and other nuclear-powered submarines, more than 120 conventionally-powered ones (SSKs), four battleships, thirty-seven cruisers, and nearly 400 destroyers and frigates. That was more than 600 major warships in all. Total manpower stood at nearly 750,000.

In the same publication, the Soviet Navy's strength was recorded at fifty nuclear-powered submarines, 350 conventionally-powered ones, twenty cruisers, and 220 destroyers, escorts, and small frigates. Total personnel numbered virtually half a million. What was more, this fleet's years of most profound expansion and transformation lay ahead.

The Royal Navy, in contrast, had a mixed bag of five aircraft carriers of varying and in some cases marginal capability. Its first clutch of three nuclear-powered submarines had been built. There were forty-three other conventionally-powered ones, three cruisers, and more than ninety destroyers and frigates. Personnel strength stood at just over 100,000. But more devastating than these bare statistics was the blow that had been inflicted on the Navy the year before, which struck at the heart of its vision of itself at this time.

In the face of harsh economic realities, the then Labour government had decided to impose a strict cap on defence spending. The RAF was the first to feel the real pain, with the cancellation of its cherished, iconic TSR2 strike aircraft in 1965. However, it received a promise of fifty US-designed F-111 supersonic swing-wing bombers as a consolation.

But that was not enough. And now firmly in the line of fire was the Navy's dream of a new generation of big aircraft carriers, the first of which carried the designation CVA-01. What ensued was an inter-service battle between the Navy and RAF which has become legendary, and has left scars that still linger in some hearts and minds. At its core was the issue of whether the two services could share the right to project British air power around the world, and whether the country could afford for them to do so.

The Navy was outmanoeuvred in the corridors of Whitehall. In February 1966, CVA-01 was cancelled, and with it all the Navy's hopes of a new generation of big carriers were also dashed. The current carriers would be phased out. The First Sea Lord, Admiral Sir David Luce, and the Navy Minister, Christopher Mayhew, resigned. There was naval outrage and recrimination. Members of the Fleet Air Arm felt desperately let down, even betrayed. But the cards were always stacked against the Navy and its carriers. It was not that the RAF's rival 'island-hopping' strategy for covering the globe really convinced either the politicians or the civil service. It was, in the end, that the amount of money the new carriers represented was just too tempting a saving to ignore. The inclinations of the then Defence Secretary, Denis Healey, and large swathes of Whitehall seemed to be against them, although the Navy was given ample opportunity to make its case.

The rationale for cancellation, never accepted in naval circles, was that the carriers were essential only for a narrow set of military scenarios with which the country could dispense – the landing or withdrawal of troops against a sophisticated opposition beyond the range of land bases, and without the help of allies. Indeed, it was decided that they only really made sense in the Far East, but maintaining a credible carrier force at that distance was deemed by ministers to be beyond the nation's means.

But the country's economic woes continued. And the RAF's triumph did not last long. The F-111s soon went too as the government faced up to a decision that it had fought to avoid or delay, which was that the country had to withdraw from a permanent military presence 'East of Suez'.

The succession of blows leading up to the East of Suez moment forced a difficult change of course on the Navy. It had to recast itself from being primarily an independent, oceangoing force charged with maintaining a protective umbrella over the country's steadily-declining colonial footprint. The accelerated imperial retreat now imposed on Britain meant that the Navy had to refocus on a core mission closer to home, derived from the country's membership of the North Atlantic Treaty Organization (NATO), as the principal anti-submarine warfare (ASW) support for the United States to counter the Soviet maritime threat in the eastern Atlantic.

There was one piece of good fortune for the Navy at this time. It was that NATO chose to switch from a strategy that no longer seemed credible – a massive nuclear 'trip-wire' response to a Soviet attack – to a policy of 'flexible response'. That at least implied the prospect of a more prolonged military build-up and confrontation that would require transatlantic reinforcements, and therefore a key naval dimension.

Despite the painful contractions, this was still an age when the services were able to shape themselves for their core functions in such a way that they retained a residual ability to act farther afield and beyond their narrower NATO missions. And that is exactly what the Navy did, albeit not without a struggle. With not a little ingenuity and deft political footwork that had eluded it earlier, it created a new fleet based around a new concept.

This was the birth of the Invincible-class carriers. For a time, they were dubbed 'through-deck cruisers' to try to throw suspicious ministers, air marshals, and civil servants off the scent. But that did not really fool anyone, and most saw them for what they were – a new form of mini-carrier. Also, they were designed primarily to operate helicopters. But always in the minds of at least the more ambitious – and one might also say far-sighted – admirals was the thought that they could be launching pads for V/STOL aircraft, ironically a concept that many in the Navy had disdained while it still had full-size carriers.

The Navy in the end managed – just – to get its way. It was helped by the fact that the difficulties of providing adequate air cover for the Fleet from land bases, even in the NATO context close to home, became quickly apparent. It got its new mini-carriers as the centrepieces of new formations, the ASW task groups, to perform its primary role. But these ships, plus a new generation of destroyers and frigates, and the RFA support train that the Navy was able to sustain, all meant that the Navy still had a significant residual ability to roam the further oceans independently when required. And, despite the East of Suez decision, it made a point of continuing to practise how to do that on a regular basis, by initiating 'out-of-area' group deployments beyond NATO's boundaries of responsibility to 'show the flag'.

Thus, by imagination and initiative, and some luck, the post-1966 Navy was able to mitigate much of the impact of what had been a traumatic moment in its modern history. But it would take the better part of a decade for the enforced change of course to take full effect. And barely had the Navy's new concept started to take concrete shape, and its new generation of warships started to arrive, than another crisis hit. It was 1981. The backdrop again was economic recession. The government was a new Conservative one this time under Margaret Thatcher, determined to rein in government spending. And, after a less-than-co-operative stance from her first Defence Secretary, Francis Pym, Thatcher appointed a new one, John Nott.

As the government grappled with strained defence commitments, the trouble for the Navy was that there were no cast-iron treaty commitments setting out the scale of Britain's maritime contribution to NATO, as there were in the case of the country's land and air forces in Europe. Numbers in the Fleet had continued to dwindle. But, at the time, its strength stood at two V/STOL carriers, including a brand new HMS *Invincible*, four ballistic missile submarines and a dozen other nuclear-powered submarines, sixteen conventional submarines, and more than sixty destroyers and frigates.

What turned into the Nott defence review was to rank as one of the most contentious of modern times. He concluded that the defence programme was unsustainable. The government had decided, at the highest political level, that neither the nuclear deterrent nor the British commitment to NATO's Central Front could be seriously cut. What was then a fragile Western alliance might not take the strain. The same was true of the home defence capability. That left only one source for real savings – the maritime commitment.

As if that were not enough, John Nott took on the Navy over how it went about its business. In this, he and his aides were encouraged by what they contended was a real difference in perspective between the admirals in Whitehall and more operational senior commanders at the Fleet's headquarters in Northwood. There would be yet another shift in focus, to give less emphasis to the surface fleet and more to submarines and long-range maritime patrol aircraft. Most notably, only two rather than three Invincible-class carriers would be kept in service, and the number of operational surface escorts would fall dramatically to forty-two, with a further eight in reserve. Thus, in the decade-and-a-half since the Healey review, the size of the operational Fleet would have been halved.

The Nott review still divides opinion. For some, it was a rare attempt genuinely to tackle a strategic conundrum, challenge conventional wisdoms, and take on entrenched service interests, only for its results to be undone by a last stirring of imperial nostalgia in the South Atlantic, the 1982 Falklands War. The Navy, in this view, was clinging on to big, prestigious surface ships which would not survive under the bombardment of the Soviet naval forces.

For much of the Navy and its supporters, John Nott's review was an ill-informed and arrogant exercise which totally failed to understand the true value and significance of maritime power, either in the relatively narrow NATO context or more broadly. From this perspective, the Falklands War was the almost inevitable consequence of that.

The conflict arrested the decline in the size of the Fleet for a while, but it did not halt it. One of the immediate Falklands effects was that the government agreed to keep the operational escort force at fifty ships. But, by the early 1990s, when the government took its 'peace dividend' from the end of the Cold War, that had dwindled to 'around forty'. In 1997, the force inherited by the new Labour government of Tony Blair stood at thirty-five destroyers and frigates.

Here was another potential watershed moment. The new administration was keen to be seen to be throwing off unpopular political baggage from the past, and that included the image of being soft on and even hostile to the business of defence. The vehicle for doing that was what became known as the 1998 Strategic Defence Review (SDR).

It may not have seemed like it at the time but, with the benefit of hindsight, the SDR probably marked a modern high-point for the Royal Navy in terms of the prominence that it was accorded at the heart of British defence policy. However, if it was a victory at all for the Navy, it was a pyrrhic one.

The SDR was something of an exception in the annals of post-Second-World-War British defence reviews. Conducted at a time of relative plenty, it was initially lauded for its analysis and conclusions.

Again, there were tough choices to be made. The upheavals of the decade from the end of the Cold War in 1990 had seen the peace-dividend cut in real defence spending total some 23 per cent. It was clear that that shrinkage in spending now needed to be matched by a more fundamental readjustment of forces.

And yet, suddenly, there seemed to be an opportunity for the Royal Navy. Official defence thinking – driven by a strong Defence Secretary in the shape of George Robertson – seemed to be properly freed from the straitjackets of the Central Front, the continental commitment, and the legacy of Cold War perspectives. It appeared that the chance was there to restore the maritime dimension to a central position in the government's defence thinking.

For the First Sea Lord at the time, Admiral Sir Jock Slater, and his team, there was no doubt that it was a hard fight. The Navy itself faced difficult adjustments. Its own Cold War mission of hunting Soviet submarines had vanished, and along with it the chief justification for large chunks of the Fleet.

But, throughout the 1990s, a lot of thinking in the Navy and the Royal Marines had gone into considering the role of maritime forces in 'the new world order', not least the role of key capabilities like carrier aviation, amphibious forces, and SSNs in 'joint' power-projection operations. And the agenda that emerged from the SDR read like a manifesto for maritime forces. The focus may have shifted from controlling the seas to acting as a key component of future joint operations, but maritime forces were described as 'inherently suited' to the expeditionary, power-projection vision set out. There was the added spur of the as-yet not fully-formed – or at least not fully-articulated – Blair doctrine of 'liberal interventionism'. This was at least in part heralded by the declared SDR ambition that the British military should seek 'to be a force for good'.[2]

In the settlement that was reached, the Navy would lose three destroyers and frigates, down from thirty-five to thirty-two, although there was the promise of a dozen powerful new air defence destroyers. The submarine force would come down from twelve to ten and mine warfare ship numbers from twenty-five to twenty-two.

But that was, to the Naval Staff, an acceptable package in return for the key victory, endorsement of a plan to build two new big aircraft carriers as replacements for the Invincibles, and to maintain a much-enhanced amphibious capability. The new carriers, the review predicted, would likely be around 30-40,000 tons, deploy around fifty aircraft including helicopters, and enter service from about 2012. It cannot have harmed the carrier case that, in early 1998, at the time of the SDR deliberations, HMS *Invincible* was rushed to the Gulf to play a prominent part in the naval reinforcement there to stare down the Iraqi leader, Saddam Hussein, in the latest row over UN weapons inspectors.

All in all, the Navy proposed in the SDR still looked like a force that had real shape and substance. The carriers and amphibious ships would become more central and prominent in the make-up, the numbers of ocean escorts less so. But it remained what the modern Navy had always striven for, a balanced fleet.

The government portrayed the review as a thoroughgoing effort to reshape and modernize the armed forces for the challenges of the twenty-first century. George Robertson himself called it 'radical'. Indeed, it would be trumpeted as a model to be emulated by many other governments which were grappling with strategic readjustments of their own. There were, of course, critics who saw it as a political surrender, a New Labour document to soothe the services and silence any residual mutterings that the party was 'unsafe' on defence. Those criticisms would only get louder as time, the tide of events, and the tensions inherent within the SDR began to make themselves felt.

At first, things went well for the Navy. The 1999 Kosovo crisis saw the first employment of its new capability to launch Tomahawk land-attack cruise missiles (TLAMs) from submarines – a key part of its new armoury to project power. The following year saw the Sierra Leone intervention, seemingly a textbook case of naval power projection, employing a task force centred on a carrier – HMS *Illustrious* – and amphibious ships to stabilize a crisis.

Even the early stages of the interventions in Afghanistan and Iraq appeared to reinforce the naval case. The first direct British military action in Afghanistan after the al Qaeda attacks on the United States on 11 September 2001 came from the sea. TLAMs again from submarines, and a carrier – HMS

Illustrious again – rapidly switching roles from flying Sea Harriers and Harriers in a major exercise in Oman to acting as a launching pad for special forces and Royal Marines. Carriers were there again at the outset of the Iraq invasion in March 2003 – *Ark Royal* this time and the helicopter carrier HMS *Ocean* plus frigates providing naval gunfire support to forces ashore for the first time since the Falklands. And more submarine-launched TLAMs.

But the problems were already brewing. As with so many of the defence reviews of the past, the financial assumptions on which the SDR had been based quickly proved to be illusory. Almost from the outset, it became clear that the MoD would not be receiving the future funding that it had been expecting.

For the Navy, the SDR 'package deal' soon began to unravel. In 2002, it was announced that its force of Sea Harriers would retire early in 2006. In 1998, they had been seen as a critical link to the future and to the arrival of the new carriers. More than that, they were a significant part of the Navy's stake in a historic bargain with the RAF, which helped win backing for the carriers themselves but also created a joint Harrier force that it was planned would eventually be transformed into a new generation of aircraft to be shared by the two services.

More would follow with what was, in effect, a mini-review in 2004, to try to address pressing budgetary tensions. Dramatically, the Navy would lose another half-dozen destroyers and frigates. Submarine numbers would drop by a further two. The then First Sea Lord, Admiral Sir Alan West, clearly saw as his chief priority the preservation of the carrier programme. There was also a critical upgrade of the hugely valuable new Merlin ASW helicopter to be protected, as well as the amphibious force. He knew that he had to give up something. He felt that destroyers and frigates were a sacrifice that might be recovered at some point, in a way that the carriers could never have been. But he would face criticism from within the naval community that he did not fight his corner hard enough. He did publicly warn of the risks involved in the reductions that were announced. But still, for many in the Navy, the cuts were a nasty shock.

It was around this time that opinions within the naval community started to diverge on 'the vision thing'. What did it mean to be a strategic navy? In one camp, an increased concern on preserving those key elements like the carrier strike capability, the amphibious ships, and the SSNs. But, among others, a dawning worry about the cost to the rest of the Fleet. The focus on high-end, potentially high-impact contingencies, but with a low probability of materializing, was robbing the Navy of its ability to respond to those tasks which most connect with people, and make a difference most of the time.

And even the prized carrier programme still seemed tantalizingly out of reach, with no firm orders in the offing. Its forward momentum was slowing as the price attached to it started to rise, and the attention focused on it was starting to become ever more critical and questioning.

On the ground in Iraq, the military operation was evolving into a draining and difficult garrison-style commitment, countering a developing insurgency. From 2006, Britain also took on a further commitment in the southern Afghan province of Helmand that would quickly become far more challenging than originally predicted. The scale and length of these operations would far exceed the assumptions in the SDR about potential commitments. It became ever clearer that overall defence funding could not sustain both the ongoing operations and the long-term equipment modernization programmes. The armed forces were descending into crisis.

Despite the mounting strains, the feeling in the Royal Navy was still that no other fleet save that of the United States could project power as far or as convincingly. It continued regularly to muster task groups for extended deployments to practise the art and make the point.

But many were not convinced. The gaps were beginning to show, and the disquiet in the wider naval community was beginning to grow. The withdrawal of the Sea Harriers robbed the Fleet of an element of air defence capabilities. The limitations of its other main air defence assets, the increasingly elderly, 1970s-vintage Type 42 destroyers, compounded the problem. More generally, the Fleet was ageing as new major warship orders were not forthcoming, and the Navy was finding it increasingly difficult – with funding priorities elsewhere – to maintain key equipment. In common with other navies, the Royal Navy's ASW skills – previously a great strength – were declining. Despite new amphibious ships, its real ability to conduct amphibious operations was certainly less than advertised. It struggled to muster the vessels or the personnel to train on any scale and with any regularity, as the Royal Marines took their share – and some would say more than their share – of the ground commitment in Afghanistan.

Like other navies, it made a virtue of necessity by filling gaps in its deployments with ships from other nations – specifically France and the United States – under the banner of increased international co-operation. But the impression was growing that, despite the undoubted skills and depth of capabilities that the Royal Navy was displaying in sustaining these deployments at all, the actual military power which these formations represented seemed increasingly in doubt. The suspicion was growing that the Navy would face some serious problems if it suddenly had to mount a major task force for real, that it risked becoming a 'hollow' force. Nor, many argued, did it have enough ships any more for all those routine tasks of maritime security requiring presence and patrolling in key waters.

Expressions of concern were starting to appear regularly in print. In one particularly noteworthy paper, in the Journal of the Royal United Services Institute for Defence and Security Studies (RUSI), the respected but some would say rather turbulent duo of naval commentators, retired Vice-Admiral Sir Jeremy Blackham and Professor Gwyn Prins of the London School of Economics, warned that the Navy 'risks losing irretrievably the capacity which it has had since before Nelson but especially from the time of Trafalgar to the present, to be a decisive force across the globe'.[3]

The authors followed this up with a similar article, entitled 'Storm Warning for the Royal Navy', in the influential Proceedings of the US Naval Institute. And across the globe, others were also noticing and commenting on the perceived malaise. The journal of the Navy League of Australia had already carried an article entitled 'The Terminal Decline of the Royal Navy'. In March 2008, in another article in Proceedings, a retired Indian naval commodore directly challenged the image presented by those extended deployments, that the Navy still retained a full-scale, long-range, open-ocean, 'blue-water' capability, by suggesting that 'the Royal Navy today, with twenty-five major warships, cannot claim to be a blue-water navy'.[4]

Part of the Blackham/Prins line of attack was clearly critical of the Navy itself for being too wedded to too few high-capability ships, and not embracing cheaper vessels as a way of filling the order books, increasing the size of the Fleet again, and sustaining a presence on the oceans. Others rallied to the Navy's defence. In a direct riposte to the Blackham/Prins salvoes, and the murmuring of others, the respected naval historian Professor Eric Grove rejected 'the totally spurious sense of crisis, a highly misleading proposition that can only have the most negative effects on the perceptions of our closest allies of what is still a world-class navy'.[5]

Grove certainly offered a useful corrective, accentuating some of the more positive aspects of the Royal Navy's condition, not least an SSN capability unmatched in any other medium-sized fleet, plus the prospective carriers. And he suggested that the Navy's then future frigate plans promised to answer some of those criticisms of gold-plating, and the need for a mix of both higher-end and more basic capabilities. In fact, he was trying to accentuate the positive when he himself saw the situation as only just acceptable, but also feared the consequences of too much gloomy talk. Subsequent events – especially the aftermath of the SDSR – would force him firmly into the concerned camp.

By this time, the strains within the MoD over funding, and therefore between the services, were spilling out into the public domain. The then Chief of the General Staff, General Sir Richard Dannatt, had already started stirring the pot with comments on the pressures facing the Army. In February 2007, the then First Sea Lord, Admiral Sir Jonathon Band, had made his public pitch for more funding, suggesting that Britain risked turning into Belgium without additional investment in its maritime capabilities. And he called for a clear commitment to the two carriers. It was a typically pithy intervention. He was forced into a partial retraction. But he had made his point.

Admiral Band was clearly fighting hard for the carriers in particular, which had still not been ordered, as well as the case more generally for long-term defence investment. His predecessor, who became Lord West and a government security minister, was also still exerting his pro-carrier influence within the government. But, not surprisingly, given the immediacy and intensity of the struggles in Iraq and Afghanistan, it seemed that the Army had very much seized the initiative in terms of framing the debate both on immediate defence priorities and also on what the future character of conflict would be, and therefore how the armed forces should shape themselves for that future.

Band, like West, took the view that what made a difference, and what set the Navy apart, were those key elements including carriers, an amphibious capability, and the SSNs. Frigate numbers could be addressed when needed. But he also fought on a broad front to make the case for investment in the future, despite the growing urgency of current operations.

But there was a growing sense – at least in much of the commentariat – that somehow the Army 'got' the complexities of modern warfare in a way that the other services did not, and that it was indisputably the most important of the armed forces. It has, undoubtedly, been the busiest and most committed of the armed forces in recent times, even if it might be argued that these engagements have been the result more of political choice than long-term strategic interest. But it had certainly learned painful lessons, and at considerable cost transformed itself into an army better able to conduct the arduous missions of counter-insurgency, 'war among the people', and nation-building. The argument clearly gained traction that this was the shape of things to come, with an added dose perhaps of cyber and information warfare. Naval arguments that the campaigns were but distractions, of strategically dubious long-term significance, clearly faltered and fell on deaf ears against the background din of, by then, nearly a decade-and-a-half of prolonged land commitments not just in Iraq and Afghanistan, but previously in the Balkans too.

In this climate, calls for even more of a shift in resources towards the Army, and away from the Navy and RAF, seemed to grow louder. In 2009, the Institute for Public Policy Research produced a report by its 'Commission on National Security in the 21st Century' proposing an increase in the size of the Army of 15–20 per cent, and questioning – among other things – the continuation of the carrier programme. Among other commentators too, there seemed to be growing public support for the argument that 'the government is lavishing billions of pounds on weaponry that ignores the nature of modern wars'.[6]

The debate was not confined to Britain. In the United States, the new Defence Secretary, Robert Gates, complained about what he called 'next-war-itis', the propensity of much of the defence establishment to focus on what might be needed for a future conflict. The priority had to be winning the current wars, he argued, and even prospective state-on-state conflict in the future was more likely to see opponents using unconventional 'asymmetric' means to neutralize expensive, high-tech Western capabilities. So, at least for a long time to come, 'the kinds of capabilities we will most likely need in the years ahead will often resemble the kinds of capabilities we need today'.[7]

Still, there was no appetite among ministers for what many increasingly regarded as essential – a new defence review. Instead, they continued to try to juggle the finances. But mounting operational costs were being matched by a growing realization of the scale of the structural crisis in MoD funding – with projected budgets falling far short of the levels needed to maintain the equipment programmes that were envisaged. This was what would become 'the black hole' at the heart of defence – and which would ultimately be estimated to total some £36 billion. The remedy being adopted, of deferring major projects to ease the MoD's cash flow, would equally come to be seen as a major part of the problem, as it raised ultimate costs and produced a growing 'bow wave' of bills still to be paid. This was one of the key findings of the highly critical and highly influential Gray report on MoD procurement, published in October 2009.

Just as troubling for the Navy, in all the critiques of the MoD, defence procurement, and defence policy generally, the precious aircraft carriers were becoming the poster children of all that was wrong with how things were being done. It seemed as if hardly a commentary went by without the carriers being described as 'behemoths', in a way clearly not meant to be complimentary.

The onset of global financial and economic meltdown in 2008 had only added to the sense of inevitability. In July 2009, the then Defence Secretary, Bob Ainsworth, announced that there would indeed be a new defence review. But it would not take place until after the next general election, then less than a year away. However, since all the major parties were committed to one in some form or another, it would certainly go ahead.

As it turned out, it would be the new Conservative-Liberal Democrat coalition government which would actually carry it out. The new review, which finally got under way just days after the May 2010 election, was different from its predecessors in two key respects. First, it was a defence *and security* review. So it was meant to join up the issues of defence and security across the government in a way that had not been done before. That also meant that the MoD, rather than being the main driver of the process, was but a participant. The centre of gravity was the newly-created National Security Council (NSC). The other key difference was that the government committed itself to holding regular reviews in the future, about every five years.

The first strategic choice which the government made was that cutting the public deficit quickly was an absolute priority. This coloured all the SDSR deliberations, not least the hurried nature of them. The other associated political choice was not to ring-fence defence spending. In the end, the government would impose a financial settlement on the MoD less harsh than that forced on other ministries. But, coupled with the need to address the MoD budget black hole, that still meant that the financial context for this review was as bleak as it had been for any previous such undertaking since at least the 1960s, and perhaps since the end of the Second World War.

However, the political context was very familiar, in the sense that the coalition government was as reluctant as any of its predecessors to acknowledge that there would be any diminution in Britain's role in the world. So the political rhetoric of ministers, of 'no strategic shrinkage' and 'no East of Suez moment', was going to have to be squared with a prospective real reduction in defence resources. The other familiar element of the SDSR was that, almost immediately, it sparked an intensified new round of inter-service infighting, played out in part with leaks and counter-leaks, but also pursued behind closed doors.

For many, the Navy seemed strangely absent from the public debate, except as a target. In this atmosphere, the Blackham/Prins double-act weighed-in again with an imploring attempt to make the case that a strong maritime stance remained fundamentally in Britain's long-term interest, that its 'core strategic challenges are naval', and that the Royal Navy had already become 'dangerously weak'.[8]

The NSC offered ministers three recipes from which to choose for the decade ahead: a 'vigilant' Britain, retrenched and concentrating on the home front; an 'adaptable' Britain, ready to engage but reluctant to get stuck into long-term commitments; and a 'committed' Britain, carrying on much as it had done for a decade.[9] These options may have appeared more like convenient brands than thorough strategic analyses. However, ministers predictably chose the middle way.

To the Naval Staff, Adaptable Britain seemed tailor-made to its own vision. The problem was that there was still a legacy of Committed Britain. The new government had already set the clock ticking for an end to a British combat role in Afghanistan by 2015. But, when the political decision was made at the highest level that there would be only limited cuts to the Army's manpower until then, the calculations changed dramatically. That was inevitably going to leave the Navy and the RAF to shoulder most of the burden of immediate cuts. There was no money, so there was no room for manoeuvre. And everyone, it seemed, was gunning for the carriers.

In the end, the overall exercise was presented as two documents on two successive days in mid October 2010, a new National Security Strategy (NSS), and the SDSR – the context and the choices. The component parts would be widely criticized both individually and in combination. In mitigation the government could argue that it faced the harshest of economic backdrops, a legacy of problems, and a strategic outlook of exceptional uncertainty.

The NSS set out two broad ambitions, a secure and resilient nation at home, able to deal with immediate threats, especially terrorism, but also a continuing desire to shape international events and promote a stable world. But the SDSR proposed a military force structure that would reduce the country's ability to project power by about a third compared to the scale of operation which it mounted for the 2003 Iraq invasion and which it was sustaining in Afghanistan. The government would make up the difference by being 'smarter' about the deployment of force in the future, and more focused on narrower national interests and efforts to anticipate and prevent conflict. But, to the critics, it did not add up.

The government insisted that the SDSR would produce a coherent capability by the end of the decade – Future Force 2020. It would be smaller but balanced and more suited to future threats. However, there would be turbulence, severe cuts, and acknowledged risks on the way to achieving that. Again, the critics attacked the cuts for being political and financial rather than strategic, and claimed that the specific choices made undermined the flexibility, adaptability, and range of options that the government professed to be pursuing. The government's retort was that there was no money and that the legacy of mismanagement that it had inherited would take time to sort out.

And so it went on. One of the most telling objections to the SDSR came in the House of Lords on the day of its publication. In an allusion to a famous television exchange in the 1980 US presidential election campaign, the author of the SDSR's predecessor, Lord Robertson, remarked: 'I know a strategic review, I have done a strategic review, and this is not a strategic review.'[10]*

In the Navy and among its supporters, there was a clear sense that the maritime cause fared worst when the final judgements were made. For some, that feeling was accompanied by a belief that, in the circumstances, it was perhaps inevitable, and it could have been worse still. In others, the mood was more of bewilderment over how it had happened ... again.

The First Sea Lord, Admiral Sir Mark Stanhope, led the Navy case. A serious, clever, and thoughtful officer, he was blamed for what were seen by some as ineffective tactics by the Navy in the Whitehall battle, and for the fact that the Navy was not more publicly vocal in defending itself as the debates unfolded. But he was also in an unenviable situation, and clearly under siege over the carriers.

A repeat of 1966 loomed. There is little doubt that, were the move to have yielded significant savings, the coalition government would have chosen to scrap one or both of the new carriers. But, this time, the ships were already under construction. And the specifics of the contractual arrangement with the builder, BAE Systems, meant that it would be entitled to compensating work if the ships were scrapped. In the end, to the consternation of senior ministers it seemed, it turned out to be cheaper to carry on building them.

---

* This was a reference to the famous television put-down by Democratic vice-presidential candidate Lloyd Bentsen of Republican rival Dan Quayle, during the 1988 US presidential campaign. The youthful Quayle had played up comparisons between himself and John F. Kennedy, and Bentsen responded, 'Senator, I served with Jack Kennedy, I knew Jack Kennedy, Jack Kennedy was a friend of mine. Senator, you're no Jack Kennedy.'

Options were considered. Accelerating design and building work on the new frigate programme was rejected as impractical in the timeframe required. Building five corvettes to an existing export design was also investigated. In one telling intervention, the First Sea Lord rejected them as 'snatch frigates'. (This was a reference to the vulnerable 'Snatch' Army Land Rovers that had become so notorious in Iraq and Afghanistan and which were themselves so named because of the original purpose for which they were designed in Northern Ireland: to 'snatch' rioters off the streets.) And it was by no means clear whether these limited-capability vessels would be additions to, or substitutes for, the Navy's existing future frigate plans.

Clearly, the Naval Staff faced some dark days. As well as the pounding over the carriers, there were also some other nightmare scenarios placed on the table as the MoD contemplated worst-case financial settlements. These included a surface escort force reduced to eight or nine vessels, and the complete scrapping of the amphibious force.

And yet, for much of the SDSR process, the Navy seemed to feel that it was winning much of the argument. Indeed, for a good part of it, the RAF looked like ending up the biggest loser. A key decision was that the number of fast jet fleets would be reduced from three to two. The Eurofighter Typhoon was inviolate. That left a battle between the older, more expensive Tornado, favoured by the RAF because it was ultimately more capable in the long-range strike role, and the Harrier, operated jointly by the RAF and the Navy, and favoured by the latter because it was Britain's only carrier-capable combat aircraft.

And, for a long time, it looked as if the chief victim would be the Tornado. In the end, the decision went the other way. The reasons were murky. But many in the naval community were convinced that it was down to a last-minute ambush by the RAF which swayed the opinion of the Prime Minister, David Cameron, on what they would repeatedly contest were spurious grounds.

The *Ark Royal*/Harrier decision both overshadowed and shaped attitudes towards the other elements of the SDSR's naval package. Of the two new carriers being built, one would be kept in service and operated, but the fate of the other was uncertain – it might simply be mothballed or sold. For many of the Navy's supporters, these decisions were disappointing enough by themselves. The amphibious warfare capability, which the Navy had fought so hard for so long to restore, was also cut.

And, but for the carrier controversy capturing attention, the further cut in the Navy's escort force to just nineteen ships would surely have provoked more international comment. As it was, it raised eyebrows in Washington. Compared to the SDR target of thirty-two destroyers and frigates, the Navy had shrunk again in barely more than a decade by more than a third to what for many was a breathtakingly low number of escorts. And even the other big, eye-catching cut, scrapping the long-delayed and deeply-troubled Nimrod MRA4 surveillance aircraft programme, while nominally an RAF loss, had its chief impact in the maritime sphere.

The Naval Staff would argue that, save for the unhappy carrier gap, it had essentially preserved the key elements of a balanced fleet – just. It could, for example, have seen the entire amphibious capability scrapped. There were also some possible compensations. One concerned the aircraft that would operate from the new carrier, or carriers. The plan had been to purchase the F-35B version of the Joint Strike Fighter, the most direct successor to the Harrier, designed for short take-off and vertical landing (STOVL). But it was largely unloved in the Fleet Air Arm, because it had less range and payload than the conventional carrier version, the F-35C. The SDSR switched to the latter, which will be less expensive. And its adoption will increase commonality and the potential for co-operation with the US and French navies. There was also the confirmation that the order for a seventh new Astute-class SSN, which had been in serious doubt, would go ahead.

But many in the naval community were unconvinced. The Navy's situation appeared precarious. Much of what was proposed that was positive seemingly remained hostage to fortune, including – still – the new carriers. For some, the Navy was looking even more like a hollow force, less a fleet as such, more just a collection of assorted vessels, and not many at that.

CHAPTER TWO

Britain, the Navy, and the World

When Prime Minister David Cameron stood up in the House of Commons on 19 October 2010 to present the conclusions of the SDSR, he spoke approvingly of how Britain had traditionally 'punched above its weight in the world'. Not surprising, perhaps, from a Conservative leader. And the country should continue to aim to do so in the decades ahead, he said. The NSS and the SDSR both expounded at length on the complexities of the modern world, Britain's different types of engagement in it, and the different levers of influence. But it was also clear that a large part of the weight that David Cameron was referring to was military.

And yet, just a few hours earlier, Cameron had faced an awkward encounter when he visited the country's Permanent Joint Headquarters at Northwood in north-west London, as an overture to his statement. He was confronted by an unhappy Harrier pilot, contemplating the possibility of redundancy as the aircraft that he flew faced the scrapheap. The officer in question was Lieutenant Commander Kristian Ward, a veteran of combat sorties over Afghanistan. He was a chip off the old block. He was the son of Commander Nigel 'Sharkey' Ward, a former naval aviator celebrated as the leading Sea Harrier pilot of the Falklands War, and himself a stern and longstanding critic of official policy towards the business of aviation at sea.

The two episodes highlighted what many saw as the contradiction on display that day. It was of a government declaring 'no shrinkage' in Britain's influence, while it was revealing real and significant reductions in the country's military clout. There was another paradox outlined by Cameron and his Liberal Democrat deputy, Nick Clegg, in their foreword to the NSS on the previous day, that 'Britain today is both more secure and more vulnerable than in most of her long history'.[1]

There was at least one more paradox. The SDSR was simultaneously too late and too soon. It was overdue in the sense of dealing with the compounding overstretch and overheating of the armed forces and the defence budget, which had been plain for all to see for years. But it was premature, because it was inevitably overshadowed by the continuing, straining demands of Afghanistan. So the SDSR could never be a clean-sheet assessment of Britain's long-term security and strategic requirements. As a result, it seemed to settle nothing. But then, in a way, it was never meant to. It was not meant as a final destination, but as a starting-point for a process of five-yearly reviews that would continue to refine British defence and security policy. Already, much of the focus is on the next one. That may or may not coincide approximately with the end of the British combat mission in Afghanistan and some kind of economic recovery at home, and thus – perhaps – produce a somewhat different set of calculations.

There was no doubt that, as far as the SDSR was concerned, the accumulation of pressures – the almost perfect storm of financial meltdown, a rush to cut, the demands of current operations, a more than usually unfocused future, played out on the unfamiliar terrain of coalition government, with an inexperienced ministerial team, and a largely disengaged public (at least where foreign policy, defence, and security were concerned) – was a challenge in itself. In those circumstances, a genuinely strategic review, providing a new global vision and balancing immediate needs – budgetary and operational – against a genuine consideration of future risks and responses, was always going to be a tall order.

So the expectations being placed on the SDSR, and indeed the claims that were being made for it in advance by ministers, may always have been unrealistic. But there was another problem of timing. To many, Britain appeared exceptionally exposed and vulnerable at a moment of potentially dramatic change, uncertainty, and insecurity. For many, the stakes for the United Kingdom appeared exceptionally high. In the world of the think-tanks and academia, as the SDSR process unfolded, a constant refrain was that Britain had to tackle the fundamentals, and decide first and foremost what kind of country it wanted to be.

In the aftermath of the Second World War, the British experience was one of trying to mitigate relative decline, maintain its own security, and keep an influential place in the world. It was not an easy task, encapsulated famously by the former US Secretary of State, Dean Acheson, in his observation that 'Britain had lost an empire and failed to find a role'.

The country managed this effort through its involvement in key relationships, alliances, and international organizations. In addition, both because of the direct perceived Cold War threat to its own territory and independence and as a lever of influence, it continued to place emphasis on one area in which it still retained a comparative advantage over most of its would-be peers, that of military power. It consistently spent more on defence as a proportion of national income than any of its neighbours except France, and continues to do so.

But, of course, the world has changed, and continues to do so dramatically. The post-Second-World-War world evolved into that of the Cold War. That evolved further into a post-Cold-War world that was also the 'uni-polar moment', when Britain's most critical ally, the United States, enjoyed unprecedented geostrategic dominance and freedom of international action.

Now the post-post-Cold-War world is upon us, a multi-polar one – or some would say a non-polar one – of a more constrained United States, with emerging powers feeling and testing their own growing strength, and with the global balance of power shifting measurably from West to East.

A case could have been made that now was the time for the country finally to give up its global pretensions. Britain should move closer to the European norm, exercising any influence through soft rather than hard power. For some, there was no paradox about the country's security situation. Britain has never been safer. Such threats as do exist – of terrorism, cyber security, or organized crime – have nothing to do with defence. They are about intelligence, policing, the legal system, and international regulation. In other words, it is time to stop clinging to an illusion of big-power status, and for Britain's centuries-long global odyssey –and with it that of the Royal Navy – to come to an end.

Clearly, the mainstream political judgement remains that this is not what Britain wants, or what the British public would support, at least for now. In January 2007, in one of his parting public shots as Prime Minister, Tony Blair argued (in a speech aboard HMS *Albion*, moored in Devonport) that Britain should retain the ability to project hard power.[2] Indeed, he maintained that it was a false choice, that British soft power would be devalued without a hard-power foundation.

And that was clearly endorsed in the NSS and SDSR, albeit in more straitened circumstances. For all the painful cuts, Britain would continue to spend more on defence than all its European neighbours except France. The new government still listed as one of its 'tier one' risks 'an international military crisis between states, drawing in the UK'.[3] However, there were also multiple references to the smarter employment of a range of options. And there was a narrower focus for future interventions than in the Blair years: 'we will be more selective in our use of the armed forces, deploying them decisively at the right time but only when key UK national interests are at stake.'[4]

And for the British defence and security establishment, so much hinges on Afghanistan, and especially the extent to which the scheduled end of British combat operations there in 2014–15 will mark any kind of watershed. What the long-term strategic benefits and costs of the conflict will be for Britain are far from clear, not least because its outcome is still far from certain. The security situation will remain very difficult. There will be a continuing commitment to Afghanistan from the United States, Britain, and others for a long time. But it will be of a different nature. The resources devoted to it will be far less. The Afghans will be doing the fighting. In the United States and the United Kingdom, as well as in the rest of NATO, the political and public desire to move on will be huge.

The extent to which the Afghanistan campaign will be considered any kind of success will matter to the armed forces, especially after the uncertain judgement on the adventure in Iraq. The way that the British forces have seemed to struggle in Afghanistan has been a further blow to public confidence in the military's prowess and capacity, at least in that kind of grinding land campaign.

It has been an unpopular and confusing commitment, and the British public has never really seemed to buy the argument that it was helping to make the streets at home safer. The public has supported the armed forces and acknowledged their sacrifices. But the use of the military in pursuit of policies that do not have popular backing will inevitably threaten the forces' relationship with the rest of society in the long term.

That risk is compounded when conflicts like Afghanistan have raised questions about the actual utility of force in finally resolving them. The remark has regularly been made that the military alone cannot resolve such crises. Politics and development must also play their part. That may have blurred people's understanding of how and when the armed forces can and should be used, and their value as an instrument of security.

But do those qualifications apply only to the kinds of conflicts that Britain has been fighting in Iraq and Afghanistan? And is Britain as a result suffering from a kind of strategic tunnel-vision? At great cost, the British Army has learned, or relearned, how to fight such campaigns, and remodelled itself in the process. But has that process gone too far? Is Afghanistan the shape of conflicts to come, or already being overtaken?

There will certainly be an ongoing need to tackle the threat of terrorism. There will be the continuing challenge of first trying to prevent but if necessary dealing with the consequences of fragile and failing states in unstable but vital parts of the world. But there is also the evidence of a re-emergence of a classic geo-strategic and geo-political global environment, with the frictions brought on by the rise of new powers, all flexing new diplomatic and economic muscle, and all doing what rising powers traditionally do, investing in new and significant military capabilities. The threat of state-on-state confrontation has not disappeared.

Judging where the balance in all this will lie, or perhaps more pertinently how quickly it might shift, remains a great challenge. The word 'uncertainty' pervaded the 2010 NSS and SDSR, and they do not make a judgement over which way the trend may veer. Many who have devoted great time and effort to identifying the lessons of Afghanistan see a future still dominated by persistent, messy, low-level conflicts. On the other hand, one of the most energetic strategic thinkers about the future, the former director of the MoD's Development, Concepts, and Doctrine Centre (DCDC), Rear Admiral Chris Parry, rejects the notion which he characterizes as 'the future will be like the present, only more so'.[5] He sees instead a world in which – within a decade – there will be a serious return to regional rivalries between states, that much of that will be played out at sea, and that by the mid-2020s 'the world will again begin to resemble an armed camp'.

Future conflicts and confrontations will be complex and confused, but they may not look much like either Afghanistan or conventional wars of the past. Non-state adversaries will take on more and more of the characteristics and capabilities of states. Meanwhile, states will use more asymmetric, guerrilla-style, unconventional means, but also asymmetries of a different kind, on the high frontiers of space and cyberspace. And there is no denying the proliferation of high-end capabilities. Also, while complexity may be a given, the environment of confrontation and conflict is not. It will not always be deserts or mountains. Even when those are the battlefields again, the political choices that will be made about the methods of intervention may be very different, given what has unfolded in the last decade. For much of the rest of the world, the anguished debates in some Western war colleges over the future character of conflict have probably looked rather insular and parochial, and of barely marginal relevance to their view of the future strategic outlook and challenges. It will not be a future of wars among the people, but 'wars among the fishing fleets', or between the islands and over the undersea gas fields.

For both Britain and the United States, first Iraq and then Afghanistan have been salutary lessons about the limits of their military power. They will certainly restrain their appetites for future such prolonged nation-building exercises. Limited liability – the 'long and light' approach to counter-terrorism in failing states – may be more the order of the day. That would involve special forces, UAVs, and other methods of precision strike. And, as the navalists point out, that will so often be most effectively deployed from the sea. After all, it was a close-run thing even back in December 2009, when the Obama administration was thrashing around in its strategic review of Afghanistan. As it was, the decision went in favour of the comprehensive counter-insurgency strategy, troop surge and all. But it might easily have gone the other way, in favour of the limited counter-terrorism approach of drone strikes and special forces. The decision might well go the other way next time.

Indeed, Robert Gates, he of the 'next-war-itis' remarks of just three years earlier, would comment in early 2011 that any future Defence Secretary who advises the President again to send a big American land army into Asia or into the Middle East 'should have his head examined'.[6] He may have subsequently suggested that he regretted that comment, because of its implied criticism of the Afghanistan mission. But he also remarked for good measure at West Point that, looking ahead, 'the most plausible, high-end scenarios for the US military are primarily naval and air engagements – whether in Asia, the Persian Gulf, or elsewhere'. It seemed like something of a change of tune.

Of course, this leads on to another aspect of how Britain will see its role and influence in the future. In many ways, the most strategic element of the British decisions to weigh-in in both Iraq and Afghanistan was to do with being seen to be the closest and most dependable ally of the United States. Maybe, some would say, that has backfired, at least to a degree. But the NSS and SDSR both remained attached to the relationship with Washington as the most significant for Britain, and perhaps inevitably so.

But there is also a universal acknowledgement that it will have to be recalibrated. There has been much paranoid discussion (at least in British elite circles) of the health or otherwise of 'the special relationship'. Beyond instinctive and emotional links, there have been tangible pillars to it. Nuclear co-operation is one, although its value may be in decline. Intelligence-sharing is likely to remain a key connection, so long as the intelligence community in Britain remains alive to changing US priorities. That only highlights the fact that the real gauge of the relationship's value to Washington in times of need has always been the pragmatic one of what Britain – or anyone else come to that – can bring to the table.

The relationship, therefore, is likely to be less emotional and instinctive, and more pragmatic. It will be less exclusive. Washington's attention is going to be drawn elsewhere. It will be a United States more self-conscious about its power and its limits, and more likely to have to pick and choose its engagements around the world. For Britain, as for everyone else, the calculations about how best to have an influence with Washington will change, and will become more complicated.

The problem in London is that the transatlantic bridge is going to become a less strategic structure for Washington. And that will also have implications for the value of some of the traditional levers of British influence – not least its status as a leading member of certain international institutions. NATO is one of them. It clearly faces an uncertain future. Even permanent membership of the UN Security Council may not have quite the cachet or clout that it has had in the past, as other informal partnerships and new institutions come more to the fore. For the United Kingdom, other institutions may take on more strategic relevance than they have before, not least the Commonwealth.

And, of course, the new strategic fluidity, plus the age of austerity, has already been forging, or at least burnishing, other relationships closer to home. Most notable has been the further strengthening of Anglo-French defence ties. The two countries may be being forced together by reduced circumstances. Professor Julian Lindley-French was one of those to pose the question of whether this was 'a dialogue of decline',[7] as each sought to help prop the other up to maintain what both see as their rightful international places. But the *force majeure* of cruel economics may also provide the foundations for a broader future European capacity for influence, should it choose to pursue one.

The financial meltdown has accelerated the drift of power from West to East. It has deepened European defence retrenchment. But it might yet be the catalyst to a more co-operative and co-ordinated defence reappraisal in Europe, especially since the real limitations of European capability – even collectively – were exposed over Libya in early 2011. Libya, however, also highlighted a less than consensual approach in Europe to such a crisis, and was perhaps another sobering illustration that the alliance ties that bound during the Cold War are not as strong in the current international climate. At the same time, Europe has been waking up to the challenge of how to adjust to a world in which the key dynamics are being forged in Asia, with and between the United States, China, and India.

Another challenge for Europeans, though, is that, as well as a relative decline in their political and military power, the future may also see the potency of their much-touted soft power diminished as well – cultural as well as economic. And the debates over the relative values of hard and soft power have all been conducted against the backdrop of an international system largely guaranteed by the ubiquity of US hard power. Indeed, that is what has provided much of the room for manoeuvre for soft power to have an effect at all. That may be less the case in the future, and that may colour the argument over the relative merits of hard and soft power, and the definition of that hybrid, smart power.

The SDSR, perhaps unavoidably, fell back on something of a wait-and-see approach to how future conflict might shape up. Of course, the upheavals that almost immediately erupted across the Middle East were seized on by the critics as ammunition for their assault on what they saw as the strategic shortfalls of the review. In other words, the post-Afghanistan future had arrived rather inconveniently too soon, before Afghanistan itself had run its course.

The appetite for committed nation-building may be limited in the future, and political and public resistance to prolonged stabilization operations much increased. But it may be too soon to proclaim the end of interventionism as such, in an age of instantaneous, accessible, and indeed relentless global communication, as events over Libya in early 2011 appeared to demonstrate. Indeed, the continuing diffusion of power through communication and information will – again paradoxically – make it more difficult for governments to predict and control the impact of unfolding of events, and therefore be able to control how to react.

But what does what unfolded over Libya represent? Is it a sign that a new phase in interventionism is developing, the impulse of humanitarian concern leading to a limited type of international military response? Was it a sign that the lessons of past interventions had been learned, or that none had? What to make of the fact that, for whatever reason, the British Prime Minister, the leader of a government that only a few months earlier was proclaiming that his country would be much more discriminating in future about the use of the military, should suddenly find himself in the vanguard of calls for the establishment of a no-fly zone over Libya.

So, is the Libya example a possible formula for the future, or a strategic dead end? What did the rather limited and reluctant US leadership role at the outset represent? Was it a sign that a new, genuinely multilateral approach to such crises is emerging, or was it the first sign that a more inward-looking United States will produce an international leadership deficit, to go with all the other deficits with which the world is having to contend? Either way, Washington's semi-detached approach to the Libya crisis was one of its most significant aspects, even if its behind-the-scenes practical support was vital, given the Europeans' capability shortfalls.

The unfolding of the international response and, in particular, the failure once again of intervention limited to air power to have a decisive early effect, was also a stark reminder of the shortcomings of the long and light approach to intervention. In the end the military outcome may have been satisfactory for NATO. But there was some luck involved, and, before that, doubts and some worries about prolonged stalemate. For the Navy, there was the added frustration that its not inconsiderable contribution in Libya failed mostly to attract the limelight, or had to remain largely in the shadows. At the very least, Libya suggested that a lot more needs to be done to develop a new doctrine of intervention that satisfactorily identifies when and where action can and should be taken, can limit the military liability of outside powers, can match achievable ends to deliverable means, and has a sufficiently well-developed set of other levers of influence to be able to produce the desired effect in reasonable time before the pressures for 'mission creep' assert themselves.

Despite or because of all this, will the British political and public impulse post-2015 in fact be to turn inwards, to worry only about dangers closer to home? If, as is planned, the final British combat troops have by then wended their weary way home, will the public call be for a new peace dividend, a further reduction in defence funding, to reimburse the middle classes for years of belt-tightening, or to help pay for public projects elsewhere that have had to be shelved in the years of austerity? Or will events by then have produced a dawning realization that the wider world beyond Afghanistan has become a more dangerous and unpredictable place, that Britain has chosen to make herself weaker militarily just as this trend has begun to take tangible form, and that something needs to be done to address this? All these issues will have an impact on the future for Britain's armed forces, and most particularly on the future fortunes of the Royal Navy.

Clearly, the Navy's hopes rest on the British political establishment and public raising their heads from the arena of Afghanistan, 'smelling the strategic coffee', and seeing a very changed environment, and most particularly one that will underscore how the country's maritime capabilities have been undervalued. For some, though, nothing short of a calamitous 'event', in the Harold MacMillan sense, will produce any kind of sea change in political or public outlook in Britain. For others, even that may not be enough, as they see the Navy ill-prepared to respond, to 'seize the day'.

After all, even the Royal Navy's recent most glorious moment, the Falklands War, might have been different but for the intervention of one individual. The former First Sea Lord, Admiral of the Fleet Sir Henry Leach, died on 26 April 2011, aged eighty-seven, as the arguments over the fallout from the SDSR for the Navy continued to reverberate. The obituaries highlighted that he is widely credited with persuading the former Prime Minister, Margaret Thatcher, that the despatch of a naval task force to recapture the Falklands was not only possible but necessary.

The details of his intervention on 31 March 1982, with the Argentine invasion imminent, have become the stuff of modern naval legend. They included the fact that, despite being dressed in the full uniform of First Sea Lord, his path to the Prime Minister's office in the House of Commons was initially barred by a duty policeman.

Henry Leach had the Navy running through his veins. And yet he had been no more successful than some of his predecessors in fighting off cuts to the Fleet. He had briefly contemplated resignation following the results of the Nott review the year before. The government had briefly considered firing him for some of his lobbying tactics. Because of this unhappy preamble, some initially questioned his advice on the Falklands.[8] But there seems little doubt that his initiative changed the mood of senior ministers, and especially the mood of the Prime Minister, and thus also altered the course of the crisis. Without it, the task force might never have sailed.

Of course, it is one thing today to ask whether the Navy, the Naval Staff, and the naval community more broadly are in the right state of mind and condition to make the maritime case. But another is whether politicians and the public are in the mood to be at all receptive to it. Yet another is what that case might be exactly.

The Royal Navy's leadership has revived in recent years the question of whether Britain has become 'sea blind'. Is there a political or public indifference to or – perhaps more to the point – ignorance of the importance to Britain's safety, prosperity, and general well-being of the sea? And if so, why?

Statistics are paraded to illustrate the fact that the British economy is as reliant on the sea as it has ever been. There is also the oft-repeated observation that the 'just enough, just in time' global trading culture, which aims to minimize stocks held at warehouses on land and turns ships at sea into a global conveyor belt, leaves the whole system immensely vulnerable to any kind of interruption. There has even been a remarkable revival in aspects of British merchant marine activity, such as a trebling in the size of the British-owned fleet since 2000 and a six-fold increase in the British-flagged fleet, albeit from a low base.

And yet this has not resonated with the political establishment or the public, at least as far as a frustrated naval community is concerned. Even a couple of generations ago, Britain's reliance on the sea for survival was an unquestioned universal truth, with vivid experiences of the Battle of the Atlantic fresh in minds and memories. As a result, national identity remained closely connected to the sea.

Of course, the fact that the system at sea has worked virtually uninterrupted for decades has meant that, for most, it has long ceased to be interesting or relevant. Recently, clearly, attention has been focused elsewhere. Another factor is that many of the threats at sea of which navalists warn remain nebulous or nascent rather than actual. The maritime trading system, for the most part, continues to function smoothly. The one threat that does grab attention, of piracy off the Horn of Africa, appears containable at least, and does not seem to justify the kinds of investments that the Royal Navy sees as its priority. And so long as all that remains the case, engaging people in issues of security at sea will remain a challenge.

Of course, as the 2007 US Maritime Strategy points out, peace does not preserve itself, and that is true at sea. But, for now, the US Navy remains the ultimate guarantor of the maritime system. No realistic amount of extra funding would enable the Royal Navy to protect all Britain's maritime trading interests. What is more, precisely because the world is so globalized now, all trading nations – even landlocked ones – are critically dependent on the workings of the great global domains, including the sea. All states are, to a degree, maritime states. For that reason, even Britain's position as an island nation may be less special than it has been historically.

It remains an element of British national identity. But, as the world has got more complex, and as society has become more sophisticated, so the identity issue has become more intricate, both for the nation and for the Navy. When the Navy was at the heart of national identity, it was a simpler time. British society has evolved, and questions of identity have become more intricate. It has been argued that the Navy's malaise has deep-seated roots in how Britain perceives that identity now, its island status, and what confers status in the modern world.[9] It is not just a matter of messaging.

Navigating this particular conundrum is a uniquely difficult problem for the Royal Navy, precisely because of its special historical status and its tradition. For some, it is just the past. And then there is the question of whose past. For some, there is no attachment even to that historical legacy. Britain is a different country, more mixed ethnically. It is also a Britain in which the Navy is simply much less visible. Part of that is because it has become so small now, concentrated around three widely-dispersed bases with little or no footprint beyond, the smallest of the three services. Its total personnel strength is some 35,000, which is being reduced by a further 5,000 under the SDSR. So the entire Royal Navy could fit into one mid-size Premier League football stadium. It is significantly smaller than, for example, the Arcadia retail group which owns Top Shop.

Having said that, one path to the future for the Royal Navy may be to reduce its footprint on British soil still further, if in doing so it can increase its profile at sea. But that, again, will not be easy. For navies the world over there is a structural problem in the age of continuous news, instantaneous global communications, and short public attention spans. Maritime power is by its nature often slow to have an effect, out of sight, over the horizon, and is very often about deterrence – about preventing things from happening.

Images of counter-piracy patrols off Somalia are one thing. Reports on drugs-busting successes in the Caribbean are a reminder that the Navy has plenty to do. But, much of the time, they have served only as a contrast to the grim realities of Afghanistan. There are always challenges, of course, not least because of the basic operating environment. And the Royal Marines and Royal Navy personnel have played their part, and more, in Afghanistan. But it has been hard for the Navy to counter the impression that it has gone a little soft, and perhaps lost something of its fighting edge.

The culture at sea is different. The images of a navy going about its business are not the same as those from Helmand province in Afghanistan. The threat is different. The relationship to the enemy is different, and harder to capture in a simple and straightforward way. But it has not always been like that. For much of history, naval war was very close-up and personal. After all, the greatest naval hero, Horatio Nelson, was done for essentially by a sniper. And even at sea, the threats are changing and becoming more complex, especially in the shallow coastal waters where navies have often found themselves in recent years.

Perhaps it was a combination of these elements which came together in one disastrous moment for the Royal Navy. It was in the northern Persian Gulf in March 2007. It was the capture by Iranian Revolutionary Guards of fifteen members of the crew of the frigate HMS *Cornwall*, while they were detached in boats carrying out boarding-party duties. The incident and the subsequent controversy over the authorized sale by crew members of their stories to the newspapers all produced some desperate headlines for the Navy.

There may have been mitigating circumstances. The political and operational guidance under which the ship was operating may have been blurred, in congested and confused waters in a period of tense but uncertain relationships, neither at war nor really at peace. But maybe the Navy was at fault for allowing such circumstances to prevail, for not being attuned to the level of risk in such circumstances in the climate of the times. There were other failures as well. It was certainly a damaging hit below the waterline for a service whose prospectus for the modern world is that it is flexible and adaptable, and poised to deal with the unexpected.

It has had a corrosive effect. There have been further instances that have hinted that maybe the Navy has lost some of its edge. And, unfortunately, unwelcome headlines have not been relieved by much in the way of good news that has really grabbed the public's attention.

In a provocative article in The Naval Review, an author writing under the pseudonym Cincinnatus saw the *Cornwall* incident as a symptom of a greater malady, of a Royal Navy that had lost touch with its traditional ethos and its history:

For the past few years, it has been adrift, and is unprepared intellectually, conceptually, and morally for the challenges and risks of the future. Indeed, in its determination to demonstrate relevance and reflect the latest social and political fashion, the Royal Navy has mislaid what its real role and purpose are.[10]

That may have been strong stuff, but it was by no means an isolated suggestion that somehow the Navy had lost its bearings. On the policy front too, in the weeks after the SDSR, Professor Lindley-French, in the guise of a frustrated friend, offered the observation that 'the Navy has become too technically focused on tactical process, too concerned about the Army and Air Force and has in effect forgotten its place at the core of British national strategy'.[11]

There has been more. It was 1 December 2010, just a couple of days before HMS *Ark Royal's* mist-shrouded last entry into Portsmouth harbour, and – again – just a few weeks after the publication of the SDSR. The venue was HMS *Collingwood*, a shore establishment near Portsmouth with a venerable and revered name that is the Navy's main training school.

The then Defence Secretary, Liam Fox, stood before a group of senior naval officers, commodores and above. The occasion was what is known as the First Sea Lord's conference. Alluding to the widely-held view that he was particularly sympathetic to the naval case, he joked that he had been accused by some of being 'the only dark blue suit in the SDSR apart from the First Sea Lord'.[12] But he went on. He felt, he said, as if the Navy was somehow 'less successful, even less willing' than the other services when it came to selling itself.

Maybe the Navy does need to tell its story better. Perhaps more importantly it needs a better story to tell than its recent routine. Trying too hard to make too much of yet another drugs interception in the Caribbean can, in the end, be counterproductive, as it contrasts with the real and extreme dangers of Helmand. And the participation of the naval services in Afghanistan does not bolster the maritime case as such. For the Navy, this all may mean being more creative, and taking more risks, in being 'out there', in deploying the Fleet, trying to anticipate events, and being ready to remind those who need reminding – politicians and the public – about what the Navy is ready and able to do.

Of course, the Navy's leadership responds that it has never been more 'out there' in the sense of having ships deployed on the essential tasks that they are assigned. What is more, there is less room for manoeuvre in the era of jointness and ever-more-centralized political control. But there is a sense that the Navy as an institution has allowed itself to become too constrained by this.

The Navy is hamstrung, as indeed are the other services, by the fact that Britain remains more perplexed and self-conscious, and self-critical, about its role and its aspirations than other countries, like France. It is a particular handicap for an institution that has seen itself as the embodiment of a self-confident and ambitious nation, as indeed most strong or expanding navies are. But a population for whom the predominant question is why are we still doing so much, rather than why are we not doing more, is one that will be hard to persuade of the virtues of a stronger fleet. So the Navy's hopes must be pinned on the British being a people who will rebound, rather than recoil, from the current rather downtrodden mood brought on – in part – by prolonged war and profound economic slump.

As has been suggested, being an island nation may not make quite the qualitative difference any more to the case for the level of naval ambition that it once was. But, for a country like the United Kingdom, even if it supposedly suffers from sea blindness, an island history has bequeathed a legacy of skills, of global financial interests, trade links, and presence in terms of citizens living abroad, which add up still to an exceptionally high level of global engagement and therefore exposure.

But until that is palpably put at risk, grabbing people's attention will be a challenge. And the maritime domain will remain in many people's perspective an issue of history, of Nelson and Trafalgar. It is not uniquely a British issue. The US naval community may feel similarly overlooked. It may be that attention will begin to switch again. The Navy will need to be ready for when it does.

CHAPTER THREE

What are Navies For?

In April 2007, on the twenty-fifth anniversary of the Falklands War, John Nott reflected for the Royal United Services Institute on the lessons of that conflict. He acknowledged that, while all the services performed admirably, the principal credit for the operation fell to the Navy. However, he also mused, 'I find it hard to see what role the Navy should play in the twenty-first century, apart from evacuating civilians and acting as a poor relation of the Pentagon.'[1]

No doubt many of the Navy's Falklands veterans will have felt that this was the then Defence Secretary, and mastermind of the Nott review, coming back to haunt them and the Navy itself. Nott himself ruefully observed that 'fortunately for the Royal Navy, its role is for others to decide, not me'. But he did also venture that, as far as he was concerned, the Falklands was a one-off, and expressed regret that – in his view – it had distorted British defence policy ever since.

And the question implicit in those Nott remarks – what are navies for in the twenty-first century? – dogs many of the major fleets, not just the Royal Navy. How do they contend with the assertion that this is a post-naval era, since the Falklands has been the only major naval conflict since the end of the Second World War? While many regard 'sea blindness' as the affliction that needs to be overcome, it may be that the phenomenon is really 'naval invisibility', exacerbated by the prevalence of land-focused operations for so long, at least as far as the perspectives from London or Washington are concerned.

Navies around the world, and especially the major fleets, protest that they are as busy as they have ever been. And the challenges presented by that fact are compounded by a reality that the numbers of ships available have been dwindling. The other problem is that the tasks which have been keeping them most occupied of late have not been those for which they seem chiefly to have been designed. Indeed most of those missions, by themselves, do not justify the level of investment in the kinds of equipment that the top navies, including the Royal Navy, most seek and most value.

Of course, warships tend to last a long time. Navies change slowly. But then so too, navalists assert, do the principles of maritime power.

Naval strategic thinking remains dominated by theories of just a handful of individuals. Indeed, many people would name only two. One of those is the

US Navy captain Alfred Thayer Mahan. In his *The Influence of Sea Power on History* in 1890, he made a causal link between national power and prosperity and sea power, exercised through naval superiority and command of the sea achieved as a result of decisive action by battle fleets.

The British writer Julian Corbett, in *Some Principles of Maritime Strategy* in 1911, offered a more qualified and nuanced perspective on the ability of fleets to command the sea, and how. But he chiefly made the critical link between sea power and the achievement of broad national objectives by having influence on the land.

The works of these men have themselves been worked on over the decades since. In the 1970s, in the light chiefly of technical change and its influence in the maritime arena, the US Navy refined the idea of sea control into one limited both in area and time, an exercise of power to achieve particular ends.

So, historically, navies have sought to exercise sea power through the decisive fleet battle, the direct protection of shipping, blockade, commerce raiding, the possession of a fleet-in-being, and the direct maritime defence of territory. The outcome of the contest between sea control and sea denial either opened or closed the door to the other key objective, the maritime projection of power.

Decisive fleet-to-fleet actions have been infrequent. But are they definitively a thing of the past? How many were there in the last century? There was the Battle of Tsushima. Jutland counted, and Midway too, but how many others?

But the sea was a critical arena in both world wars. That was especially so in the Second World War, when the conflict became both total and truly global. There was the Battle of the Atlantic, the role of the Royal Navy in protecting the United Kingdom from invasion, the influence of sea power on the prosecution of the land campaigns in North Africa and Europe, and in sustaining the strategic partnership between Russia and its allies, and of course in the unfolding of the war in the Pacific.

Moving on to the Cold War, there was a great battle of nerves between the US and NATO navies on one hand and the Soviet Navy on the other through the latter half of the twentieth century. If the Cold War had ever turned hot, it might have produced a fiery, and perhaps rather short, conflagration in the waters north-east of the Greenland–Iceland–United Kingdom (GIUK) Gap, between assembled American carrier groups and the massed ranks of the missile-armed Soviet ships, submarines, and bombers. The odds for that increased as the US Navy adopted a much more aggressive maritime strategy in the 1980s. But that will forever remain conjecture because, of course, the Soviet fleet disintegrated, along with the state itself, in more ways than one.

It is not difficult to assert that Western maritime power, and especially that of the United States, and their preparation for the most demanding of potential conflicts, played a crucial part in the outcome of the Cold War. But is there an equivalent deterrence role that major navies can play now and in the future, or are they clinging on to legacy thinking as well as legacy forces?

The end of the Cold War certainly brought a shift in strategic focus. The ability to use the sea was no less critical. But, as the world passed through its uni-polar moment, US naval supremacy was such that there was no real contest. The use of the sea was taken for granted. The preoccupation of navies became not the exercise of 'blue-water' sea control, since that seemed largely assured. It was instead the ability to project power from the sea.

Some may criticize navies for not changing enough, but it is certainly not the case that they have not changed at all. There has been a clear shift among the established Western navies, and others besides, to acquiring shipping designed more for projecting power. And the ability of navies to project power and influence ashore has also increased significantly with the development of new technology. It is no longer chiefly a choice of blockade, naval gunfire, or putting troops – including special forces – ashore. Carrier air power has gained dramatically from the developments of precision weaponry across the military aviation spectrum. Land-attack cruise missiles have transformed the capabilities of surface ships and submarines. Technology has also dramatically increased the intelligence-gathering capabilities of fleets.

Legacies certainly remain in the make-up of fleets. But there have also been costs as well in the change in strategic focus. The skills of navies in key aspects of open-ocean warfare – like ASW – have withered dramatically.

Some berate the US Navy that, for all its talk for two decades now of 'littoral warfare', it remains essentially a blue-water navy. That may be an unfair complaint, given the prominence and power of its amphibious groups, and the way its carriers have played significant roles in a succession of interventions. But it is also true that the maintenance of the US Navy's blue-water dominance remains the critical element of the maritime picture.

The critical issue in the next decade or two is whether and how that might change. There may be no other navy on the horizon that will be able to challenge the US fleet head-on, not even China. But the US Navy has been shrinking. Others are rising, and more particularly are acquiring more advanced technology. The balance is shifting. More generally, the proliferation of what the US Navy has dubbed anti-access/area denial (A2/AD) capabilities, not least the new generations of modern submarines and potent anti-ship missiles, will mean that major fleets may have to concentrate significant high-end forces either to exercise influence or send a credible message if they want to, or – if there is a real confrontation – in order to prevail and preserve their freedom of manoeuvre.

The US Navy certainly seems to fret over what it sees going on around it. And even a passing perception of US vulnerability might make some sort of renewed tension on the high seas all of a sudden plausible.

The sceptics tend to argue that the number of fleets that might have both the intent and ability to be seriously disruptive at sea is small, and likely to remain so. And the potential scenarios in which they would want to act in that way are remote. In this view, those who are pursuing powerful new fleets are doing so more in a search for prestige than as a result of real strategic calculation. Therefore other traditional navies which argue for the retention of high-end war-fighting blue-water capabilities are merely reinforcing a strategic fallacy.

And yet, it seems something of a stretch of credulity to conclude that those emerging powers which are pursuing their naval ambitions are doing so just for the sake of national pride. Just because their strategic perspective does not align with that in the West, say, does not make it any less valid. Indeed, the way the world is changing, perhaps the reverse may be truer. The shifts that are under way in the global balances of economic power clearly have their corollary in a shift in the balance of military power, including naval capability. The background of growing strains on the energy and resource supply chains could quickly snuff out all the talk of a post-naval era.

Of course, just because certain nations are building certain types of fleets against each other does not mean that others should follow suit. Likewise, there are questions over what constitutes an effective modern fighting navy, on the basis of strategy and tactics. But, given the interconnectedness of the modern world, it is also a risky judgement simply to ignore or dismiss naval developments elsewhere that could represent a real challenge.

The United States still enjoys huge margins of superiority of military and naval might over any other individual nation. But it also has huge and dispersed responsibilities. Gaps are growing in its ability to range across the oceans, just as they are narrowing in terms of its margins over others in specific regions and ranges of capabilities. As such, they are already starting to change strategic calculations.

After a traumatic and indecisive decade in Iraq and Afghanistan, against the backdrop of economic and political travails at home, the aura of American power is under threat. And nowhere is that likely to become more suddenly obvious than in the domain where Washington has most confidently exerted its influence, at sea.

A general decline in the level of order at sea may be an early symptom of this trend, and an early sign that the freedoms enjoyed in the maritime domain for so long may be breaking down. There has been so much talk about the risks of growing ungoverned space on land. Almost unnoticed, the ungoverned spaces at sea have been expanding as well. The inability of failed or failing states to exert their authority on land applies equally to the waters that they claim as well. Mix in growing population demands and the competition for resources, and stronger and more aggressive states. There could be a growing assertion of restrictive national rights in what have been open international waters.

One of the key differences between navies on one hand and armies and air forces on the other is that warships have a day-in, day-out job every time that they go to sea in a way that soldiers and jet fighters do not. But how should that influence how navies shape themselves? The dilemma is highlighted, of course, by the image of billion-dollar destroyers and frigates tearing around in the expanse of water that is now dubbed 'the Somali basin' off the Horn of Africa, bearing down on pirates or would-be pirates in open skiffs with little more to wave in defiance than a few AK-47 assault rifles or rocket-propelled grenades.

In terms of the range of tasks that navies now perform, one could easily start at home. The defence of territory, and the patrolling of home waters remain critical missions. For a country like Britain, the focus for the moment may be more on countering terrorism and organized crime from and at sea, of securing ports and their use, and likewise critical coastal or offshore assets, and simply of helping to maintain the basic safety of increasingly crowded home waters and the coastline. The tapestry of potential threats and risks has become more intricate, and so to the overlapping responsibilities of different agencies. Information – 'maritime domain awareness' – has become an even more critical tool in tracking potential or developing problems. The United Kingdom has established the National Maritime Information Centre, to paint a broad picture that is as widely accessible across a range of agencies as possible.

The scale of the military challenge that most of these threats close-to-home represent may be relatively limited. Mostly, in naval or coastguard terms, they require simple patrolling, a limited degree of military clout, but mainly timely information and intelligence, communication, and co-ordination. Navies will be but a part of a tapestry of other enforcement and civilian agencies, forming a comprehensive approach to security, surveillance, and regulation.

While the threat of direct military attack on a country like the United Kingdom may be remote, there are still maritime tasks close to home which require significant capability. One is the protection of one's own strategic assets, like a submarine-based nuclear force. There is also the need to watch for and guard against the probing of one's own military capabilities and the collection of strategic intelligence from the United Kingdom, for example from submarines.

There is also one prospective direct military threat to the United Kingdom which equally could give rise to a potential new military task. This is the threat of ballistic missile attack and the need to defend against it. It is a task already being embraced by some navies – notably those of the United States and Japan. And, for a country like the United Kingdom, a naval approach to ballistic missile defence (BMD) may be the most obvious one, whether for a national system or as a national contribution to a multilateral system, whether for direct territorial defence or for the protection of forces deployed abroad. But, potentially, it could be hugely demanding, and hugely expensive.

To stray further afield in terms of the check-list of tasks for navies, 'gunboat diplomacy' is not dead. On the contrary, in an age of fluid strategic relationships and shifting geo-political balances, and increasing interconnectedness, naval diplomacy is growing in importance. Of course, in the modern world, the military plays only a part in the broad range of political, economic, and cultural connections between nations and peoples. But, because they are flexible, mobile, and independent, and able to operate at long range for long periods at relatively little expense, naval forces remain ideal tools – so the naval argument goes – for building and maintaining partnerships, and for making statements of political intent and commitment while limiting exposure and not being unnecessarily provocative or menacing. Warships and navies are consummate 'networkers' in a networked world. And it is a world in which those who are on the 'up' seem to place significant store by the maritime domain and maritime capabilities.

As part of that equation, there is the role of navies in 'soft' power projection. Whether it is fully-fledged hospital ships, or amphibious vessels with medical or other support facilities, navies can and do mount humanitarian missions as a matter of routine, and provide the platforms from which a range of other agencies and soft-power players can operate, in the cause of conflict prevention.

The US Navy's Global Fleet Station (GFS) concept may be the best example of that. It sees US ships establish a limited presence in certain areas to provide different types of local assistance. It might be focused on humanitarian assistance, or – as in the case of Africa Partnership Station – on maritime security co-operation and the development of local capabilities. GFSs or their equivalents could also be platforms for broader engagement to assist wider local development. There is also the utility of naval forces in responding to major natural disasters.

Some might question whether military forces are appropriate or really cost-effective in providing any of this, or whether it is a political option to provide the same capabilities through purely non-military means. But the fact is that such capacity is inherent in a whole range of naval assets, and in some instances only a military capability will do.

Moving further up the scale, there is the task of providing maritime security. The one area where what navies do consistently gets public attention at the moment is at the low-end of this mission of pursuing maritime security, whether it is countering pirates, seizing drugs at sea and rescuing desperate and adrift migrants and trafficked humans, or patrolling for terrorists in transit on the high seas with illegal weapons, including possibly weapons of mass destruction (WMDs). And, as far as the latter is concerned, the potential for a further cascading of WMD proliferation around the world's trouble-spots presents another area where navies – especially in partnerships – may find their attention increasingly focused in the future. There are also other continuing challenges where specialist naval skills and capabilities will still be required, like mine warfare.

For many, it is in the dirty brown waters off troubled shores, in the littoral regions, where navies will continue to find their most regular and relevant employment, and by this reasoning they should plan accordingly. It is here where order at sea will most likely dissolve, where the contests over resources will most likely flare, and where the spill over from the failing of states on land

and the persistence of low-level conflicts there can be most easily addressed and if necessary cordoned off. It is here where the principles of deterrence, presence, and patrol should be focused and practised.

It is also here where the eternal arguments over presence and ultimate fighting power, quantity versus quality, and what is the correct balance of a fleet begin to assert themselves. The unfocused instability of the modern world means that the list of potential trouble-spots is a long one, and the ability to predict where danger will occur is limited. This, according to one school, argues in favour of ubiquity at the expense of ultimate potency.

Presence, and 'showing the flag', is one element of the mission of deterrence and its corollary of maritime coercion. Deterrence is at the heart of what most naval advocates would argue navies do. The key phrases in the 2007 US Maritime Strategy underlined that message: 'preventing wars is preferable to fighting wars', and 'peace does not preserve itself'.[2] It was also not for nothing that Blackham and Prins entitled their main pre-SDSR contribution in the RUSI Journal, arguing for a predominantly maritime strategy, 'Why Things Don't Happen'.

And a plethora of patrolling craft, whether cheap frigates or corvettes, can deter and coerce in a certain way, whether it is pirates or terrorists planning an attack at sea or from the sea. In what is essentially a constabulary role, they are the 'bobbies on the beat'. But their capabilities are narrow and their impact is limited. It is negligible when it comes to impressing more significant entities like states, unless such vessels are seen as the tokens or heralds of much greater capabilities held in reserve.

Operating in the littorals is also in itself challenging, and likely to get more demanding. Even major high-tech navies have found themselves embarrassed and worse in the complicated littoral environment. For the US Navy, there was the devastating attack on the USS *Cole* in the Yemeni port of Aden in 2000. There was the Royal Navy's *Cornwall* debacle. A swarm of speedboats, whether packed with pirates, high explosives or irregulars determined to send a message on behalf of a rogue or client state, present a real challenge.

Such low-tech threats will continue to present an asymmetric challenge to the status quo. But there have also already been warning signals about how the threat could quickly become more sophisticated. The attack by the Hezbollah group on an Israeli warship off Lebanon in 2006, using an anti-ship missile, was the most notable example so far. The use of submersibles is an obvious next step. Both ashore and at sea, the tactics and capabilities of non-state actors are beginning to resemble some of those used by states.

So a warship that is both cheap and effective for the job of policing maritime security in the littorals may prove to be even more elusive than might now be supposed. The ability of such a vessel to have influence ashore is also significantly constrained. It could play a role in overseeing that modern-day equivalent of the blockade, the internationally-mandated sanctions regime. But in most cases of extending influence on land, something more eye-catching and capable, and thus expensive, is needed.

The piracy problem off the Horn of Africa highlights some of the dilemmas. To some, it is a showcase of the utility of navies, to others a dubious diversion. Somali pirates may be a new incarnation of an age-old problem, and thus an obvious candidate for naval action. But the persistence of the piracy problem in the Somali basin and beyond continues to pose questions for navies and the maritime community.

It has to some extent been a phenomenon that has been partially tolerated and tempered rather than truly tackled, the costs to some extent absorbed. But, as it has escalated, so the calculations have been changing. And among those questions is how much navies will end up being the main part of the answer. Ship owners are becoming more tempted to buy protection of their own. With the number of attacks and the number of hostage seafarers on the rise, the International Chamber of Shipping (ICS) was moved in early 2011 to clarify its position that, while the use of private armed guards was not recommended, it acknowledged that many shipping companies had concluded that arming their vessels was a necessary option.[3] The ICS also noted that the estimated cost of piracy to the global economy was already $7–12 billion a year and, if ship owners started diverting their vessels, that action too would have a major impact on the entire mercantile supply chain.

Naval commanders insist that the intervention at sea of some two dozen or more nations in various multinational formations has had an effect, albeit that the problem has continued to grow. One answer may be that more stringent tactics may be needed – even mandatory convoying of merchant ships – or changes in the agreed rules of engagement for the patrolling warships. The critical constraint may be the legal framework for dealing with the problem.

But it is also acknowledged that piracy in the Indian Ocean is only the symptom of a malaise that starts on land, in the dysfunction of Somalia. And this is where the issue of what level of capability and commitment to apply to a problem comes into play: how to influence events and actions on land, including the projection of actual power ashore, or at least the threat of it.

This is another step up the ladder of maritime tasks, but it still spans a spectrum of contingencies from deterrence and conflict prevention to coercion and intervention, with possible stabilization operations somewhere in the mix. Navalists are never tired of arguing that, in most of these cases, maritime forces are the most flexible of tools, offering persistence and poise, limited liability and minimum vulnerability to attack, and the fewest political problems. Most of the operations and contingencies that are likely to be considered or undertaken will be joint with other services. But naval forces can uniquely add to the flexibility and utility of the others, or so the Navy likes to suggest.

As has been mentioned, in terms of projecting direct military power ashore as an instrument of coercion, the capabilities available to maritime forces are as potent and flexible as they have ever been. They range from the traditional naval gunfire option to land-attack cruise missiles fired from surface ships and submarines and precision strikes delivered by carrier-borne aircraft or UAVs. In a post-Afghanistan world, the attractiveness of such an arms-length, light-footprint approach will surely increase.

But, as has been mentioned, the events in Libya in 2011 have also been a reminder of some of the limitations of such an approach, in terms of the ability to be fully in control and be able to shape behaviour and events on the ground. Even for more limited contingencies, there are question marks. With sufficiently accurate intelligence, maritime forces can be the launching pads for a cruise missile strike or even a special forces raid, against a pirate camp or a suspected terrorist base. Indeed, this has been tried on more than one occasion in Somalia. But how enduring an effect such an intervention might have is another matter, as is the risk of unintended consequences. There may be nothing to stop whoever was the target of a strike taking their revenge on, say, the local population, or any foreign nationals to hand.

At the very least, gauging what force to use and how to use it in order to have the desired effect – while also keeping one's distance – is a difficult calculation. The land-based critics of the maritime approach argue that the strategists' recipes for power projection work only up to the point where deterrence fails. From the point where action is required, the premium value of a presence of some sort on the ground – despite all the attendant costs involved – rises dramatically.

The poise and positioning of maritime forces can, of course, delay that point as much as possible. Critically, amphibious forces also provide the option of putting 'boots on the ground' for specific missions of limited duration if necessary. As such, their value may be significantly increased as the major powers adjust to a post-Afghanistan world of continuing instability. And maritime forces can provide the extraction method should an intervention on the ground look at risk of turning sour. A British naval task force was despatched to the Adriatic in 1993 to be ready to perform just such a role for the British military contingent deployed in the Balkans.

Those capabilities would also apply to a post-conflict stabilization mission. And, of course, there is the Nott scenario of civilian evacuation. The circumstances of the recent such operations in Lebanon in 2006 and Libya in early 2011 were relatively benign. They might not be on another occasion, and for the Royal Navy that might also be in a far more remote location. But, again, the advantages of maritime forces are that they can pre-position and loiter for a considerable period, and – with the right shipping available – have very considerable capacity.

But the key for the future for maritime strategists in terms of power-projection doctrine will be to marry the concept of limited liability with that of enduring effect in the light of the experiences of the last decade. Certainly, for the foreseeable future, not even the United States will have the appetite for much more in the way of fully-fledged nation-building. For all the hard-won lessons, counter-insurgency may give way to light and long counter-terrorism, including from the sea. The lessons of the Libyan intervention, perhaps coupled with those of the initial campaign in Afghanistan in 2001, may yield a new doctrine of how to leverage local forces and other actors in a more effective way without exposing one's own forces.

Of course, so much of the discussion on projecting all that power has presupposed the free use of the sea. And for much of the interventionist era, that has been largely taken for granted, at least by anyone other than navies. The two biggest interventions of the last two decades, both in Iraq, required massive build-ups by sea. The fact was that there was little or no interference. But in 1991 there was a fear that Libya might make a nuisance of itself, so naval forces were deployed to the Mediterranean. And two US ships suffered serious mine damage in the Gulf itself. In both operations, the key navies concerned clearly took serious precautions. In both 1991 and 2003, the Royal Navy deployed significant supporting naval forces into the Gulf, including critical mine warfare vessels.

But the maritime environment may not be so benign in the future. And a potential adversary like, say, Iran may be both wiser to the potential vulnerabilities of maritime supply lines, and more capable of doing something about it.

That may be one reason why there may need to be a reassessment of the range of maritime capabilities in the major fleets. Another is the more general proliferation of weaponry that could shift the balance in the sea control and sea denial stakes, and raise the capability bar for those navies wishing to maintain their freedom to operate. For such navies which do aspire to range the oceans independently, that will mean the need to continue to invest in the top-of-the-range war-fighting capabilities, and maybe to refocus on neglected skills like ASW.

And then there is the emergence of strong new states which have their own views of what the global system should look like in the future. And some of them, like China, are investing in military capabilities – not least maritime ones – in order to be able to exert an influence at least in a regional context, and ultimately farther afield as well.

The revival of real inter-state competition is already evident, plus the first inkling that it might be gathering pace. There is no inevitability about it, let alone of it taking primarily a military form. Nor is it clearly determined that it would lead to actual armed confrontation between any of the major powers. But a glance at the likely friction points, and where the likely main contenders in this competition are focusing their attention and efforts, suggests that the sea will be one key arena where this competition will find expression.

In a recent study on the prospects for the US Navy, the Center for Naval Analyses (CNA) usefully portrayed the world as one which, in the future, will be increasingly fluid (the report was entitled 'The Navy at a Tipping Point: Maritime Dominance at Stake?'). It will involve a mixture of global competition (the United States and China, the rise of other emerging powers and the development of new geostrategic relationships and coalitions, and the continuing shift of economic, military, and diplomatic power from West to East), continuing chaos (terrorism, further failing states, and political fragmentation), and new and sometimes overlapping opportunities for co-operation (new global economic institutions and relationships, and a developing international legal framework).[4]

In a slightly different way, Professor Geoffrey Till has written of the future of sea power in terms of modernist and post-modernist navies. Defending the globalized system as expressed through the use of the sea is at the heart of both visions. But the modernists focus on a revival of nationalism and the threat of renewed inter-state rivalry. The post-modernists see more limited threats – such as terrorism and lawlessness at sea – which would not endanger the system as such, but rather its efficient working. Hence, the modernists see more need for continued high-end, high seas navies, while the post-modernists would argue that the focus should be more on the lower-end threats closer to shore. Likewise, the former would be motivated to act more by narrower national interests, the latter by a more co-operative desire to uphold the system as a whole.[5]

For the US Navy, as the sole superpower navy, there is no real choice but to take on the range of these challenges. The only question is how, since the US Navy itself acknowledges that it can no longer cover every eventuality without help and partnerships.

Obviously, for medium-sized and smaller navies, the calculations are rather different. They, or rather the governments of their respective states, can choose at what level they wish to contribute on the maritime front. Will it be to provide a full war-fighting capability and, if so, in what way? Or will it be a more limited, constabulary role? In other words, will it be a hard-power or essentially soft-power contribution? Is a mixture of a bit of each a feasible option on limited budgets, or will the end result of that be tokenism on both counts, and not enough of either? Some would argue that that is the trap into which the Royal Navy is in danger of falling, if it has not already.

Does a navy have merely regional aspirations, or global ones? How much does it wish to be able to exert influence on allies, or potential adversaries, or simply to offer capabilities to safeguard certain interests? Does it aspire to a leadership role within coalitions, or merely a supportive one? In an uncertain world, is it clear which capabilities would be most useful to which potential allies? And how would shaping a fleet to suit those goals fit in with national interests and objectives?

Whatever the choices that are made, the waters of the world's oceans look set to become choppier and more crowded.

CHAPTER FOUR

A Maritime Century?

In 2007, Professor Paul M. Kennedy, he of *The Rise and Fall of British Naval Mastery* fame (and of course *The Rise and Fall of the Great Powers*), observed what he described as a 'remarkable global disjuncture'. It involved, as he put it, 'massive differences in the assumptions of European nations and Asian nations about the significance of sea power, today and into the future'.[1]

This was, Kennedy observed, a mirror image of the events of the early fifteenth century when China, with an incomparable navy at the time that had crossed even to the eastern shores of Africa, turned its back on the sea. At that moment, Europe's mariners were reaching out to create dominions in a dynamic process that appeared to cement the idea of maritime power as a key to prosperity and global influence.

Not all is what it may seem in terms of the current trends. But the shifts – the relative fall of the European navies and the rise of Asian ones – are undeniable. And Asia's interest and investment in the maritime sphere is also extending well beyond just navies.

For many navalists, what beckons in the coming decades of the twenty-first century is the further embedding of the notion of the sea – or the maritime domain – as the true super-highway of the globalized world. Beyond that, trends in population growth and patterns of settlement, and energy and other resource demands, will both change the way the maritime environment is exploited and increase still further its significance.

Many of the bare statistics of the case have become familiar. The international shipping industry is responsible for carrying around 90 per cent of world trade. The trends in economic development and trade liberalization saw a four-fold increase in seaborne trade in the four decades from the beginning of the 1970s.[2]

Of course, the global economic downturn brought on by the financial crisis of 2008 had a huge impact on the global shipping industry and the demand for merchant shipping. But the expectation in the long term is for continued significant growth, in a world whose population is forecast to increase by another two billion to nine billion by 2050, and whose demand for energy is anticipated to double in that time.

The terms 'trade routes', or even the 'sea lines of communications' (SLOCs) that were such a familiar part of Cold War naval jargon, feel as if they are from bygone eras. And yet, from a naval perspective, the sea easily takes its place as one of the great enabling commons of the modern era, along with space and cyberspace. Human activity is moving offshore in the search for resources, and beginning to inhabit the maritime domain, or at least the shallow waters of the littorals, as never before. The Deep Water Horizon disaster in the Gulf of Mexico in April 2010 was just one stark illustration of one set of risks that that entails.

Even in traditional merchant shipping terms, the surge at sea has taken on very tangible form. In February 2011, the Maersk Line placed an order with South Korea's Daewoo shipbuilders to construct a fleet of the biggest-ever container ships, which should be the biggest ships afloat when they enter service. Dubbed 'Triple-E' ships (for economy of scale, energy efficiency, and environmentally improved), their scale – at 400 metres in length and with a capacity for 18,000 containers – is astonishing. The order was hailed as a signal that the shipping industry was emerging from the doldrums of recession, and that global trade was growing again. Other shipping lines are already following in the wake of this particular sign of resurgence and a further extension of the limits and scale of maritime trade.

Even more than that, this was another step in the relentless growth of ships, perhaps the most tangible, massive, and visibly impressive evidence of the potency of the driving power of global economic growth and the significance of seaborne trade as an enabler of that growth. Maybe the supertankers carrying crude oil have passed their peak, as has that energy source, but the liquefied natural gas carriers that are now the conveyor of so much of the world's energy resources are taking on an economic and strategic significance all of their own. And, just as the growth of the containers ships underscores the world's burgeoning appetite for the goods of Asia, and especially China, so the ballooning size of bulk ore carriers is evidence of China's and India's growing appetite for raw materials.

The motor of economic demand is also likely to increase not only the importance of the maritime domain but also its complexity, particularly along the oceans' shores. In 2007, the MoD's Development, Concepts, and Doctrine Centre (DCDC), produced a vision of maritime developments over the forthcoming couple of decades, under its director, Admiral Chris Parry:

The littoral regions of the world already contain the bulk of the world's population and human activity. The next 20 years are likely to see a massive increase in urbanisation and settlement in the littoral regions (including into the sea), as well as a substantial proliferation of artificial structures, energy farms, power generators, and aquaculture. Gas and oil pipelines and port facilities are also likely to increase in complexity and footprint. As well as the consequences of climate change, the effects of extreme weather and other natural events will also impact heavily on heavily-populated and developed littoral regions ...

The high seas, the deep ocean, and the Polar regions are likely to become areas of increased competition as advanced technology, increased accessibility, and resource pressure encourage more intensive exploitation by states and commercial interests. Competition will centre on fishing, deep sea mining, and the extraction of oil and gas, but may possibly extend to transportation and rights of passage.[3]

To add one other detail to the maritime picture, the sea has become a massively busier environment for human recreation. In 1996, for the first time, a cruise liner exceeded the gross tonnage of the Cunard Line's former transatlantic ocean liner RMS *Queen Elizabeth*, ending that ship's reign of five-and-a-half decades as the world's largest passenger vessel (although the liner herself foundered in a fire in Hong Kong in 1972). In the years since, dozens of cruise liners larger than the old Cunarder have been built, in an unprecedented explosion of construction to supply a transformed market in the pursuit of leisure at sea.

So the significance of the sea to human activity is destined to increase further, as probably will the competition in, and the congestion and complexity of, the maritime environment. But what does that really mean from a strategic point of view? Where and how are threats at sea likely to emerge? And how will they fit into the other potential stresses and strains in the international system? Are they more likely to be limited asymmetric disruptions to the smooth working of the maritime network, or more challenging big-power stand-offs for larger stakes? The DCDC analysis under Admiral Parry clearly leant towards the latter in terms of the weight of risks. Others are not so sure.

And precisely because it will be an even more interconnected and complex world, the calculation over how much individual nations should invest in policing the oceans, or projecting power on and from them, is far from self-evident. Virtually all developed trading nations may have a stake at sea, but none will be able to secure that stake by their own means alone. Even the United States' admittedly much-criticized 2007 Maritime Strategy places a huge emphasis on co-operation, and not just between nations and navies but also a whole range of other international entities.

With the definition of security now seemingly so elastic, and potential threats so diverse, judging what precautions to take for a nation to feel at least moderately safe at sea has become more complicated. The basic facts of geography may mean that the points of vulnerability of the maritime network may be largely unchanging. There are the two strategic canal routes, Panama and Suez, the chokepoints of the English Channel, the Straits of Gibraltar, the Red Sea, the Straits of Hormuz and the Malacca Straits, and the two Cape routes. But their relative importance shifts with the changes in the balance of power and economic activity.

Clearly, to follow up on Professor Kennedy's observation, for Europe, for some time, immediate threats at sea have appeared limited, albeit with a potential to cause some disruption. The preoccupation with the transatlantic bridge has been fading for a while. The potential for instability across and through the Mediterranean may be growing, and require added precautions. There has been the particular disruption caused by piracy in the Somali basin and the Indian Ocean, which has provoked a limited, co-operative response. The most tangible and looming maritime threat from Europe's perspective has been that of a major confrontation with Iran, which would close the Straits of Hormuz. And that would clearly be an issue that would engage the United States and most other major powers as well. So Europe's practical ability to influence events in such a situation would be far from clear. Otherwise, from a European perspective, the threats to the maritime trade routes may look more latent and theoretical rather than actual. And even where they might be brewing, they have appeared geographically rather remote.

But that may be changing. First, climate change and the opening up of the Arctic, its possible resources and potential sea routes, have between them produced a flurry of edgy concern and excitement. Assessing the true strategic significance of these developments, and ensuring orderly adjustment to the possibilities that they may offer, will require attention. Whether they really raise the spectre of some kind of new 'cold war', requiring significant military and particularly naval precautions to be taken, is another matter. But these waters are in many cases contested. The same is true of the potential new northern sea routes which could cut more than a third of the distance off voyages from Europe to the Far East. And there are other ways in which Asia suddenly seems far less remote from Europe, as the pendulum swing of economic power to the east has suddenly accelerated.

For most Europeans, the sea and its routes had really come to be seen not essentially in security terms as an arena of risk. Instead, they had become much more conduits for projecting whatever limited power and influence European countries – individually or collectively – might wish to apply. Now that perception of risk may be changing. There is also a realization that the tide of power projection might just be starting to flow in the opposite direction. For the first time in 2011, a Chinese warship ventured into the Mediterranean to support the evacuation of Chinese citizens from Libya.

The International Institute for Strategic Studies (IISS) sees 'persuasive evidence that a global redistribution of military power is under way'.[4] From the Middle East, through the Indian Ocean, and into the western Pacific, significant military investments have been underway. And, as Professor Kennedy suggested, a large proportion of those investments are focused on the maritime sphere. Perceptions of growing Chinese military power and assertiveness may be among the key drivers, but there are many other interlocking regional dynamics as well.

It is here where there is the most volatile mix of increased competition for resources, plus neighbourhood frictions and an increasing struggle for influence. The increasingly obvious tensions in the western Pacific have been a special focus of attention. But, in the mix of dynamic change, the Indian Ocean too is becoming a strategic link which could be increasingly contested. Its sea lanes will only grow in importance, and with them the choke points that are the funnels of trade to and from Europe and East Asia. Complicating the picture in this arena will be the continuing conflicts and tensions which have been a source of prolonged instability on its edges, in Afghanistan, along the southern edge of the Arabian Peninsula, and in the Horn of Africa. Here, too, the manoeuvring for dominance is well under way. And, of course, the ripple effects go farther, down the eastern coast of Africa and around the ever more significant Cape of Good Hope into the southern Atlantic and across to South America.

What may be developing into something like a modern-day arms race may be dismissed as the pursuit of national pride and prestige. But this investment is still a strategic reality. Europe, including Britain, may not yet have made up its mind about the extent to which it wants to involve itself in the new dynamics of Asia, including the maintenance of maritime order, let alone the potential flashpoints of the Korean peninsula, Taiwan, and the South and East China Seas. But crises on any of these fronts could potentially produce the equivalent of a strategic tsunami, and at the very least would have serious effects on the international trading system. Any decision either to have influence or to be able to offer anything other than token intervention, at least in terms of hard power, to sway the strategic balance, deter conflict, or affect the outcome of any confrontation, will surely require serious maritime capabilities.

As it is, Europe occupies an uncertain place in the global naval stakes. Fleet sizes have shrunk dramatically. They are likely to do so further as the fallout from the financial and economic turmoil of the global recession – which has hit large parts of Europe especially hard – continues to be felt. And yet European navies have continued to make forays farther afield, and have most notably sustained a large part of the international counter-piracy deployment off the Horn of Africa. The various leading fleets also have between them a reasonable collection of quite modern vessels for limited power projection, task forces operations, and maritime patrol, as they have each transformed themselves in subtly different ways from their Cold War days.

It is arguable that, as a result of the decision made in the 2010 SDSR, Britain decisively passed naval leadership in Europe to France, at least for a while. The Royal Navy would contest that, pointing to key advantages still in, for example, SSNs. But others would point to the French Navy's nuclear-powered aircraft carrier, its three helicopter carriers, and a mix of destroyers, frigates, and corvettes, which many would argue should be a model for the Royal Navy.

Apart from numbers of destroyers and frigates, perhaps the starkest shift in the European naval stakes has been in large aviation ships. For years, the British and French had the strongest forces of such vessels, between two and three each, different but roughly equivalent. The Italians and Spanish had one mini-carrier per navy. Now, the Royal Navy will soon be down to just one such vessel for a while at least (without any fixed-wing aircraft), while the new French force of four such vessels might yet be joined by a fifth, and the Italians and Spanish have two each.

But, wherever the balance of the argument lies over European naval leadership, the stronger case is that this is strategically of much less relevance than it has been for a century. The similarities of the British and French navies will matter more in the future than their differences. The key benchmark navies of the future will be elsewhere, and how the Royal Navy will relate to them – either individually or with its European neighbours – will be a large part of what matters in terms of its strategic significance. Will either the British or the French, let alone any other Europeans, be able to keep up with and compete with those emerging major maritime powers?

Setting aside the US Navy for a moment, the two key fleets are those of China and India, and most particularly Beijing's. As the US Navy of the early twenty-first century is to what the Royal Navy was at the beginning of the twentieth, so the Chinese navy is to the navy of Imperial Germany. That is not to say for a moment that an armed confrontation is inevitable. But the attention being focused on the growing Chinese fleet by the rest of the world – and particularly by the current leading naval power – is of a similar order.

So much has been written and discussed already about the rise of China and its navy. The topics fill more and more pages of the US Naval Institute Proceedings. For both nation and navy, the transformation in the past two decades has been dramatic. On the global scale, China does not come close to matching the United States either economically or militarily, and its potential on both fronts, while huge, remains uncertain.

However, the nature of China's naval development is already forcing Washington to recalculate strategically, and that is already having and will have a ripple effect both around the region and beyond. And such is the psychosis now surrounding the rise of China economically, politically, and strategically – and, indeed, surrounding debates over relative US decline and vulnerability – that the region seems almost on a knife-edge already.

China insists that its military modernization is not directed at, and does not represent a threat, to any other country. And it may not be building a navy to mirror that of the United States. But it is building a maritime capability that could potentially neutralize the US Navy in the western Pacific and Washington's ability to project power into the region, and therefore raise doubts in the minds of all those regional states which have sheltered or would expect to shelter under the US security umbrella. It is also a navy and maritime capability that will, over time, give Beijing an increasing ability to project its own power. And it has already started practising that art. Add to that a sense in the region of growing Chinese diplomatic assertiveness and, again, the strategic dynamics could be changing quite rapidly.

At one level, China's naval growth is both natural and logical, with a massively long coastline, but more importantly its mounting needs for energy, metals, and other strategic materials. That is a classic impulse to greater naval strength, to protect access to such necessities, as well as to spread influence and find markets. But such developments have invariably challenged established orders. If the United States has been the indispensible nation, China is becoming the unavoidable one. For everyone, that means a complex set of relationships with Beijing. The United States insists that it does not see China as an adversary. But it remains concerned about the extent and nature of its ambitions. China says that it is in favour of a stable, orderly international system. But not necessarily the current one, with the existing values. China, in its efforts to grow and develop, has been described as an 'uber-realist power',[5] and that surely promises frictions of one sort or another.

In such a fluid and frankly somewhat fraught atmosphere, relatively minor incidents take on greater significance. And there have been no shortage of those, which have reverberated around the region: the theatrical surfacing of a Chinese submarine in the midst of the USS *Kitty Hawk*'s carrier battle group in the waters off Japan in October 2006. Beijing's increased assertiveness over its claims in the South China Sea; the way it faced down Tokyo in 2010 after Japan arrested the captain of a Chinese fishing vessel for ramming a Japanese patrol vessel, close to the disputed Shenkaku/Diaoyu islands in the East China Sea; and the fact that China chose to carry out its first test flight of a prototype stealth fighter in January 2011, while US Defence Secretary Robert Gates was visiting Beijing.

Of perhaps greatest strategic significance in terms of the Chinese naval build-up so far has been its force of submarines, already topping seventy boats. This includes a growing number of SSNs, the sophisticated and quiet Song class of conventionally-powered submarines, and the Russian-designed Kilo class of SSKs. The Chinese navy also now comprises nearly eighty major surface warships. Between them, these submarine and surface forces include in their armoury very potent Russian-designed SS-N-22 and SS-N-27 anti-ship missiles, giving them already a significant A2/AD capability.

What has provoked most agitated debate, however, has been the status of China's DF-21 'carrier-killer' anti-ship ballistic missile. How close is it to being operational? And to what extent does it represent a 'game-changer', at the very least forcing the US Navy to think twice about deploying its carrier strike groups?

All these capabilities – plus a large flotilla of missile-armed fast attack craft – give Beijing a significant capacity to flex its muscles close to home. That has significant implications for key disputes like that over Taiwan, and for the security of strategic SLOCs running through the region. The announcement in May 2011 that it is to boost the size and capability of its marine surveillance fleet was another signal of its increasing attention on the sea.[6]

The other development that has been making most waves in the region and beyond has been China's long-suspected ambition to deploy its own aircraft carriers. In December 2010, the Financial Times reported final official Chinese confirmation – in an obscure maritime planning document – of a programme to build a carrier.[7] It had hardly been the best-kept of secrets.

The speculation mounted in the early months of 2011 that, finally, China's first carrier was about to emerge. In 1998, Beijing had purchased from Ukraine the incomplete hulk of the Soviet-era carrier *Varyag*. The Chinese had been tinkering with the ship for more than a decade, slowly modifying and equipping her for service. She reportedly was renamed the *Shi Lang*, after a seventeenth-century Chinese admiral who conquered Taiwan, and set sail on preliminary sea trials in August 2011.

The *Shi Lang* herself is a potent symbol rather than a sensational new capability. She is likely to be used mainly for experimentation and training in the techniques of carrier aviation. One second-hand, worked-over, experimental carrier hardly equates to eleven established carrier strike groups. It will be years before China will be able to deploy a carrier operationally. But the direction of travel seems clear. Because of what carriers represent the world over, embarking on the carrier path is very tangible reinforcement of the message that China is intent on acquiring big-power status.

The steps that the Chinese navy has taken already to extend its reach have provoked enough interest. The most noteworthy deployment, on the counter-piracy mission in the Gulf of Aden, commenced in December 2008. It has been conducted in a co-operative spirit with the other nations present. It has also shown up some serious shortcomings. There were other notable formation deployments beyond China's strategic 'first island chain' in 2010.

But, for those who have been keeping a watchful eye on China's spreading influence, it has been what has been labelled its 'string of pearls' strategy that could have the most repercussions in the near future. Beijing's financing of port developments in Pakistan, Sri Lanka, Bangladesh, and Myanmar looks like an initiative to help secure both its supply lines and its diplomatic leverage out into the Indian Ocean, looping around the shores of India. And the Indian government, for one, does not like what it sees in this development.

And this is where the latent maritime ambitions of one emerging great power start nudging against those of another. China and India seem destined to share and affect, and maybe increase, each other's growing pains, and this will in turn have an impact on the rest of the region and beyond. India's vision of itself as a maritime power of growing weight is hardly hidden. India has been bolstering its own maritime outposts on the remote Andaman and Nicobar island archipelago. It has been boosting its ties with the African states on the Indian Ocean's western rim[8], in part as a counter to Chinese influence there. And, as China has raised its naval profile in the Indian Ocean, so India has stepped up activities in East Asia with the likes of Singapore and Vietnam.[9]

For some years, the Indian navy's warship construction programme has seemed like the stuff of dreams for most other naval powers around the world, with – at various points – some thirty-plus vessels under construction. But it has had its share of teething troubles too, not least with its most ambitious programmes. The navy's efforts to create a modern and significant aircraft carrier capability have been especially fraught and protracted. The purchase of the much-modified ex-Russian navy carrier *Admiral Gorshkov*, to be called INS *Vikramaditya*, has been a troubled affair, with delays and cost increases. So too has India's effort to build its first indigenous aircraft carrier. A ship of about 40,000 tons, construction started in 2006, and it may be ready some time between 2015 and 2020. So the Indian navy has struggled on with the veteran INS *Viraat*, formerly HMS *Hermes*, with a dwindling number of Sea Harriers.

There have also been delays in India's submarine plans, both in terms of modernizing its conventional-powered force, including with new and sophisticated French-designed Scorpene-class boats, and in getting a nuclear-powered force properly under way. It will be some time before the reality of India's maritime strength catches up with its vision. But the navy's trajectory towards becoming one of the great fleets of the twenty-first century seems pretty clear.

These developments in China and India would be noteworthy enough in themselves. But they are just part of – and in part are the catalysts for – much wider maritime stirrings. In late 2010, Japan carried out a long-overdue overhaul of its defence strategy, switching from a northern focus that was a hangover from Cold War worries about the Soviet Union to a more southerly one mindful of China, the potential for instability on the Korean peninsula, and concerns about the security of its southern offshore islands and main trade and supply routes.

It reinforced its maritime outlook. The only significant enhancement was in submarine numbers, to be boosted from sixteen to twenty-two. But Japan already has a sizeable surface force of nearly fifty warships, and their capabilities have been increased significantly. As well as its impressive force of Aegis-equipped destroyers capable of ballistic missile defence, its sea control flotillas are being bolstered with a new breed of mini-carriers. In an echo of the Royal Navy's initial description of its Invincible-class carriers as 'through-deck cruisers', these 18,000-ton vessels with full-length flight decks are described as 'helicopter-carrying destroyers'. A larger, 24,000-ton version is on the way.

The South Korean navy has also been turning itself into a significant regional blue-water force on the back of its now-formidable maritime industrial base. Its surface flotillas now comprise an impressive collection of destroyers, the largest of which – at 10,000 tons – are the equivalent of heavy cruisers of the Second World War. They are equipped with the Aegis combat system, and are bigger than anything similar in any other navy save that of the United States. The South Korean navy has also taken delivery of a 19,000-ton amphibious assault carrier. And it has been building up a formidable submarine force, with the latest design of conventionally-powered boats with air independent propulsion (AIP) to extend their range of operations.

The sinking in March 2010 of the South Korean corvette, *Cheonan*, apparently in an attack by the North, further focused attention on the maritime element of security and stability in and around the Korean peninsula. Whether or not the attack was an act of deliberate policy, it further underlined the potential volatility of the region. The responses to the incident also emphasized the maritime nature of the strategic and diplomatic dance that is being played out. The United States ostentatiously despatched an aircraft carrier, the USS *George Washington*, to show solidarity with Seoul. Beijing complained, and held tit-for-tat manoeuvres of its own.

All around the region, there is further evidence of a maritime scene that is stirring significantly. Vietnam, Malaysia, and Singapore have all announced naval plans including the purchase of new submarines. Indeed, it has been estimated that the nations of the region will be purchasing up to ninety submarines over the next decade.[10]

The other country in the region which has attracted most attention for its strategic statement of intent has been Australia. Its 2009 Defence White Paper set out an avowedly maritime strategy to respond to the changes that it is observing in the region. Of course, Australia faces a unique set of circumstances, including one of the three largest maritime jurisdictions in the world (along with the United States and France). But the strategic course that it has set out on over the next two decades is noteworthy, not least from the perspective of Whitehall.

First, it was initially driven from the highest political level by the then Australian Prime Minister, Kevin Rudd. Secondly, it should see a significant enhancement of the Royal Australian Navy's capabilities by 2030. There will be two new, 27,000-ton amphibious assault carriers, advanced air warfare destroyers, new frigates, a new class of oceangoing patrol vessels, and – most significantly – a plan eventually to double the size of the submarine force with twelve new, larger, and longer-range boats. Thirdly, and perhaps most strikingly for the Royal Navy, this maritime strategy is one that seems to have been embraced across the Australian defence establishment, and indeed relies on a joint approach.

Whether this will all come to pass is another matter, but it has certainly put Australia firmly back on the strategic map in the region. The Australian model is also clearly designed to be complementary to and compatible with US forces, in the context of the unfolding Asia-Pacific strategic scene. And that, as well as the broader picture at sea, hinges crucially on how the United States views its maritime future.

There are other actors on the maritime stage whose future roles are uncertain, but potentially significant. One is Russia. Moscow retains big-power pretensions and a mercurial political leadership. The plan to buy four French-designed Mistral-class amphibious helicopter carriers will significantly increase the Russian navy's amphibious capability. That has provoked considerable unease in Russia's neighbours on the Baltic and Black Seas, as well as elsewhere in NATO. But some of the ships could equally be deployed to the Pacific, where Moscow clearly still feels that it has a significant stake.

Whether this presages the long-promised revival of Russia's general naval fortunes is another matter. Its naval activity has certainly revived in recent years. It is still potentially a major player, with more than thirty major warships, including the aircraft carrier *Admiral Kuznetsov*, and more than forty submarines, not counting ballistic-missile-carrying boats. But the fleet is still reliant on major vessels from the Cold War. Ambitious talk of a major new carrier programme seems to have been just rhetoric. Modernization is proceeding slowly.

In Europe's south-eastern corner, commanding access to the Black Sea, bordering on Asia, and in a crowded, tinderbox neighbourhood around the eastern shores of the Mediterranean, Turkey is another country quietly establishing its maritime credentials. Another potentially significant player on the move in another region of growing interest and importance is Brazil. It has long-term plans for a major submarine force, including nuclear-powered boats, as well as plans to modernize its surface fleet which have attracted the interest of numerous potential international suppliers. At Africa's southern tip, the South African navy is showing its potential to become a regional force of note in a strategic location.

Against the backdrop of all of this, the US Navy remains peerless at sea. Again, as the then US Defence Secretary, Robert Gates, pointedly observed, in tonnage terms the US battle fleet exceeds that of the next thirteen navies combined, of which eleven are US allies, and in terms of missile firepower outmatches the next twenty largest navies.[11] Gates was gently scolding the US Navy for being preoccupied with its shrunken numbers.

It is this perspective on US maritime predominance that has been one of the greatest challenges to the Royal Navy and its supporters in making a case for stronger British maritime capabilities. Why, the sceptics ask, does the Royal Navy need carriers of its own, or even nuclear-powered submarines, when they are most likely to be used in situations in which the United States will also be involved, and has such vessels in abundance? Why not just leave it to the Americans?

That is not the perspective of either country's naval establishments. The question, rather, may be whether the US Navy will be there in the coming decades? Can it from now on be relied upon always to be the maritime shield of last resort?

Just as a matter of statistical comparison, two new Royal Navy aircraft carriers – should both become operational – would represent a larger fraction of current US capabilities (ten or eleven carriers in all) than British land forces amount to relative to their US counterparts (108,000 versus 840,000). Of course, the political value of British 'boots on the ground' to successive US administrations in recent conflicts has been significant. But so, too, have been the costs to the United Kingdom. And, in the light of Robert Gates' remarks at West Point about Washington's future maritime and air focus, 'ships at sea' may become a more valuable strategic currency in Washington than those boots.

What is more, much of the debate on US maritime power in the United States itself is tinged with alarm, despair, and a sense of crisis, almost on a par with that surrounding the arguments over the state of the Royal Navy. Many of the points aired in the US debate echo those that have been constantly rehearsed in the United Kingdom, albeit that the forces at issue are of an altogether different scale, as are the US Navy's missions and global responsibilities.

Relentless articles, chiefly from the Right, have decried what is seen as a dangerous slump in US maritime power. No one in this camp, or in the US Navy's own senior ranks, sees ten or eleven aircraft carriers as plenty, even if the rest of the world does. Hence the talk of a navy at the tipping point. Yes, the US Navy is unique, but so too are its responsibilities and breadth of tasks. It has never, in recent decades, felt more under pressure or undervalued.

Equally, attacks from other quarters citing the costs of new carriers, SSNs, and indeed the Navy's whole shipbuilding programme, have grown louder. Again, American admirals, like their British counterparts, are accused of not having updated their thinking since the Second World War. These complaints will only grow in the era of austerity. The storm front of potentially hundreds of billions of dollars of defence cuts by the early 2020s is beginning to hit home. Significant defence programmes will be in the line of fire for cancellation, some of them close to the US Navy's heart. This atmosphere has only sharpened the debates within the US naval community over the relative merits of carriers and cruise missiles, Aegis-equipped cruisers and Littoral Combat Ships (LCSs), or amphibious forces versus UAVs.

When it emerged in 2007, the US naval establishment's new vision for twenty-first century sea power attempted to show that the US military maritime services – the US Navy, Marine Corps, and Coast Guard – were responsive to the perceived new security environment. To the traditional core US naval tasks of forward presence, deterrence, sea control, and power projection, it added maritime security and humanitarian assistance and disaster response. But many saw in the strategy's emphasis on co-operation, coalitions, and partnership an admission of essential weakness and vulnerability. Even the mighty US Navy was unable to undertake alone such a wide range of tasks unaided.

At the heart of much of the debate has been controversy over the chances, and indeed the advisability, of the US Navy achieving its declared goal of rebuilding its diminished battle fleet to a force of 313 vessels. The more than 600 warships of the 1960s dwindled through the 1970s. The fleet approached 600 ships in the Reagan build-up through the 1980s. It had slipped to around 280 in 2010. Much of the blame for many of the difficulties that the US Navy has encountered in making headway towards its goal have been laid firmly at its own door, for its failures of planning and acquisition.

One response by the United States to the challenges that it faces has been to get the US Navy and the US Air Force to explore a new AirSea Battle

Concept, to see how they can combine to take on the most demanding threats, like the growing A2/AD capabilities of China.

By itself, though, that is not going to be enough. The proliferation of modern submarines and advanced anti-ship missiles across Asia, combined with the even more towering concerns for the United States over its economic competitiveness and international indebtedness, will force tough choices on Washington. The CNA's tipping point report offered a numbered of options for the US Navy's future make-up, in order to sustain its influence, including prioritizing areas of operation at the expense of others, and reshaping the fleet to concentrate on high-end operations at the expense of maritime presence – choices that, at a lower level, the Royal Navy has been forced to address.

In the evolving strategic picture, the land, air, space, and cyberspace will remain vital domains. The drivers of climate change, population growth, and economic demand will lead to dramatic changes in the landscape. But it is the seascape that is likely to be most affected, and where there could be the greatest change, driven by the added factor of great strategic shift. The rise of China, and the Asian century, may not materialize in the way now so widely predicted. The current rates of growth in the region may be unsustainable. But this will produce its own set of frictions. And it all adds to a challenge for a country like the United Kingdom, if it wishes to exert influence over whether the international scene will be more chaotic, competitive, or co-operative. And for the Royal Navy, if it is to play the part that it believes it can and should.

CHAPTER FIVE

New Ship Shapes and Technology Horizons

In 1906, the advent of the first modern all-big-gun battleship, HMS *Dreadnought*, revolutionized naval thinking. The ship was conceived by the radical First Sea Lord at the time, Admiral Sir John 'Jackie' Fisher. And, while the basic idea for such a ship may have originated elsewhere and been around for a while, part of the impact of *Dreadnought* was that her design and construction were completed within two years, and by its actions the Royal Navy decisively grabbed the initiative in the global naval race that was under way.

Dreadnought herself was quickly overtaken as the race unfolded. And the reign of the dreadnought battleship as queen of the seas was also a relatively brief one, lasting barely three-and-a-half decades. Its supremacy was literally blown apart in the crucible of the Second World War, as the giants of the age succumbed in one way or another to the threats from below the surface or, more definitively, from the air – *Bismarck*, *Arizona*, *Prince of Wales*, *Tirpitz*, *Yamato*, and *Musashi*, to name only some of the most prominent. In contrast, the battleship's successor, the aircraft carrier, or more particularly the US Navy's unique fleet of super-carriers, has enjoyed uncontested supremacy at sea now for more than sixty-five years. And, judging by shipbuilding schedules, the mainstream of thought in the US Navy does not see that changing for decades to come.

But many see that longevity as an historical illusion. When Japan signed the surrender on the quarterdeck of the battleship USS *Missouri* on 15 August 1945, in Tokyo Bay, to bring the Second World War to a close, it marked the end of the last conflict in which general naval forces were engaged in a general war.

The carriers' proponents point out that no weapons have been successfully launched against any carrier since the Second World War. Their detractors argue that that is irrelevant, since there has been no confrontation of the kind for which the ships were primarily designed. They are, so the argument goes, hugely expensive white elephants, designed to carry equally expensive aeroplanes, and are massively vulnerable to the latest exotica of advanced anti-ship missiles, and the US Navy in particular will get a shock one day.

Of course, navies have not been idle. Western naval forces did what navies traditionally do in terms of applying deterrence effect and exerting strategic influence during the Cold War. And they took part in limited actions throughout that period. The Falklands War was, of course, a naval action in large part, and perhaps the most significant of the missile age so far. But it was of a very particular kind, involving forces of a specific character and capability. It had painful lessons for both sides involved. But they were more in terms of particular equipment shortfalls for the navies concerned than as general principles.

The Falklands War spurred a flurry of public debate about what it said about the fundamental vulnerability of surface ships in the era of precision-guided weaponry. After the shock of the destroyer HMS *Sheffield* succumbing to an air-launched Exocet anti-ship missile attack, a Newsweek magazine article at the time posed the question in its headline: 'Are Big Warships Doomed?'[1] That particular event and the conflict more generally were certainly a rude awakening for the Royal Navy in terms of some of its own weaknesses and vulnerabilities, and some of the assumptions that it had made about the design of its ships. The US Navy, in contrast, appeared in large part comforted, reassured that the breadth and scale of its capabilities, and the more generous design of many of its ships, would have avoided the alarms and reverses that the Royal Navy suffered. Whether the events in the South Atlantic were really much of a guide for either country's naval establishments about how their forces would have fared in a full-on encounter with Soviet naval and air forces in the North Atlantic is another matter.

There have been serial naval skirmishes and incidents since then, notably in the Persian Gulf. Naval forces have had significant parts to play in the conflicts with Iraq, operations in the Balkans, and particularly the early stages of the conflict in Afghanistan (with US naval air power continuing to have a significant part to play subsequently as well). The United States has regularly employed its carriers in particular to make points in limited actions around the globe.

But revolutions in missile technology, electronics, computing power, and communications have unfolded, and the global Cold War stand-off has given way to an uncertain and seemingly rather less stable new world order, without most of the naval technology at sea and in service around the world ever having been truly tested in the circumstances for which it was primarily developed. In many ways, designers are rather in the dark about how the ships and weapons that they have created, and are conceiving now, would perform in major combat, or indeed in a range of future, rather unpredictable scenarios in which they may be called upon to act. They have their theories and models, but little real experience. The same is also true for those charged with devising tactics and doctrine, and deciding the make-up of fleets.

Of course, major navies regularly conduct elaborate and supposedly realistic exercises. There is any amount of computer-generated assistance available in the modelling process now. And the basic designs of warships, and how they stand up to the harsh basic environment in which they operate, are being tested in the routine of operations around the world. But the passage of the decades has also left much fertile ground for debating the effectiveness of warships and their weapons, those inevitable calculations and trade-offs between such factors as sophistication and numbers, reliability and redundancy, and speed and sustainability.

It all also makes the major navies and those who run them easier targets for the detractors. When naval fleets look at least superficially very similar to those that have gone before, it is simpler – in the absence of the example of recent major naval warfare – to deride admirals as living in the past. It also makes it more difficult to discern the merits of any potential technological leaps that might be out there, on the horizon or just over it, which might dramatically alter the calculations about what navies – and particularly the Royal Navy – might look like in the future. Is there an equivalent of a *Dreadnought* out there, which could change the naval game?

One key point about the world into which HMS *Dreadnought* was born in 1906 was that there was a very focused strategic concern, and a very specific set of questions for the Royal Navy about how it was to maintain its position in the world. *Dreadnought* provided a technical answer to some of those questions, a new type of battleship that would make those that existed already immediately inferior and obsolescent.

But such conditions currently do not exist. There is no overwhelmingly clear strategic imperative. Instead there are endless debates about how enduring the current threats from terrorism and failing states will be and how to respond to them in the future, and whether and how the spectre of strategic competition between the United States and China might take solid form. Recent trends towards maritime operations in the littorals, with a focus on basic patrolling, have led to an emphasis on producing smaller, simpler vessels, hopefully in larger numbers. But will that be sustained? Could events, having changed direction in one way following the end of the Cold War, change again? There is at least flickering evidence that they are already. Clearly, major navies continue to plan for the possibility of renewed operations of a more challenging nature against more sophisticated foes. But have they got the balance of investment right? What, in fact, are the pressing and precise questions to which a new *Dreadnought* might provide the answer?

The major navies have certainly become more thinly spread as warship numbers have declined, and they have had to look at ways of compensating for this. The factors driving ship design have evolved, with cost becoming an even more pressing one, but issues of adaptability, sustainability, crew accommodation, and environmental impact have all imposed themselves. And, of course, there is the technological change in terms of information, computing, sensors, and weapons.

The environment has certainly become more complex, and that is a trend that is unlikely to be reversed. The numbers and types of potential threats that major navies face have been expanding. In coastal areas, fast attack craft which could be manned or unmanned, and may be increasingly stealthy, could engage in 'swarm' attacks and be used essentially as floating improvised explosive devices (IEDs), as with the attack on the USS *Cole* in the port of Aden in 2001. There could be the increased use of guerrilla-style attacks against ships themselves, or in ports and against targets ashore, as in the attack on the Indian city of Mumbai in November 2008.

Mines are an old threat, but have become attractive again. The submarine challenge to naval formations has proliferated, even as the anti-submarine skills and capabilities of established navies have dwindled away. Modern conventionally-powered submarines are exceptionally quiet, have become significantly more sophisticated, and can deploy a much greater range of potent weaponry. And the shallow waters in which navies have increasingly been operating of late are exceptionally challenging for the conduct of anti-submarine warfare. Mini-subs are also looking increasingly attractive to both state and non-state actors. Just how navies are able to cope with such threats will dictate how the constantly shifting balance between offensive and defensive capabilities unfolds, and how the A2/AD war of nerves develops.

There is the missile question. The Royal Navy – and others – learned from its bitter Exocet experience in the Falklands War. But the missile game has also moved on substantially. Modern weapons make the Exocets used in the Falklands look like fireworks in comparison.

Among the most daunting is the Russian-made SS-N-22 'Sunburn', in service with China and India, and capable of Mach 2–3, compared to the subsonic Exocet. There is the similarly fast Russian/Indian Brahmos, with a hypersonic version capable of Mach 6 reportedly on the way. And there is the SS-N-27 'Sizzler', whose supersonic final sprint to its target and extreme terminal zigzag manoeuvres have provoked intense debate as to whether there is indeed any defensive system that can stop it.

The real attention grabber, though, has been China's DF-21D/CSS-5 long-range anti-ship ballistic missile, the 'carrier killer'. It has a range of more than 900 miles, and hypersonic speed. But is it a game-changer? Has the game moved on sufficiently that China has been able to overcome the tracking and targeting hurdles that defeated Soviet efforts to develop a similar anti-carrier weapon? The US Navy is certainly concerned, but insists it is not going to change its fundamental operational plans. The debate has been heated. The sceptics argue that the issue is not of one weapon against one ship, but of a whole array of defences against a system that will have its own vulnerabilities, including its detection and guidance systems.

Carriers have never been quite the sitting ducks that the detractors suggest. But equally, the more resources that have to be put into defences, the more costly the projection of power by sea becomes. The defence-versus-offence battle goes on.

Beyond all that potential pyrotechnics, there are also those much-talked-about asymmetric threats in space and cyberspace. How much might they threaten the asymmetric advantages of established navies in communications, sensors, and networking? Will they force a change in the direction of naval warfare in the future, a back to basics approach perhaps?

One of the great topics of debate always, of course, is the actual shape of future warships, and whether radical new hull forms offer a way forward. In the aftermath of the Cold War, as the Royal Navy began to contemplate the requirements for its next generation of frigates, it seemed almost self-consciously determined to demonstrate a break with the past. Many of the design concepts that were published featured concepts with unconventional hulls, particularly trimarans.

Among the notional advantages of trimarans are better sea-keeping and lower costs, and greater upper deck space for helicopter flight decks and hangars. The MoD even commissioned a trimaran trials ship, the *Triton*, ordered in 1998, launched in 2000, and operated until it was sold in 2005.

The very existence of the *Triton* suggested that the option of an unconventional hull shape for future warships was taken seriously. But, at least in Royal Navy terms, interest has subsided. The new generation of frigates looks set to have a largely conventional hull form.

In the US Navy, however, developments progressed further. Whether they will prove any more successful may be more open to doubt. But, during the 1990s, thinking started on a new design of warship which, for a time, looked as if it might just make all other vessels of its type seem obsolete, rather as *Dreadnought* had done.

The DDG-1000 Zumwalt class began life as the DD-21 project, or a destroyer for the twenty-first century. In November 2001, it was re-designated DD(X) before it became DDG-1000 in April 2006. The programme aimed to produce a ship that could fill the specific gap in naval gunfire capability that was left when the last battleships finally retired in the 1990s. It was also intended to be able to operate in dangerous littoral areas. But, crucially, it would deliberately be used to introduce several new technologies, including much greater automation, and thus open the way to a dramatically reduced crew size of 142. That is less than half the number on existing destroyers, on a ship that would be substantially bigger.

Its appearance was certainly going to be radically different, in a rather 'back to the future' sort of way. The striking shape of the DDG-1000 includes a new hull form with tumblehome sides and a wave-piercing bow meant to reduce the radar signature. It recalls the design of old ironclads with their ram bows. There is also a massive block-like superstructure, like a steel citadel, again for stealth reasons. There is a new design of propulsion, integrated electric drive, to help provide massively more power to run a host of new systems and weapons. There is an advanced gun system, and a new concept for missile installation, distributed about the ship rather than in one magazine to improve survivability.

Taken together, all these attributes add up to a vessel that has the appearance almost of a comic-book fantasy of a future warship. And yet the hope that it might be the shape of things to come currently looks like a forlorn one. On the contrary, it may for now be a dead end in design. It could turn out to be a lesson that too many radical ideas in vessels whose mission had become confused are not a recipe for success, let alone ground-breaking change.

The US Navy had originally hoped to build thirty-two DDG-1000s. As costs spiralled to more than US $3 billion per ship, and questions were raised about aspects of its capabilities and whether some of the design's new technologies really worked, the programme was eventually reduced to just three vessels. Maybe the alarms should have been sounded earlier over the viability of a new destroyer design that would end up at close to 15,000 tons.

Instead the US Navy has decided to revert to new orders for admittedly heavily-modified versions of its Arleigh Burke-class destroyers, a design dating back to the 1970s. In its desire to make a technological leap, and actually overreaching, the US Navy may end up having to take a step back.

The other focus of radical ship design has been the US Navy's Littoral Combat Ship (LCS) programme. The Navy had been carrying out studies on possible future small warship designs as far back as the 1980s. But the LCS really grew out of an idea championed by the Pentagon's former transformation guru, the late Vice Admiral Arthur Cebrowski, for what was dubbed the 'streetfighter', a vessel – or rather a family of vessels – that would be able to operate and survive in the crowded and dangerous offshore waters of the littoral, or – as he put it – 'baby-sit in the petri-dish of festering problems we have around the world'.[2]

What emerged as the LCS may have departed somewhat from the original concept, particularly in terms of size. But it is still being viewed by the US Navy as critical to its ability to deal with the shallow-water, near-shore threats of the future. Just as importantly, the hope still is that – despite major programme difficulties – it can be afforded in sufficient numbers to make a major contribution to the Navy's target for the future size of its fleet. It looks set at the moment to supplant completely the more traditional frigate in US Navy ranks.

Two different LCS designs were produced for a US Navy requirement for a type of ship that would be relatively small and affordable by modern US warship standards, have high speed and agility, and be of modular design so that it can be reconfigured with mission packages to fulfil a range of different tasks – chiefly mine countermeasures, anti-submarine warfare, and surface warfare. So included in the concept is the 'mission bay' to house the different sets of specialist gear. The ship design itself is, in the jargon, simply a 'sea frame' in which modules of equipment would be inserted, and specialist crews assigned, as required.

A key factor in the design, and something that has set the US Navy apart from most other fleets, was the requirement that such a vessel should have the ability to sprint at very high speeds for a major warship, of 40 knots and more. A key conceptual issue for future warship designs will be whether such high top speeds yield benefits worth the undoubtedly high costs of achieving them – costs that are likely to get even steeper in the future.

The first of the rival LCS designs, USS *Freedom*, was what is known as a semi-planing monohull, and – at just over 3,000 tons – has the appearance of a giant speedboat. The second design and the second ship to be built, USS *Independence*, of 2,800 tons, looked even more radical. A trimaran with sloping sides for stealthiness, it really did seem like the manifestation at long last of so many of the advanced concepts that had seemed for so long destined to be nothing more than sketches or computer graphic images. And yet, the *Independence* was actually based on an established design for a high-speed commercial vessel, used to transport passengers or cargo.

There was another speed aspect to the LCS programme. One of its distinguishing features was the rapidity, once the official go-ahead was given, with which the idea was turned into actual hulls in the water. For some, that was a welcome break in the practice of prolonged gestation periods for so many programmes, a development that might herald a more flexible approach to future warship design. And, yet, one of the criticisms of the LCS project has been that some of the shortcomings of the ships are down to insufficient analysis of the details of their design.

The LCSs remain controversial. Much will depend on the US Navy's experience as more are brought into service. It is still planning for up to fifty-five of them. But, for the moment, the idea does not really seem to be catching on elsewhere. Instead, other navies seem to be heading in the opposite direction, certainly in terms of ultimate speed and simplicity of construction. Clearly, for the Americans, speed is important, not least in terms of being able to deploy quickly to operational areas. But it comes at a price, and most other navies have been asking how often they would need to operate at high speeds, and whether it was worth it.

Perhaps the most appealing part of the LCS concept will turn out to be that of the basic sea frame, that ships are essentially 'garages' with modular equipment packages added when necessary, and a small core crew that would be supplemented by specialists in the different missions to be undertaken. Modularity has been around for a while. The Royal Danish Navy has been one of the standard-bearers with its StanFlex ships. The LCS takes the concept a step further. And technology may take it further still.

One of the key features of Britain's Falklands operation was the extensive use of requisitioned merchant shipping in auxiliary roles. In the aftermath, there was a surge of interest in the idea of developing containerized weaponry and other systems to give such vessels genuine capability and utility in conflict in the future. The idea did not get very far initially. The Americans developed the 'Arapaho' concept for using prepared containers to equip merchant ships at short notice to operate helicopters. After the Falklands, the Royal Navy bought the 23,000-ton container ship *Astronomer*, and operated her for a while in the 1980s as a helicopter support ship, renamed RFA *Reliant*, with a version of the Arapaho system. But the experiment was not considered a great success.

Modularity, however, did not die. And technology now may be sufficiently mature to be able to produce genuinely capable building blocks of command systems, sensors, and weapons capabilities in containerized form. Most strikingly, the Russians have been marketing a containerized version of their SS-N-27 as the 'Club-K'.

That initially looks more like a threat than an opportunity for major navies. The spectre of a concealed anti-ship missile that could be launched against an unsuspecting warship along any shipping lane from an anonymous merchant ship represents another asymmetric danger. But the concept could offer the prospect, at the very least, of spreading more capability around traditional fleets, to compensate for the shrinking of first-rate warship numbers. Modules could be deployed on existing auxiliary ships, or even aboard standard commercial vessels that could be purchased or leased. Thus the technology focus would be the systems, rather than the ships that would accommodate them.

Clearly, in an era of austerity, that should have appeal across many naval staffs. The analysts Philip Pugh and Norman Augustine have been key luminaries in exposing the dangers of the phenomenon of defence cost inflation, the historic trend whereby the cost of key defence equipment rises substantially faster than the general inflation rate.[3] Making more of modularized capabilities may be one way of breaking, or at least easing, the upward curve of defence cost rises.

As it is, shipyards continue to produce radical warship designs, hybrid hull forms, and elaborate new concepts. In the US Navy, as well as the LCS, they are finding their place in fulfilling specific tasks, such as for high-speed, short-range troop and equipment transports. And in other navies in smaller warship designs, for fast attack craft for example. But, for the moment, the designs for the specific requirements of actual navies for their major warships tend still to be more evolutionary, rather than revolutionary. Cost is an important factor.

The incorporation of stealth technology is becoming a growing priority, and that is clearly affecting ship shapes. The French Lafayette-class of frigates, and the Swedish Navy's Visby-class corvettes, are perhaps the most notable examples. But the trend that they represent is spreading among fleets.

For many established navies, particularly in the developed world, a key determinant of future warship design will be crew requirements, and these are changing faster now than they have done for a significant period. These requirements are connected with the developments in modularity, system packages, and networking.

Over perhaps the last two or three decades, the demand for increased crew space, with sailors requiring ever more creature comforts and facilities, has been a factor driving up the size requirements of warships. For example, the differences between the accommodation on a Royal Navy Type 42 destroyer of the 1970s and its successor, the Type 45, have been likened to those between a two-star and a four-star hotel.

But, as well as representing a significant capability in itself, the crew of a warship is also a huge chunk of the lifetime cost of a warship. Hence, the drive also to reduce actual crew numbers. That is also evident in the Type42/Type45 example, with crews of about 270 aboard the early ships, and around 190 on the newer, much more capable ones.

How far this drive towards 'lean manning' can go is a matter of intense debate. Some argue that Royal Navy ships, and indeed warships generally, remain significantly over-manned, especially when compared to the latest trends aboard merchant ships. Others argue that doctrine, particularly in the Royal Navy, dictates that there must be sufficient numbers aboard to cope when the ships go into action. Then the issue is not that of routine operational demands but of the urgent need for inevitably manpower-intensive damage control.

Other technological advances also have implications for the crewing of future warships. The trend in combat systems will be to increase the sophistication of what the systems can do, but also change dramatically the challenges of essential maintenance and fixing faults. The new generations of sailors joining up will be perfectly comfortable with operating the latest technology, but far less inclined than earlier generations to pull circuits out of computer cabinets, diagnose a problem, and rectify it. There will be even more repair by exchange.

But the level of technical expertise that a navy actually needs to take to sea in its ships will change. Increasingly sophisticated data and diagnosis links will make it possible to keep the really deep systems expertise at home, ashore, maybe in industry rather than in uniform, at a central technical support hub, rather than be duplicated around a fleet at sea.

This will have significant implications for how a navy like the Royal Navy organizes its personnel, its specialist training, and its groupings of technical expertise in the future. And there are doctrinal tensions again. Traditionally, when a Royal Navy warship goes to sea on operations, it is as self-sufficient as it can be when it leaves its berth. How much would a new maintenance philosophy undermine that? Will it tie future warships too closely to the shore? Or will it be a change in practice too beneficial to spurn?

It may add another potential vulnerability. In an age when the threat of cyber attack has come to the fore, this further attachment to the shore could simply be another area in which a ship at sea has become reliant on a network that could be attacked. But the amount of investment and research now being put into defending such critical networks is such that the advocates of such network-centric capabilities argue that the risks – if any – will be much greater elsewhere.

Indeed, notwithstanding the cyber security concern, further networking at sea offers perhaps the most dramatic potential for change. It could fill in the gaps caused by the reduction in overall fleet sizes. But, depending on how widely available such technologies become, they could also pose challenges for traditional fleets, and their ability to operate freely.

One of the great strengths of naval forces over the ages has been their ability to deploy and poise, unseen if necessary, to use the vast expanses of the ocean both in order to range freely and apply influence, or if necessary to hide and threaten. The nature of the medium of the sea also makes it a uniquely challenging three-dimensional arena. Depending on how cool or hot any potential confrontation might be, it is a chessboard or a battlefield, for opposing naval forces or any other agents who seek to operate – for whatever ends – on, over, or under it.

Such technology as might alter the transparency of the oceans may change dramatically the nature of navies and how they can operate and be effective. The advent of the aeroplane, radar, and underwater listening devices of growing potential have all had their effect.

The arrival of satellites looked set to provide another significant advance in the ability to scan the oceans. They offered enormous footprints of coverage, but not the ability to keep areas of sea or formations of ships, or individual vessels of interest, under persistent surveillance.

The first element of future change is the further development of unmanned, remotely-operated vehicles, on and below the sea's surface, and in the air. Such maritime 'drones' are already in use, and have been for some time. But their potential is only now beginning to be exploited.

Like so many past developments in military technology, this direction of change has been spurred on by conflict. However, on this occasion, the conflicts in question have been ones in which navies have been perceived to have had only a marginal role.

Iraq and Afghanistan have between them seen an explosion in the demand for and recognition of the critical significance of information and intelligence. Their collection, processing, and exploitation have come to be seen as key asymmetrical advantages of the West. And drones have captured the public's imagination as key collectors of persistent and penetrating information and intelligence, for transforming the surveillance picture, and for delivering devastating strikes to places that would otherwise be inaccessible.

The US Chief of Naval Operations, Admiral Gary Roughead, likened the combination of 'information dominance' and the advent of unmanned vehicles potentially to the transformational changes brought in by naval air power and the introduction of nuclear power.[4] Warships of the future will be hubs at the centre of networks of eyes and arms, spreading out over vast areas of coverage. This could dramatically alter the design, appearance, and use of warships over time. Navies could move 'beyond the primacy of the platforms'.[5] This could in turn change the balance of the arguments over quality, or at least capability, and quantity, or at least hull numbers, as it could produce a leap in the reach and impact that an individual warship will be able to achieve. The refrain has been that a warship, no matter how good, can never be in more than one place at a time. The possible new networks of the sea, of sensors and even remote weapons, with warships as the network hubs, could finally start to disarm that argument.

Unmanned surface vehicles (USVs) have already been developed and are being used to provide port and coastline security and conduct mine countermeasures. Operated from deployed mother ships, USVs can undertake similar missions in distant waters, or counter-terrorism and counter-piracy patrols off remote shores and strategic chokepoints, while reducing to a minimum the public profile of the mission and the risks to naval personnel. On the more ambitious power projection operations, they could be used as a screen to help protect the more valuable naval units in the most difficult and hostile waters, detecting potential threats and defending against, for example, swarm attacks by hostile high-speed craft of whatever description.

Unmanned underwater vehicles (UUVs) are already making an impact in changing the nature of mine warfare. They are taking both the person and the mine warfare vessel out of harm's way, and certainly changing the design requirements for the latter. But UUVs could offer the greatest prospect of changing naval warfare. Their potential to carry sensors or weapons for surveillance, intelligence-gathering, anti-submarine warfare, or anti-shipping missions is considerable. They could be the means to deploy, and the links with, new networks of underwater listening devices sown across key areas of the ocean to track maritime movements. Such networks would be particularly valuable in countering the threat of hostile submarines in the murky waters off distant coasts, without risking friendly submarines or surface ships.

Clearly such networks of sensors are not new. In a limited way, they were employed during the Cold War, when helicopters and maritime patrol aircraft scattered sonobuoys to pinpoint potentially hostile submarines in localized areas. But the precision, and data-collection and data-processing power of modern technology, dramatically increase the possibilities for their use and usefulness, making large areas of sea significantly more transparent.

The future might yield fields of underwater, autonomous sensors, submarine 'gliders' that make up part of the network, and even unmanned underwater weapons-carrying drones. Thus, hundreds of square miles of strategic seaways, at least around key maritime chokepoints, could be kept under continuous surveillance.

This could also in the end be extended into the deep oceans. There could be the development of underwater drones that could trail hostile submarines or surface ships. Of course, there is always the chance that such technology, once developed, will proliferate, and could thus be used by others to inhibit as well as enhance the room for manoeuvre of major maritime powers.

And then there is the potential at sea of everyone's traditional idea of drones, the UAV or its descendant, the unmanned combat air vehicle (UCAV). In conjunction with satellites and the other networks of sensors already mentioned, long-endurance surveillance UAVs like the Northrop Grumman Global Hawk or its specific maritime derivative, the Broad Area Maritime Surveillance System, could greatly extend surveillance coverage at sea. And whatever Northrop Grumman's experimental UCAV, the X-47B, becomes, such a weapon – with its stealth characteristics – could transform the potential of carriers of the future to project power, gather intelligence, and sustain enduring combat missions in the most difficult combat environments. The potential here is underlined by the urgency of the US Navy's efforts. Under the Unmanned Carrier-Launched Airborne Surveillance and Strike (UCLASS) programme, it aims to get a detachment of combat-capable drones to sea by 2018.

Among other technologies that could play a part in this transformation, the long-dormant airship could finally make its long-promised comeback. As a platform for a new range of sensors, able to stay aloft for days or even weeks on end, especially if piloted remotely, the airship could well find its place in the new network. Afghanistan has already provided one opportunity for a reappearance. The UK-based Hybrid Air Vehicles, in partnership with Northrop Grumman, won a US Army contract for a long-endurance intelligence-gathering vehicle. In the United Kingdom, the scrapping of the Nimrod MRA4 surveillance programme may yet provide another window of opportunity for the airship. Having abandoned the long-range maritime surveillance and intelligence-gathering capability embodied in the Nimrod, the MoD is already starting to look at ways of recreating it, perhaps with a combination of different platforms and technologies. The airship may be one of them.

In terms of weapons technology, there is one other area that feels as if it has been pending for some time, but has yet really to come to pass. That is the move beyond the missile age to the introduction of energy weapons of some description. These could finally be on the verge of making a significant appearance in the next couple of decades.

Their advocates certainly portray them as potential 'game-changers' in terms of weapons capability. One is the 'electromagnetic railgun'. This uses electricity rather than traditional propellants to launch projectiles. It is estimated that such a weapon could fire a shell more than 200 miles at a hypervelocity of Mach 7.5, so it would reach its target in six minutes. The kinetic energy of the projectile would eliminate the need for a high-explosive warhead. This, it is said, could revolutionize a warship's ability to deliver firepower inland.

In December 2010, the US Navy's Office of Naval Research (ONR) conducted a test with a prototype system at the Naval Warfare Center at Dahlgren, Virginia, which had sufficient power that it could have fired a projectile over a hundred miles.

Then there is the long-sought potential for lasers at sea. They could be used as a point defence system on ships, against missiles, aircraft, or even swarms of small boats. Of course, the ability of lasers to operate at the speed of light could make them the most effective counters to attacking missiles with high manoeuvring abilities. Thus, perhaps, they could tilt the balance again in that defence–offence leapfrog, and quell some of the concerns about the vulnerability of big ships like carriers. A laser system means, in effect, an unlimited magazine, and would eliminate the need to use expensive defensive missiles against low-value targets.

Theoretically, it will also be possible to vary the strength of the beam, and therefore have different effects on different targets in a range of situations, depending on how destructive the operator wants to be. Such a system could be at least as big an advance in ship defences as the radar-controlled close-in gun systems like Vulcan-Phalanx were when they appeared in the 1970s.

However transformational or otherwise these technologies prove to be, they will have to be integrated over time into existing fleets. The reality of modern budgets will dictate that. The new warship designs that have just arrived in service, or are about to arrive, will be modified to accommodate the changes, and that will test the theories and claims about how adaptable the new vessels really are. But it will be the next generation of warships and submarines, to enter service in the 2030s and 2040s, that will really embody any effects of these changes. Questions over future energy supplies, and the high power demands of new systems like electromagnetic guns and new types of sensors, could dictate very different types of propulsion systems. More automation could produce further dramatic reductions in crew sizes, possibly to handfuls of personnel at most. And, even more than now, future warships could simply provide garaging for future remote and autonomous systems. The ability to remain undetected will be even more at a premium. All this really could dictate some very different ship shapes.

CHAPTER SIX

The Carrier Question

A t some point towards the end of this decade, or perhaps just at the beginning of the next, the Royal Navy should be accepting into service the ship that could define its future, and perhaps to a large extent the country's position in the global military hierarchy. HMS *Prince of Wales* is scheduled to become the Royal Navy's first full-size aircraft carrier in more than four decades.

Perhaps by then she will have been renamed the new *Ark Royal* – the sixth ship to bear the name – to signify more directly the legacy that she would be reviving and upholding. That is what happened in 1978 when the third and last of the Invincibles, originally to have been named *Indomitable*, was rechristened *Ark Royal* even as she was taking shape at the Swan Hunter shipyard on the Tyne, to honour the fourth *Ark Royal*, that last true Fleet carrier, which had just gone out of service.

The Navy should already have had a hint of things to come, with the arrival perhaps three years earlier of the new ship's older sister, HMS *Queen Elizabeth*. Both vessels will be equally vast. From great, panoramic bridge windows high up in the forward island superstructure of both ships, the commanding officers of each will be able to gaze out over massive flight decks. But in the newer ship, for the first time in more than a generation and a half aboard a British warship, there will be the sight and sounds of all the paraphernalia of traditional carrier operations – aircraft catapults, arrestor gear, an angled runway and, above all, a complement of purpose-built conventional fixed-wing carrier aircraft. At least, that is how the plan looks in the immediate aftermath of the SDSR.

As has been highlighted so many times, these ships will be the largest ever to sail under the White Ensign. At 65,000 tons, they will dwarf the Navy's two previous big carrier sisters, the fourth *Ark Royal* and *Eagle*, both of around 50,000 tons. And they will eclipse even the battlecruiser 'the Mighty *Hood*', and Britain's last and biggest battleship, HMS *Vanguard*, of 48,000 tons and 51,000 tons respectively.

And yet, there is also a slightly different perspective to consider, reflecting the rather different world that they will inhabit. More so than those previous generations of warship, the new carriers will themselves be dwarfed by the biggest merchant ships of their age. Throughout the painful and prolonged process of their conception and construction, these ships' size has always been both their greatest potential asset and one of their biggest handicaps. Getting a proper perspective on that has been perhaps one of the most elusive challenges in all the arguments that have surrounded them.

More than anything else, 'the carrier question' has come to frame the issues of status and self-image for the Royal Navy in recent decades. And thus it has both reflected and been a reflection of the debates over Britain's own standing in the world. It has, as a result, been a uniquely emotional saga. But, while the arguments surrounding the carrier conundrum have been long, and generated much heat and anguish, they have rarely produced much clarity. And, although the construction of the new ships is well under way, and they could theoretically serve well into the third quarter of this century, those arguments remain largely unsettled. For that reason, many still doubt whether they will – even now – really emerge in the form envisaged, or ever reach their full potential.

The Royal Navy's aircraft carriers played a significant part at key points throughout the Second World War. After that, and into the 1950s, the Navy successfully clung on to its carriers by arguing for their utility largely in the context of limited confrontations as the country wound down its imperial legacy.

The 1960s were a much more difficult, and pivotal, period. At one level, the public still seemed to gaze favourably on these imposing ships, as reassuring symbols of Britain's continuing right to rank itself as a major power around the globe. As well as *Ark Royal* and *Eagle*, there were other famous names, like *Victorious* and *Hermes*, and they were regularly in the news, as a succession of post-colonial brushfires seemed to demand their attention and presence.

Much was made in the newsreels of the day of the new radars and weaponry that were supposedly at the cutting-edge of naval firepower, as well as impressive-looking new aircraft, like the Sea Vixen and Buccaneer, whose development also seemed to confirm that Britain remained in the aviation front rank. And, of course, Britain could proudly boast that it was behind all the key post-war developments in carrier design – including the steam catapult, the angled deck, and the mirror landing sight.

The reality was rather different. In fact, an ageing clutch of carriers was increasingly displaying its shortcomings, and the Navy was struggling to keep up with the pace and the price of change. So were its British-designed carrier aircraft. The best of its big carriers at this time, the modernized *Eagle*, was probably just about fully effective, and maybe also *Ark Royal* because of her size, but her equipment was poor. The others were too small or too old. Meanwhile, the performance of the Fleet Air Arm's aircraft struggled to keep up. The honourable exception was the Buccaneer which, at least in its later guise, was to the end of its days in FAA service probably a genuinely world-beating strike aircraft.

But the costs of staying in the carrier aviation business were mounting, and the questions surrounding whether Britain could or should afford it seemed endless throughout the first half of the 1960s. The bitter arguments over whether to build a new generation of Navy carriers would echo down the decades. Intriguingly, the first of the planned new 1960s carriers, CVA-01, would have been called HMS *Queen Elizabeth*, just like the first of the ships on which the Navy has now staked its future.

The inter-service rivalry between the Royal Navy and the RAF over this issue has become legendary. The fallout from it still has an effect. The 1966 decision to cancel CVA-01 and phase out the existing carriers was a huge blow for the Navy, as it would deprive it of what had become the centrepiece of the Fleet, its striking power, and its ability to range the oceans independently. Many in the Navy refused to accept it, at least initially, and hoped that it would be reversed. The Navy's leadership rejected that approach.

On the face of it, the solution which the Navy adopted seemed to offer only very inferior consolation. At the end of her days, that last Fleet carrier, HMS *Ark Royal*, could still operate a powerful air group of thirty aircraft and half a dozen helicopters. These included a dozen US-designed supersonic F-4 Phantom interceptors, fourteen Buccaneers, and a detachment of four Fairey Gannet airborne early warning (AEW) aircraft. In contrast, the first of the new successor-class of mini-carriers, HMS *Invincible*, with the emphasis on a specifically ASW mission, entered service with just five short-range, subsonic Sea Harrier fighters and nine Sea King helicopters.

The official operational rationale for the existence of the Sea Harrier at all was a modest one, to deal with long-range Soviet reconnaissance aircraft which might shadow the Navy's new ASW task groups, to 'hack the shad' in the jargon. In fact, the potential for more was always there, and crucially it kept the skills and capability of flying fixed-wing aircraft at sea alive in the Royal Navy.

In 1982, HMS *Invincible* went to war with twice her normal complement of Sea Harriers. The big gap, of course, was in AEW capability. That was cruelly exposed in the Falklands, but then quickly rectified, with hurriedly-adapted Sea King helicopters that would still be serving with various further updates three decades later.

The Invincibles themselves would go through various adaptations, most notably following the end of the Cold War. The increasing focus was on a return to more traditional carrier-style missions, as ASW gave way to power projection in the list of operational priorities. By the end of the 1990s, the ships had taken on an appearance to gladden the hearts and stir the memories of those who had served in carriers in the 1960s, as their flight decks were regularly packed with jets (albeit that many of them were the RAF's bomber version of the Harrier).

One way or another, the Navy clearly felt, with these developments, and with a succession of operations in the Balkans and the Gulf throughout the 1990s, that it was re-establishing the strike role of the carrier. But the maximum effective capacity of the Invincibles was about sixteen Harriers. That was a far cry from five. But it was rarely going to be enough to have a decisive impact. The real issue for the Navy now was re-establishing a carrier role for the long term.

From about the mid-1990s, studies were under way on how or if to replace the Invincibles. Among those early studies were proposals to build updated versions of the existing ships, or even to extend the lives of the current vessels themselves and stretch them so that they could carry and operate a few more aircraft.

By 1997, the options under consideration included four different sizes of air group – of twenty, twenty-six, thirty, or forty aircraft. There were three different configurations – short take-off and vertical landing (STOVL), conventional carrier take-off and landing (CTOL), and a hybrid solution used by the Russians on their big carrier, the *Admiral Kuznetsov*, of short take-off via a ski-jump but arrested landing (STOBAR). Most of the options involved building new, purpose-designed vessels. There was also still the possibility of stretching the Invincibles, or adopting a converted container ship design.[1]

These last two always seemed the least favoured approaches, chiefly because their capacities would be limited to twenty aircraft. As the focus of future strategy and operations seemed to be shifting even more towards power projection and expeditionary warfare, so the focus of the carrier plans began to shift as well. The emphasis became not so much creating *Invincible* duplicates for the twenty-first century, but rather resurrecting a full-size carrier capability. The thinking at this time was that the first of the new ships should be ready in 2010.

The full endorsement for the idea came in the 1998 SDR. And, in many ways, the carrier decision was an extraordinary coup for the Royal Navy. It amounted to official backing for the recreation of a capability that had been abandoned a generation earlier. The Invincible class were hugely important, and far exceeded their original design specification, thus reinforcing the argument that large aviation ships are inherently flexible. And, of course, *Invincible*'s presence was decisive in the Falklands. But the ships would only ever be able to provide a fraction of what a full-size carrier could offer, a window onto what that might mean in terms of political and military options, but not the full capability itself. The new carriers would mean, unusually, a step back up the capability ladder to a higher level.

For that opportunity, the Naval Staff was clearly willing to pay a price, but not too much. The timing in terms of political, economic, and strategic backdrop seemed propitious. But resistance within the MoD was considerable. A chief argument deployed by the anti-carrier camp was that of potential vulnerability, especially if there were to be only two such vessels. The Navy countered that bigger ships are inherently more resistant to damage, that the ships would have protection from supporting vessels, and that experience showed that well-operated carriers are never easy targets.

But clearly a crucial factor in getting the green light for the project – and specifically in persuading the then Defence Secretary, George Robertson, of the carrier case – was a remarkable agreement forged between the then First Sea Lord, Admiral Sir Jock Slater, and the then Chief of the Air Staff, Air Chief Marshal Sir Richard Johns. Slater has called it 'the historic document'. It was in many ways a heroic effort to try to bury the animosities and bitter memories of the past. A large part of the Naval Staff's calculation was that it had to get the RAF on board on the carrier plan. The scheme was also an acknowledgement on the Navy's part that trying to maintain its small and probably dwindling force of Sea Harriers on its own was going to become increasingly difficult, and maybe even prohibitive.

The joint proposal was developed by a small Royal Navy/RAF team. It was presented on 19 January 1998, and offered what the two chiefs described as 'a new and joint approach to the provision of offensive air power in the future'.[2] It outlined an argument for the continuing need for long-range precision air attack, an emphasis on expeditionary operations, and – crucially for the Navy – a joint endorsement of 'the need for carrier-borne air power'. Critically for the RAF, it supported its own pet project for the future, the successor to its main strike aircraft, the Tornado, in the form of the Future Offensive Air System (FOAS) programme.

The proposal was entitled Joint Force 2000.[3] 'Jointness' was the key watchword in defence now. The document said that the planned new-generation carrier should be considered a 'joint defence asset'. In addition, a joint approach to producing a future carrier aircraft, the replacement for the RAF's Harrier, and maybe even the FOAS Tornado replacement could maximise cost-effectiveness. A key plank of the argument was that this proposal offered maximum flexibility in terms of the number of future combat aircraft that could be switched between land-based and carrier-based operations. Up to that point, the assumptions had been that the Navy would need sixty future carrier aircraft, and the RAF was planning to buy sixty-five of the new Eurofighter Typhoons (or EF2000s as they were then known) to replace its Harriers.

The plan to implement the new joint approach would take place in stages. First, Navy Sea Harriers and RAF Harriers would be integrated into a joint force. The second part would be the choice of a common aircraft to replace the Harriers in each service between 2012 and 2015. Although no official choice had been made, there was a strong assumption implicit already that the US Joint Strike Fighter (JSF) programme would be the pick. The final stage of the process, and key to the RAF, would be meeting the FOAS requirement. That might involve using the same plane or something new, possibly developed in collaboration with European partners.

The existing Sea Harriers and Harriers – operated and maintained together – would be the crucial link to the future and a fully integrated joint force. At the time, the assumption was that the Sea Harriers would keep going until 2012, the RAF's Harriers until 2015, and the Tornado until 2018. At this stage, the plan for the future carriers was described as 'fully-funded'. The price tag then was put at £2.7 billion. The plan would be for two ships entering service in 2012 and 2015 respectively. There was also even – tantalizingly – the suggestion of a third, 'if required', in 2019.

There were huge misgivings and suspicion in both services, not least within the Fleet Air Arm. The agreement was instrumental in gaining a clear government commitment in the SDR to build two new big aircraft carriers. It was estimated then that they would be of 30–40,000 tons, to carry up to fifty aircraft. But, in detail, and in spirit, it would soon begin to unravel. And, of course, what was a huge coup for the Navy at the time, and perhaps a dream come true, would turn into a nightmare, and one of the most troubled and controversial of defence programmes that would display some of the worst traits of defence establishment mismanagement. The SDR decision turned out to be the easiest part of the process for the Royal Navy.

From the beginning of 1999, assessments of possible designs began. In the end, two groups, one led by BAE Systems and one by the UK arm of the French company Thales (or rather Thomson-CSF, as it still was then), were invited to put forward design proposals. In January 2003, the MoD chose the Thales design, but in a split decision picked BAE Systems as the preferred prime contractor to build the ships. The government in effect forced the companies together in what would become the Aircraft Carrier Alliance (ACA).

The chosen design called for a ship of about 68,000 tons (quite a step up from the admittedly somewhat arbitrary 30–40,000 tons of the SDR), with a length of 292 metres (958 feet), and the ability to carry up to forty-eight aircraft. The estimated budget now was £2.8 billion.

In some ways, the Thales design appeared rather conventional. But there were significant innovations. The most noticeable, and one of the most controversial, was the incorporation of twin island superstructures, separating ship control in the forward island from the air control facilities in the second island. Most aviators applauded that, believing it gave them a huge increase in operational effectiveness. Others were not so sure. But a beneficial side-effect was that it allowed the conventional power plants to be separated, improving ship survivability.

A further innovation was that the design was deliberately made adaptable to either conventional or STOVL operations. On top of that, a significant amount of automation was incorporated, such that the overall complement – of ship's company and air group – would total just 1,400, in a 68,000-ton carrier. That was only a little more than the 20,000-ton Invincibles (and, in fact, a smaller ship's company). As a further comparison, the US Navy's Nimitz-class carriers (admittedly tipping the scales at around 100,000 tons, and usually operating sixty-five or more aircraft) carry some 5,600 personnel. Even the supposedly innovative new US carrier design, for the USS *Gerald R. Ford*, while cutting overall crew numbers by a thousand, will still require some 4,600 personnel to operate. This may yet prove to be one of the most challenging aspects of the design of the future British carriers.

Pretty soon the problems started to appear. As work on the design progressed, BAE Systems told the government that the ships could not be built for less than £3.8 billion – a full billion more than the budget. A scaled-back design was urgently proposed. But that was unacceptable to the Navy. Further redesign went on. A compromise was produced that was close in size to the original, at 65,000 tons, but shorter at 282 metres (925 feet), with a smaller aircraft capacity of forty, and much-simplified propulsion and electronics. It was accepted, but still the arguments over the cost continued.

In the meantime, the government had confirmed in January 2001 that the JSF would be the choice for the new British Joint Combat Aircraft (JCA), as it was being called. In October of that year, Lockheed Martin won the design competition for the JSF. And September 2002 saw the British government pick the STOVL version as its preferred variant.

There was also, for a time, French government interest in the Royal Navy's new carrier design. The French Navy already had the troublesome nuclear-powered carrier *Charles de Gaulle*. She herself had been a long time in the making, having been ordered in 1986 and finally commissioned in May 2001. She was a replacement for the long-time French carrier double-act of *Clemenceau* and *Foch*. The French had announced that a second new carrier, *Porte Avions 2* (PA2), would be built, but with conventional propulsion.

With the coincidence of new conventionally-powered carrier requirements, the opportunities for co-operation seemed considerable. The fact that the British design was adaptable to the CTOL configuration preferred by France helped. On 24 January 2006, a formal agreement was reached between the two governments for France to have access to detailed information on the British design in order to adapt it to French requirements. But there would soon be frictions too, including a French proposal for full co-operation on the building of the two British and one French ship.

After an already protracted gestation, still there were no firm orders for the new ships. But there was a renewed promise in July 2007 to place them. The estimated cost by then had risen to £3.9 billion. And their arrival dates were now estimated at 2014 and 2016.

But, still, no contract was signed. The order for the carriers would be used by the government as a carrot as it persuaded the British warship-building industry to go ahead with the further consolidation that it favoured. When that was finalized on 1 July 2008, as a joint venture between the surface ship business of BAE Systems and the VT Group, to be called BVT, the orders were finally signed in a ceremony aboard HMS *Ark Royal* on 3 July.

But at no point had the carrier programme really managed to gain a firm footing, and the question marks remained. It seemed as if only a commitment at the highest political level, and the determination of the Navy to proceed, were keeping the programme alive. Everywhere else – within the MoD and beyond – the mood appeared hostile and in favour of cancellation. The carriers seemed to have few friends. There was clearly a strong institutional mindset in parts of Whitehall – as there was in the 1960s – to 'get the carriers'. In this climate, progress was exceptionally difficult, and the pitfalls of delay and cost escalation seemed only to increase.

Just a few months after the contract for the ships was signed, in December 2008, to deal with a mounting cash crisis, the new Defence Secretary, John Hutton, announced – among other things – a delay of one to two years in the carrier-building programme. This pushed the in-service dates for the ships back to 2015 and 2018. While achieving short-term savings thought to be around £450 million, it was estimated in 2009 that the net effect would be to increase the final cost of the programme by more than £900 million. In 2010 that estimate was revised upwards to £1.56 billion.[4] In the light of this new delay, a letter to the editor of The Times in December 2008 pointedly observed that, at about the time of the SDR and the first clear commitment to the new carriers, the Cunard Line had announced plans to build the much bigger Queen Mary 2 as its new ocean liner flagship. That ship had by then already notched up five years in service.[5]

Part of the cost controversy included the fact that the total bill included not just building the ships, but also buying the aircraft for them. And the JSF programme was also encountering delays and cost increases. For the carriers' critics, this was not a five-or-six-billion-pound issue, but something approaching a £20 billion headache.

Of course, not counting the aircraft that the ships would carry in the overall bill would indeed have been perverse. But saddling the carriers and the Navy with the total cost of the JSF programme seemed equally unjust. After all, the JSF was meant to be a joint project with the RAF. Moreover, the carriers did not seem an exceptional drain on resources when compared with other major projects, like the Eurofighter Typhoon, or even the Army's hugely troubled new armoured vehicle programme, the Future Rapid Effects System (FRES), let alone the Trident nuclear system.

The Navy probably did not help its case in the way that it tried to convey the scale of the new ships to the public, to try to capture its imagination. Flight decks the size of sixty tennis courts, and aircraft hangars equivalent in volume to multiple Olympic swimming pools, might have appeared to be quite populist comparisons. But they were perhaps more suited to the era of the 'Eagle' comic, and of a more innocent fascination with technology. Such descriptions certainly did not convey any convincing message as to why the taxpayer should want to spend so much on such ships. The most telling comparison used most commonly has been that the new ships are three times the size of the vessels that they will replace. That fact has rarely been deployed as an argument in their favour, but more often as evidence of Royal Navy extravagance.

There is also something else about carriers, beyond their size and cost, which stirs emotions. And it stirs them more in Britain than in most nations. Other countries have their carrier debates. The US Navy has had to fight for its carriers on occasions. So has the French Navy, and the Italian Navy. Part of the argument is always about what owning and operating a carrier or carriers says about a country's ambitions. It is a clear signal of that. But, in Britain, what carriers represent also seems so attached in many people's minds to what they feel the country used to be.

In some circles, the Navy's new carriers have been dismissed as 'Cold War relics'. And the Invincible-class ships did indeed start their lives as specific Cold War tools, which were then adapted for other roles. But, ironically, the Navy never made its main case for its previous full-size carriers in the 1950s and 1960s in a Cold War NATO context. It was always based on their power-projection role, to cover the contraction pains of withdrawing from empire. That may have been a rather limited and finite mission then. The new carriers and their power-projection mission, the Navy insists, have nothing to do with hangovers from the Cold War, let alone Britain's colonial past.

The British carrier debate has also been strangely parochial. It has seemed almost to overlook the fact that other navies around the world have been getting on and building their own new carriers. The carrier business has been booming of late.

After more than forty years of building Nimitz-class carriers, the US Navy is about to accept the first vessel of a new design. It remains institutionally convinced of their role, now and for the foreseeable future, even if the pages of Proceedings are often filled with articles questioning their continuing suitability and potential vulnerability in the decades ahead. The French have the *Charles de Gaulle*, and continue to mull over building a second ship, while the Russians have the *Admiral Kuznetsov*. As has been said, of the emerging big powers of the future, the Chinese have undisguised carrier ambitions, while the Indians have a definite determination to build a significant carrier force. Brazil has taken on one of the ex-French ships which the *Charles de Gaulle* has replaced. Italy and Spain have built newer, bigger ships to complement their existing mini-carriers. South Korea and Japan have joined the mini-carrier club, while the Royal Australian Navy's purchase of its two big new Spanish-designed and built amphibious ships represents a dramatic increase in its potential aviation capabilities.

In the context of these developments, size probably does matter. Some, including in the Royal Navy's own ranks, have argued that it should have gone for a more modest carrier design, similar to those of Italy and Spain, essentially updated Invincibles. The two ships that it actually chose to build look more like down-sized versions of the US super-carriers, and have thus been criticized as evidence of pretensions still to be a pocket superpower. And yet they do also potentially offer capabilities currently enjoyed by a very select few others — in fact, in serious operational terms, by only the US and French navies. It will be a very exclusive club of capability, even if and when India and China also master the art.

HMS *Ark Royal* emerges from the icy fog on 3 December 2010 for her last, sad entry into Portsmouth as an operational aircraft carrier. Her disposal, and that of the Harrier aircraft which she embarked, were the most controversial measures announced in the 2010 SDSR. (UK MoD Crown Copyright 2011)

HMS *Diamond*, third of the Royal Navy's Type 45 air defence destroyers, going through her paces on trials. The Type 45s, originally intended to have been a class of twelve vessels, will now number just six. (UK MoD Crown Copyright 2011)

HMS *Astute*, the first of what should be seven new nuclear-powered hunter-killer submarines (SSNs). The Astutes, like the Type 45s, have been a troubled and costly programme. But SSNs, while expensive, remain a hugely potent naval capability. (UK MoD Crown Copyright 2011)

The radical trimaran shape of the US Navy's second Littoral Combat Ship (LCS), USS *Independence*. The Royal Navy experimented with a trimaran demonstrator, but seemed to lose interest in the design, and such a hull shape seems destined for now to be confined to specialist vessels, with the exception of the LCSs. (US Navy)

The Royal Navy's new Queen Elizabeth-class aircraft carriers have already been a long time coming. This computer-generated image shows the design configured with catapults and arrestor gear rather than a ski-jump ramp, a switch that was announced in the SDSR. It also depicts twelve Joint Strike Fighters (JSFs), which – according to the SDSR – will be the normal complement. (BAE Systems)

Even as controversy continued to swirl around the carriers, construction of large sections of the ships was well underway. Here, major sections of HMS *Queen Elizabeth's* hull are brought together for assembly at BAE Systems' Govan shipyard. (BAE Systems)

The F–35C conventional carrier version of the JSF, which is now the British Government's preferred choice of variant to fulfil its Joint Combat Aircraft (JCA) requirement. (Lockheed Martin)

An early test firing of a Sea Viper missile from a Type 45 destroyer, on this occasion HMS *Daring*. As well as being critical to the Royal Navy's future air defence umbrella, both the missile and the ships could be modified to perform a ballistic missile defence role, if funds allow. (MBDA)

The maiden test flight on 4 February 2011 of the X-47B technology demonstrator for an unmanned combat air vehicle (UCAV). Such aircraft could be the key to the future of carrier aviation in general and play a big part in the operational careers of the Royal Navy's new carriers in particular. (Northrop Grumman)

HMS *Daring* in company with the US Navy aircraft carrier USS *Enterprise* off the US east coast in late 2010 (also with the Norwegian air defence frigate, HNoMS *Nansen*). The relationship with the US Navy will remain critical to the Royal Navy's future strategic significance. The Royal Navy also hopes its new carrier will enjoy the half-century of successful service achieved by the *Enterprise*. (US Navy)

A corvette-like design unveiled by VT Shipbuilders in response to the proposal for a C3 version of the Future Surface Combatant for the Royal Navy. A vessel like this could be capable mine warfare, patrol, surveying, and other tasks. (VT Shipbuilders)

A frigate by another name. An image of how the Type 26 Global Combat Ship might look. The programme is now perhaps the most critical for the Royal Navy's future. (BAE Systems)

A key feature of the Type 26 will be its flexible stern mission bay. (BAE Systems)

The centrepieces of the Royal Navy's one and only post-SDSR major formation, its Response Force Task Group. On Operation Cougar in the Mediterranean in early 2011, the helicopter carrier HMS *Ocean* (right) and the amphibious assault ship HMS *Albion* (left) carry out a replenishment at sea with RFA *Fort Rosalie*, with the auxiliary landing ships RFAs *Cardigan Bay* and *Mounts Bay* and the tanker RFA *Wave Knight* in the background. (Crown Copyright/MoD 2011)

RFAs *Cardigan Bay* and *Mounts Bay* again, along with RFA *Wave Knight* (centre). The Bay class have proved to be exceptionally useful and flexible vessels, as the rest of the Royal Navy has been increasingly stretched. (Crown copyright/MoD 2011)

An early conceptual image of the Royal Navy's next generation of ballistic missile submarine, currently scheduled to replace the Vanguard-class from the late 2020s. (BAE Systems)

Of course, it will never be possible to portray the new Navy carriers as a bargain. The total cost of each ship will exceed £3 billion. They were never going to be as cheap as originally estimated – a classic example of the 'conspiracy of optimism'. But, equally, they need never have become as expensive as they have, if the project had only been handled with consistency and commitment.

Notwithstanding that, the US Navy, in comparison, has estimated that the cost of buying its first new Gerald R. Ford-class carrier will be US$11.5 billion,[6] or more than £7 billion. Admittedly, the US ship will be more capable and faster, and is nuclear-powered. But the Royal Navy will still be getting two 65,000-tonners for less than the price of one US 100,000-tonner, with about the same or slightly greater overall aircraft capacity, and a smaller overall crewing requirement – which will affect relative lifetime costs as well. It is an interestingly different perspective that when, in the United States, naval commentators argue over the merits or otherwise of continuing with their nuclear-powered super-carriers, the alternatives that are often paraded as smaller and cheaper and more sensible options tend to look and sound very much like the Queen Elizabeth class.

At about the time that the orders for *Queen Elizabeth* and *Prince of Wales* finally materialized, one avenue of potential Anglo-French co-operation seemed to disappear. The French President, Nicolas Sarkozy, announced that a decision on a second carrier for the French Navy would be put off until 2011 or 2012. Even if a second French carrier is eventually built, it is by no means clear that it will be to the same design as the Queen Elizabeth class.

But the impetus towards increased Anglo-French defence co-operation would soon be revived by the pressure of squeezed budgets. After the May 2010 British general election, and against the backdrop of the continuing arguments over the Navy's new carriers, speculation about new ties emerged, including on the carrier front. By the time the new Anglo-French treaty on co-operation was signed in November, the Royal Navy's real need of help in keeping its carrier hopes alive had increased dramatically.

Before all that, a significant milestone was reached in the carrier programme at a ceremony at the Govan shipyard on 7 July 2009 when the Princess Royal performed the initial steel-cutting for the hull of the first of the ships. It was a somewhat manufactured moment in more senses than one, since work had been going on in various locations, on various bits of equipment for the ships, for some time.

Another notable feature of the carriers is their manner of construction, in disassembled blocks at six principal yards around the country, with all the pieces eventually to be brought together for final assembly in a rebuilt dock in Rosyth. By 2010, there was significant work under way across the country. By the end of the year virtually all parts of the hull of the first ship were under construction somewhere, with some close to completion. Serious work on constructing the second ship was due to begin within months. In fact, much of the equipment, like the aircraft elevators, had been ordered as sets for both ships and had already been delivered.

That may have been a crucial factor, as the SDSR storm clouds gathered around the carriers. The various carrier decisions which emerged from the review were its most controversial elements. Far from settling the carrier arguments, it seemed only to give them new life.

The circumstances of the decision also revived the inter-service frictions between the Royal Navy and RAF, or at least their respective communities of supporters and retired personnel. Certainly, the high-point of Navy/RAF accord with the Slater/Johns agreement of 1998 was but a distant memory. Of course, much had already happened since then. There was the early retirement of the Sea Harrier. The RAF had seen its own project for a Tornado replacement, FOAS, shelved. To the Navy's dismay, there had been a previous RAF attempt in 2008 to scrap the whole Harrier force early. That may have been deflected at the time, but only – as it turned out – for a couple of years.

It was the *Ark Royal*/Harrier retirement, and the 'carrier gap', that was the focus of immediate discontent in naval circles. Letters to newspapers were fired back and forth. The former First Sea Lord and Labour security minister, Admiral Lord West, wrote to David Cameron saying that he feared that the Prime Minister had been 'a victim of bad and biased briefing'.[7]

The debate was fuelled by unfolding events in Libya, which increased calls for an SDSR rethink. It was argued that Britain's contribution to the no-fly zone would have been significantly more effective had *Ark Royal* and her Harriers been available. It escaped the notice of few in naval circles that the two NATO countries with air bases closest to Libya, namely France and Italy, chose to deploy carriers for the mission. The US Navy made significant use of the large amphibious assault carrier that it had available, the USS *Kearsarge*, with her Harriers, V-22 Osprey tilt-rotor planes, and large transport helicopters.

Even if it was too late to save *Ark Royal*, perhaps a residual Harrier force could be retained, to be available to operate from the last remaining Invincible-class carrier, *Illustrious*, for as long as she was retained in service. A concerted lobbying campaign was launched. But the government resisted. Ministers argued that Libya vindicated their SDSR choices, showing that Britain could make do until the new generation of carriers arrived, albeit with fewer options and a more limited contribution in the Libyan case than it might otherwise have made. To add to the poignancy of it all, in the midst of the continuing debate and the operations over Libya, on 24 March 2011, the decommissioned former carrier *Invincible* began her final sad voyage from Portsmouth under tow to a ship-breaker in Turkey – a voyage that would take her through the Mediterranean and past Libya itself.

In evidence to the House of Commons Defence Select Committee as the Libya crisis dragged on, the First Sea Lord, Sir Mark Stanhope, was clear, 'if we had a carrier, it would be there'.[8] He also underlined, unsurprisingly, that if there was one decision that he would revisit from the SDSR, it would be the *Ark Royal*/Harrier decision.

But, perhaps more significantly, what were the post-SDSR prospects for those new carriers? On the face of it, the language of the review seemed to offer a ringing – indeed a classic – new endorsement of the underlying concept:

This capability will give the UK long-term political flexibility to act without depending at times of regional tension, on agreement from other countries to use of their bases for any mission we want to undertake. It will also give an in-built military flexibility to adapt our approach over 50 years of the carrier's working life. In particular, it provides options for a coercive response to crises, as a complement or alternative to ground engagements. It contributes to an overall Force Structure geared towards helping deter or contain threats for relatively well-equipped regional powers, as well as dealing with insurgencies and non-state actors in failing states.[9]

But the carriers' supporters were suspicious about whether those arguments had been truly embraced. After all, yes, both ships were going to be built, but the vision for how they would be employed was being dramatically redrawn. The political mood music seemed to be less of firm and enthusiastic commitment, more that the government was stuck with them, and that they were white elephants. And the SDSR declared that the government could not now 'foresee circumstances in which the UK would require the scale of strike capability previously planned'.[10]

This was a huge change. The whole rationale behind these specific ships was the scale of strike capability that they would be able to deliver. The meticulously-calculated operational requirement was for carriers that could carry thirty aircraft and deliver nearly 400 sorties in the first five days of an intense operation. And it was for two ships, so that one should always be available. Now the military advice, so the government said, had changed.

Just one carrier would be equipped to carry jets. What would happen to the other would be decided later. The operational carrier would still be able to accommodate up to thirty-six jets. But, ordinarily, it would carry only twelve. Indeed, the SDSR announced an initial plan to buy just forty JSFs. More are likely to follow if and when the money allows, but certainly never the 150 originally envisaged.

In fact, it was obvious that the protagonists on both sides of the carrier controversy felt that all options were still open. At the highest levels of the Navy, the clear belief was that the door remained ajar to a future with two operational carriers, especially in a post-Afghanistan, post-recession world. And then there were those who were confident that the longer the country managed without any fixed-wing carriers, the less persuasive the argument would become for resurrecting such a capability in the long term – both ships might be built, but both could also be sold.

For the Navy, there was another hurdle to be overcome. From an operational point of view, the SDSR decision to switch from the STOVL version of the JSF to the conventional carrier variant was widely welcomed.

The F–35C was acknowledged as offering superior range and weapons-carrying capability, plus the bonus of greater interoperability with the Americans and the French. It should also be cheaper to buy and operate in the long run. The down side was a further delay in the programme, to fit at least one of the ships with catapults and arrestor gear, 'cats and traps', and an inevitable further increase in cost.

In the early months of 2011, the likely scale of further cost increase began to become apparent. It would be perhaps another billion pounds or more.[11] But why so much? Was the design not meant to be adaptable, with inbuilt provision for such a switch, to be 'future-proof'? Apparently it was not quite as straightforward as had been advertised, or at least assumed.

However, the modifications would still require considerable work. There would have to be extensions and changes to the flight deck and runway. And, while there was provision and space to fit catapults and arrestor gear, the equipment still had to be bought. The preference was for the new electromagnetic launching system (EMALS) technology – either the US system destined for the new Gerald R. Ford–class carriers, or possibly a British-designed variation. EMALS offers the potential of much greater flexibility and reliability, and reduced maintenance requirements, over traditional steam catapults. But it is unproven technology, and would be expensive.

Meanwhile, the carrier enthusiasts were looking for ways to narrow the carrier gap. Was it too late to convert the first ship, *Queen Elizabeth*, to cats and traps? If not, perhaps Britain could purchase or lease a consignment of, say, twenty F/A-18 Super Hornets, the current mainstay of US Navy carrier air groups, for maybe just £1 billion, at least as a stop-gap. It may not be stealthy like the F–35, but the F/A-18 would be much cheaper, and for many pilots it remains a superlative carrier aircraft. This option, it was argued, could allow a return to fixed-wing flying by 2015, five years earlier than under the SDSR plan.[12]

But, with money so tight, the chances of funding the F/A-18 option – even if it was the bargain that its supporters claimed – appeared remote. And the shipbuilders were arguing that it would be impossible to modify either of the new carriers to operate the planes earlier than already planned. Even so, the F/A-18 option may not be dead, as there are still doubts over whether the F–35 will really materialize in an affordable form. In such a circumstance, the French Rafale or a navalized Eurofighter also still have their proponents. The F/A-18 also comes with an existing air-to-air refuelling capability, which could be a critical factor in the effective operation of the new carriers with conventional take-off jets. Even a limited purchase of F/A-18s for that role, alongside the F–35, could be more cost-effective than a very expensive modification of the stealthy JSF to provide that capability.

So the uncertainties continue. Critically, this is still meant to be a joint exercise with the RAF. And yet relations between the two services on the issue appear to have slumped again. The Fleet Air Arm clearly felt once more under siege. It had lost the fixed-wing capability which it had fought so long to sustain, albeit formally for only a finite period. FAA ranks, present and past, saw other exposed flanks. Was the future of the Commando Helicopter Force also being threatened in an RAF master plan to consolidate air power finally under its wing? The FAA clearly saw an existential threat forming. The chairman of the House of Commons Defence Select Committee was moved to ask the Chief of the Air Staff, Air Chief Marshal Sir Stephen Dalton, if the RAF was aiming to take over the Fleet Air Arm. Sir Stephen insisted, 'absolutely not'.[13]

The idea also seemed to be gaining hold that the operational carrier would be used mainly in a 'hybrid' role, with perhaps just a handful of jets, but also various detachments of helicopters, and maybe embarked units of special forces or Royal Marines. Thus, theoretically, it would be available for a range of roles.

For some time, the United Kingdom will not have many jets anyway, even when or if the first JSFs start to arrive. But, clearly, many in the Navy are suspicious of the hybrid concept, seeing it as a device to prevent the carriers fulfilling their true potential. It is one thing to be able to switch aircraft and roles, as the Americans have regularly done with their carriers – from strike carrier, to launching pad for special forces, to huge helicopter-carrying disaster relief platform. But it is quite another to try to configure a ship to try to be able to do a bit of everything.

For the most ardent carrier advocates, this looks like a corruption of the idea of the flexibility of such ships, and a waste of what the Navy had fought so hard to acquire.

Apart from anything else, conventional carrier jets and large numbers of helicopters make uncomfortable flight deck fellows. They make incompatible demands for flight deck space, and the rhythms of their operations are very different. There is also the issue of positioning the ship for the different types of operation. Fixed-wing flying requires plenty of sea room, while helicopter missions in support of operations ashore require a ship closer in to the coast with less opportunity for manoeuvre. The risk would be of the carrier never being in the right place at the right time for the right mission.

And yet the Navy had sought to portray the carriers as a joint defence asset, able to accommodate the aircraft of all three services. It may have been vital to winning initial approval for the ships. But did it also encourage the idea that a carrier is just a garage at sea? Is the Navy in danger of losing control of the carriers?

Clearly it is a deep-seated belief in the Navy and the FAA that there is a special skill and mindset to operating aircraft at sea, and that will need to be reflected in how the new ships are crewed and operated. It is not just about pilots. Anyone who has been aboard an operational carrier will have witnessed the symphony of skills at work – to maintain the aircraft at sea and operate them from the deck, let alone actually fly them on and off a ship, and to keep such a ship itself at peak effectiveness.

The First Sea Lord acknowledged that keeping those skills alive and resurrecting the capability will be 'a major challenge'.[14] Even before the SDSR, the Navy was going to have to turn to the Americans for help in bringing its big new carriers into service. Now, it was going to be totally dependent on the United States, as well as the French.

The carriers could be a transformational capability for the Navy, and dramatically alter Britain's ability to project power, if that is what it wants. That, after all, was the original plan. The current one, as well as the public statements which accompanied its announcement, clearly send a more mixed signal about the government's commitment and appetite. What the carriers have always needed, but have never had, has been a political message from on high that they are the number one defence programme.

And, yet, probably only if the carriers are eventually deployed regularly as real carriers will all the effort and resources devoted to acquiring them really have been worth it. Even as it is, there are those who see the carriers as having wrecked the rest of the Navy, as well as distorting the rest of the defence programme. The package for the whole Fleet might just have been acceptable at the time of the 1998 SDR. But that has long since been torpedoed. The Navy has mortgaged its future for just two ships. Even erstwhile supporters of the carriers have changed their view, seeing the price that has been paid in the Fleet as too high. Can the Navy any more contemplate even putting together an adequate task force of ships that would enable the carriers themselves to be fully effective in the kind of high-end confrontation that is their ultimate *raison d'etre*?

But what might be called the West/Band vision is still a compelling one for the Navy. As Admiral Band, as First Sea Lord, put it, acquiring such carriers 'is one of those generational decisions'. In contrast, decisions on numbers of destroyers and frigates are of a different order, and more easily altered, although that has looked an increasingly questionable assumption as budgets and industrial capacity have continued to be squeezed.

What does this all say about the carrier project as it has evolved? Is it just another example of the United Kingdom trying to maintain the appearance of great-power status without being willing to fund properly the substance of it? Or is it further evidence of a country, still deluded by the pretensions of great-power status, overreaching itself again by trying to cling on to a capability whose full cost it does not really understand, or refuses to acknowledge, and certainly cannot afford?

Part of the frustration in the pro-carrier camp undoubtedly stems from a belief that, if only the Navy can finally get its hands on HMSs *Queen Elizabeth* and *Prince of Wales*, and demonstrate their worth, their potential will be obvious, and that will change the game of political and security calculation for future governments. The problem, from this perspective, is in large part that politicians have just forgotten what it is like to have real carriers at their disposal – they simply do not understand what they are missing. Some cynics suspect that it is precisely that array of extra options to project power that carriers represent which is behind why some elements within Whitehall have been so ardently hostile to them.

The ships will never operate the full numbers of JSFs for which they were originally designed. But that, in the end, may not be a serious setback. With so many delays and disappointments in the programme, time and technology have moved on, and new possibilities beckon.

Chief amongst these is the prospect that the new carriers might soon be able to embark UCAVs. This promises a significant jump in the ability of aircraft carriers to deploy the kind of air power that has become so vital a part of the modern military campaign – the ability to launch long-range, persistent pilotless aircraft to collect intelligence and if necessary to launch strikes into environments that might otherwise be too hostile.

Drones have captured headlines and the imagination in Afghanistan and the tribal areas of Pakistan. Combat drones operated from aircraft carriers will add a further dimension.

The X-47B UCAV made its maiden, experimental flight on 4 February 2011. It is just a demonstrator. But the US Navy hopes to have a small squadron of such aircraft at sea before the end of the decade – in other words, before Britain's first fully-capable carrier is operational. Assuming the concept works, it is reported that such aircraft could carry out fifty-hour sorties, take on eleven-hour surveillance and strike missions 500 miles inland from a coast, or operate for twenty-four hours along a hostile coastline. A squadron of twelve of them could carry out five round-the-clock air patrol circuits along a coast to maintain – for example – a Libya-style air operation, with a fraction of the resources employed by NATO.[15]

So the Queen Elizabeth class could end up operating a mix of JSFs and UCAVs. Or, if the JSF project founders, as some believe it might, F/A-18s and UCAVs would offer a very powerful alternative at lower cost, and still with that 'first day of the war' capability which the fifth-generation, stealthy JSF would give to the British forces for the first time in a while, but which is also offered by the UCAV's stealth, and the fact that it does not have a pilot onboard. UCAVs could even provide air-to-air refuelling in the long run.

The other element of the carriers' repertoire will be their AEW capability. The lack of it clearly cost ships and lives in the Falklands. The solution may have appeared rather ungainly and amateurish. But the Sea King helicopters with their retractable radar in an inflatable dome that looked like a cow's udder worked remarkably well. The venerable machines were significantly upgraded over the years and designated Airborne Surveillance and Control aircraft to reflect a much greater performance, including in service in Afghanistan. But they are scheduled to be withdrawn by 2016.

At the moment, the best that the Navy seems to be able to hope for as a replacement is essentially a part-time, 'plug-in and play' set-up to be applied to some of its Merlin helicopters, under a project dubbed Crow's Nest. It would be a basic capability. And yet, the switch to a conventional carrier concept theoretically opens the door to the purchase of E-2 Hawkeye aircraft, the benchmark AEW capability at sea flown by the US Navy. The French navy also operates the Hawkeye from its carrier.

An air group of JSFs, or even F/A-18s plus UCAVs, and Hawkeyes would add up to a formidable set of influence or power-projection options. And then, of course, there is the ability of the carrier to adapt to other missions – from disaster relief to special forces operations – as required, with a flight deck and hangar packed with Chinooks if necessary.

For all the talk of the cost of the new Navy ships, some critics have suggested that, actually, corners have been cut in the design. They will not be robust like American carriers, and able to take punishment to the same degree. They will have very limited defensive systems. Some question whether they will have the necessary maintenance and workshop facilities to keep their aircraft flying. Many suggest that they will be too slow. But the designers insist that they will be impressive, even iconic, pieces of naval engineering when they materialize.

To observe a modern US carrier on operations is to witness an extraordinary capability at work. There are the thundering take-offs and landings. There is the toiling of thousands of personnel, on the flight deck, in the gargantuan hangar, and in the bewildering honeycomb of compartments around the ship. It is power projection on an industrial scale, and each carrier with an air group more powerful than most air forces. And, of course, the carrier is but the hub of an entire formation, the carrier strike group.

The Queen Elizabeth class will offer something subtly different. The atmosphere aboard is certainly going to be very different. For one thing, on a 65,000-ton ship with a total crew probably not exceeding 1,600, crew density will be about a third that aboard a US carrier. There will not be the same sense of teeming activity as on a US carrier, or even a Royal Navy Fleet carrier of old. Some crew members may get quite lonely on watch in some isolated compartments. It will not be the same level of capability as a US ship, but it will be a close approximation. And, with some more modern systems, and much more automation, it will in some ways be a more modern expression of naval aviation. But the Navy will be hard pressed to make it work.

One of the arguments used by the RAF against the Royal Navy's carrier plans in the 1960s was that, in spite of the very significant investment required, the carriers would still be able to provide only a fraction of the aircraft required for the power projection plans of the day. Even the Navy acknowledged at the time that the carriers would only complement the land-based air power that the RAF would be providing.

That is not the case now, nor will it be in the future. The fact is that a Queen Elizabeth class aircraft carrier will, in most circumstances, be able to deploy – if required – all the combat aviation that the United Kingdom will ever wish or need to project for the foreseeable future. The world into which the Queen Elizabeth class will emerge may also be one in which, instead of ten or eleven US Navy carrier strike groups, there could be only eight. It could be one in which China and India are establishing genuine and significant carrier capabilities. By then, the whole tone of the debate surrounding carriers could sound somewhat different.

CHAPTER SEVEN

The Nuclear Equation

O ne of the most profound moments in the Royal Navy's modern history occurred on Trafalgar Day, 21 October 1960. In the presence of Her Majesty the Queen, a new HMS *Dreadnought*, Britain's first nuclear-powered submarine, entered the water for the first time at the Vickers Armstrong yard, as it then was, at Barrow-In-Furness. *Dreadnought* would go to sea on trials in December 1962, and be commissioned on 17 April 1963.

That was some eight years after the world's first ever nuclear-powered submarine, the USS *Nautilus*, had famously signalled 'under way on nuclear power' for the first time on 17 January 1955. But *Dreadnought*'s arrival propelled the Royal Navy into a very special and significant club, membership of which it has been determined – if not desperate – to maintain ever since. It has been a guiding assumption of Royal Navy planning that possession of a force of nuclear-powered submarines of the highest sophistication – with their firepower and unrivalled mobility – is a crucial asset.

It may have been an act of faith at the time. It may have been an easy choice to make, with no serious question about it, given the Navy's view of itself at the time as a global force. It simply had to be in the nuclear-powered submarine business. The decision has had far-reaching consequences. Today, the Royal Navy's submarine force – although very small in numbers – is a tool of maritime power of huge potency and reach probably unmatched by any other navy except that of the United States. And, thus, it has huge potential strategic significance. But it has been bought at a very significant price.

The investment has been huge, in design, construction, operation, and support. And the costs and benefits have come into ever sharper focus. Numbers have become an issue here too, as they have dwindled to the point where the Royal Navy has been – in the view of many – teetering on the edge of what constitutes a viable submarine force.

Britain's first nuclear-powered submarine was aptly and deliberately named. The appearance of this type of vessel was at least as radical a development as that of the previous HMS *Dreadnought*, albeit that the Royal Navy was on this occasion toiling in the wake of the US Navy. Some have also compared the urgency and the focus with which the Royal Navy pursued its plan to build the new *Dreadnought* with the crash programme to build her predecessor six decades earlier.

There were problems and delays early on with the design of the reactor for the new submarine. It became clear that the reactor work could not keep pace with the urgent schedule to get the first submarine completed. But the then First Sea Lord, a great enthusiast of nuclear power, Admiral The Earl Mountbatten of Burma, exerted his considerable charm on the United States, and especially on the notorious father of America's nuclear navy, Rear Admiral Hyman Rickover, to gain access to US submarine reactor technology.

The purchase of the US reactor design to hasten *Dreadnought's* arrival meant that she was seen as something of a hybrid, with a novel – and advanced – British-designed front end grafted on to a US-designed rear. The first 'all-British' nuclear-powered submarine, HMS *Valiant*, would be commissioned in July 1966. That should not diminish the sense of achievement. In some ways, the British – while reliant on US help with the power-plant – felt they had a thing or two to teach the Americans in terms of hull design.

It was a remarkable team and an extraordinary project. One of the key players in the hull design team for this first, ground-breaking new submarine, Louis Rydill, would go on to lead the design team for the Navy's ill-fated programme for a new full-size aircraft carrier, CVA-01, which would be so controversially cancelled in 1966. However, the reliance in *Dreadnought* on a US reactor would sow the seeds for a controversy which has still not gone away over just how reliant British nuclear technology has been on the United States for crucial know-how.

The next great challenge would be the Polaris programme to create a force of ballistic missile submarines (SSBNs) to take over the role of providing the country's nuclear deterrent. For all the controversies and questions, it was an extraordinary period of leaping technological and industrial hurdles. The country and the Navy committed to a set of undertakings which taxed the capacities of both to the limit.

Dreadnought and the boats which followed her were nuclear-powered but conventionally armed. These SSNs, the 'hunter-killer' attack submarines, were officially dubbed Fleet submarines in Royal Navy parlance and unofficially hailed as the capital ships of the future. The force began to build slowly but steadily. But various constraints meant that they struggled to take the place in the Fleet that their unofficial title seemed to imply.

One of those constraints was the Polaris programme, which inevitably diverted resources into an urgent effort to build a force of four SSBNs, the Resolution class. They would each carry sixteen Polaris missiles acquired from the United States. That was an enforced move, triggered by the US cancellation of the Skybolt air-launched missile programme, on which Britain was hitherto relying to provide its new strategic nuclear capability. It caused much anguish at the time, diplomatically, politically, and in terms of inter-service envy. But, in retrospect, and setting aside the broader arguments over deterrence and disarmament, the submarine route as the way forward for its deterrent force seems such an obvious one to have pursued for a small, crowded island like Britain, wishing to deploy a first-class strategic nuclear capability of its own, that it hardly seems worthy of debate. Again, the costs would prove to be considerable, but whether they were in the end dramatically higher than the likely costs of the alternatives is doubtful.

It was inevitable that the resources needed to build and maintain a force of SSBNs would have an impact on how fast the Navy's new fleet of SSNs could be built and put into service. For a time in the early days there were at least two shipyards building the submarines – Vickers in Barrow and Cammell Laird at Birkenhead. Now that there is only one yard capable of building these submarines, at Barrow, under the corporate banner these days of BAE Systems, the choreography of building SSNs and SSBNs is even more inextricably intertwined.

Still, it is difficult to imagine just what the challenges and strains were back in the 1960s, and the scale and intensity of the effort, as technological and industrial frontiers were constantly being breached. If it was not quite the British equivalent of the space programme, as the shipbuilding industry strained to meet some very exacting deadlines, and overcome some huge technical hurdles, it was pretty close.

There was also, from the earliest days, the problem of equipping the new, true submarines with a really effective set of weapons. Simply providing these supposed new capital ships with adequate torpedoes proved to be a challenge. That undoubted weakness was eventually remedied with the arrival of the Spearfish heavyweight torpedo, albeit developed at huge expense – another aspect of the huge resources that sustaining an effective submarine capability implies.

The great power of the SSN was demonstrated most dramatically and controversially in the Falklands War. First, there was the speed with which the Navy's SSN force was deployed, far in advance of the surface task force, and its ability subsequently to remain on patrol unsupported.

Then there was the dramatic and controversial attack on and sinking of the Argentine Navy cruiser, the *General Belgrano*, on 2 May 1982, with the loss of 323 of the ship's crew. HMS *Conqueror* remains the only known SSN ever to have sunk another warship on operations, albeit that she did so with antique, free-running Mk 8 torpedoes, chosen by her commanding officer, Commander Christopher Wreford-Brown, and his number two, Lieutenant Commander Tim McClement, because of the explosive punch of their heavy warheads. Massively controversial as it was, the impact of the attack, and the suspected presence of the other British SSNs around the Falklands, forced the Argentine Navy's surface forces back to port and removed them from the military equation for the rest of the conflict.

It was also subsequently revealed that the British SSN force in the South Atlantic deployed to carry out surveillance just outside Argentina's territorial waters, to provide early warning of Argentine air attacks against the Royal Navy task force and British forces ashore.[1] It was one crucial tactic employed by the British to make up for the huge gap in their defences resulting from the absence of an AEW capability aboard the carriers. More generally, it was a pointer to the very significant intelligence and surveillance potential of SSNs, which was crucial in the Cold War, and has been of great significance since as well. The British SSN strength in the conflict eventually totalled five boats – HMSs *Conqueror*, *Spartan*, *Splendid*, *Valiant*, and *Courageous*. Apart from *Conqueror*'s dramatic contribution, their presence went largely unnoticed by the outside world, but was critical to ultimate British success.

It was also a demonstration of the unique endurance of such submarines, limited mainly by that of the crew aboard. When HMS *Conqueror* sailed from Faslane on 4 April 1982, she went to sea with supplies for ninety days. On day fifty-two Wreford-Brown and McClement put the boat on half rations. Wreford-Brown had concluded that *Conqueror* would be required to remain on station for as long as the fighting lasted. McClement calculated that, if the conflict was still under way on day seventy-five of the patrol, the crew would have to go on to quarter rations. It did not come to that. When *Conqueror* returned home to Faslane on 3 July, day ninety of the patrol, the submarine still had supplies for three more weeks.

As it built up its SSN force, at an early stage the Royal Navy identified the need for a submarine-launched guided missile. It took until 1981 for that to arrive in the shape of the US-designed Sub-Harpoon anti-ship missile.

The other great leap in the capabilities of Britain's SSNs came with the decision in 1995 to equip some of them with the US Tomahawk land-attack cruise missile (TLAM). It was this decision that dramatically changed the potential value of the SSNs in the post–Cold-War environment, and would help to justify their very considerable cost. Initially, seven of the boats would be fitted with the weapon. HMS *Splendid* became the first British SSN to sail with an operational load of TLAMs on 1 May 1998. She also became the first British boat to fire them operationally in March 1999 during the confrontation with Serbia over its breakaway province of Kosovo.

The true strategic potency of the SSN was demonstrated just a couple of years later. On the day after the 9-11 attacks on the United States, HMS *Triumph*, which had been involved in an anti-submarine exercise off Iceland, was ordered to deploy east of Suez. Less than three weeks and more than 8,000 miles later, she was on station in the North Arabian Sea, along with two other British SSNs, to launch cruise missiles against targets in Afghanistan.

No other unit with such a strike capability could have deployed so far, so fast. And *Triumph*'s voyage included a brief stop in the eastern Mediterranean to take on Tomahawks flown out by transport plane. That particular part of the operation was a planned contingency designed to increase the flexibility of the submarines to deploy quickly, anywhere in the world.

So, from its beginnings at the start of the 1960s, the Royal Navy's SSN force grew. By the mid-1970s, the plan was for a total fleet of sixteen boats, together with fifteen conventionally-powered submarines (SSKs). This was, of course, still very much the height of the Cold War.

Studies at the time considered whether the number of SSNs could be raised to twenty. That may have been possible only if the Navy and the country had foregone the intention to build a second-generation class of SSBNs. But one fleet study of that time proposed an even higher, and perhaps unrealistic, ideal of twenty-four SSNs – a very considerable force.

In fact, the controversial Nott review added one to the long-time SSN goal, up from sixteen to seventeen. The pinnacle was actually reached in 1990. For just a few short weeks between the arrival of the brand new HMS *Talent* in May of that year and the paying-off of HMS *Conqueror* in August, the Royal Navy did indeed achieve a grand total of seventeen SSNs in commission.

But 1990 was also the year when the Cold War came to an abrupt end. As a succession of older boats was retired, the force quickly fell to twelve over the next four years. Crucially, as the effects of the post-Cold-War search for a peace dividend began to bite, the Navy took the critical decision to give up its last conventionally-powered submarines in order to retain an all-nuclear force. This meant retiring the brand-new but troubled Upholder class of four SSKs, which were very sophisticated and in some ways virtually the equivalent of a conventionally-powered SSN.

As a weapon of the Cold War, against a potential adversary whose own submarine forces were vast, the SSN's role was clear. For many submariners, it was still an undervalued asset. The Royal Navy's submarines may have been relatively few in number, but in capabilities their crews were confident that they compared with the best, not least in their stealthiness. The crews' exploits in developing their own anti-submarine skills, and in stealing into the heart of the opponent's sanctuaries to garner vital intelligence, were considerable.

But what value to place on the capabilities of the SSN, and how to develop them, for the post-Cold-War world? After all, the nuclear-powered submarine seemed almost synonymous with the Cold War, like the ballistic missile or the long-range jet bomber. SSNs were and are also the most complex platforms in the British armed forces, and about the most expensive.

So it must have been something of an incongruous sight at the end of March 1993 when HMS *Triumph*, then almost brand new, surfaced off the coast of Abu Dhabi, having become the first Royal Navy SSN to deploy to the Arabian Gulf. But it was a clear signal of intent.

Indeed, the concept and capabilities of SSNs seemed remarkably adaptable to the emerging new world order. In a new age of uncertainty, with strategic eyes raised to much more distant horizons than the European Central Front and the north-eastern Atlantic, the SSNs' unmatched ability to deploy at great speed over great distances, and covertly if necessary, in response to an unpredictable threat that might occur almost anywhere, suddenly had perhaps enhanced strategic and tactical value.

Add to that the submarines' intelligence-gathering capabilities, their suitability as a stealthy platform for the deployment of special forces off a coast, and their unmatched potency in any purely maritime confrontation that might arise. And they were also now, for the first time, equipped to project military power ashore in a limited confrontation with the TLAM.

Indeed, by the 1990s, the cruise missile had become the US weapon of choice for mounting coercive actions to punish whichever rogue state or group that it happened to be confronting. Thus, the Royal Navy's TLAM-equipped SSNs became the most effective, and on occasions the only, instruments with which Britain could join such enterprises in an active military sense if it wished, at least in the early stages. Again, the country was part of a very exclusive club.

Even so, there was and is the matter of the price. The planning exercises which accompanied the 1998 SDR apparently indicated that a force of fourteen SSNs would be ideal, actually greater than the then current force.[2] But that was not to be. Reluctantly, the First Sea Lord, Admiral Sir Jock Slater, accepted an SDR verdict that the SSN would reduce over time from twelve to ten boats, although all of them would be equipped with cruise missiles, instead of just the seven in the original plan.

During the 1990s and early 2000s, the Navy's Invincible-class carriers saw action in the Balkans and in the Gulf. But, in terms of projecting firepower from the sea, the Navy's SSNs with their Tomahawk cruise missiles – in Kosovo in 1999, Afghanistan in 2001, and Iraq in 2003 – added a significant extra dimension to British military options. And yet, by 2004, the decision had been taken to cut the force further to just eight boats.

It was against this evolving background that the new hope for the submarine service had been slowly and painfully taking shape. In the late 1980s, with the Cold War apparently still stretching out into the future, plans began to be laid for an all-new class of advanced SSNs to replace the then latest model, the Trafalgar class, seven of which were either in service or being built, with the last set to enter service at the end of 1991. As its successive new designs of submarines had entered service, the Royal Navy had made a steady and deliberate journey through the alphabet in naming them. The Swiftsure class had been succeeded by the Trafalgars, which were followed by the Upholder class, and after them had come the huge Vanguard-class Trident-missile-carrying SSBNs. Inevitably, the planned next generation of SSNs became known as the W class, or SSN-20, as the first of the class would have been the twentieth British nuclear-powered attack boat.

The intention at that stage was that the first of the new class would enter service in about 1997. But it was never to be. The potential costs of this elaborate new design were looking eye-watering even early on. The end of the Cold War put paid to the plans. Thinking switched to producing a less ambitious, lower-risk and lower-cost development of the Trafalgar class instead, at least as an interim step to replace the aging Swiftsures, and to keep both the Fleet and the industry in business. Between three and five submarines would be built, and these would then be succeeded by another new design, the Future Attack Submarine (FASM). This was the genesis of what would become the Astute class (back to the beginning of the alphabet again).

But the new plan itself soon began to veer off course. With a new, much more advanced reactor design to accommodate, from the Vanguard-class SSBNs, the idea that the new vessels would just be modest updates of the Trafalgars quickly started to look unrealistic. Size was increasing dramatically. The submerged displacement of the Trafalgars was 5,200 tons. The design displacement of *Astute* quickly rose to 7,200 tons, and it would rise further to 7,800 tons.

There were forlorn hopes that increasing the size of the new submarine would actually make it easier to build compared with the earlier classes. New modular construction techniques would also simplify things, as well as the introduction of a computer-aided design process (CAD). All of this, it was anticipated, would help to hold down costs.

In fact, it did not. On the contrary, the Astute class would turn into one of the most notorious and troubled of MoD programmes, much to the Navy's embarrassment. Initial plans for an in-service date of 2005 would never be met. Such were the difficulties that the contract had to be renegotiated. There were times when the programme was described as in 'crisis'.[3]

Part of the problem was clearly created by the loss of skills and experience in the industry in building submarines, due to the gap that developed in SSN orders. The last Trafalgar-class SSN, HMS *Triumph*, had been completed in 1991, the last Vanguard-class SSBN, HMS *Vengeance*, in 1999. Another factor in the troubles was the switch to the CAD process.

Official figures in 2010[4] suggested that the average cost of the first three boats of the class would be more than £1.3 billion, and that that represented an increase of more than a third (37 per cent) over the original estimate. The defence that this still probably made the Astutes less expensive than their American or even French equivalents did not seem to sway much opinion. The price tag has certainly fuelled a heated debate over whether the country can or should afford to maintain such a capability.

When *Astute* rolled out of her assembly hall at the BAE Systems yard at Barrow-in-Furness for her naming ceremony on 8 June 2007, she certainly made a breathtaking spectacle. It was a brilliant summer's day. And yet her great bulk and girth seemed to carry a greater menace and impression of power even than is usual with modern submarines. She may have been a linear descendant of the Navy's previous submarine classes, but it was as if a generation of development had been missed out. In the long, spreading, sculpted shape of her huge fin or conning tower, and the intriguing kick-up swelling of her aft deck, she had none of the simple, smooth appearance of her predecessors, with their more flowing lines and almost knife-like fins. She was like a massively-muscled super-heavyweight bruiser to their simple but impressive elegance and athleticism.

Given that the intention at one stage had been to produce a relatively modest, low-cost, low-risk improvement on the Trafalgars, an understandable reaction among those who gazed up at *Astute* as she was rolled out for the first time would have been, 'what on earth happened?' But given all the tribulations that the Navy had been going through at the time, a beaming First Sea Lord, Admiral Sir Jonathon Band, was unrestrained in his welcome of *Astute*, and what she represented. Still the question was being asked, was she too big and too ambitious for what her likely roles would be? Despite her traditional dark submarine drabness, the phrase 'gold-plating' again came to mind.

In fact, the idea of a relatively basic interim design simply to replace the Swiftsures had long ago been abandoned as the delays mounted. The separate FASM proposal to replace the Trafalgars was axed. The Astutes would be the replacements for all the remaining – and indeed ever reducing numbers of – Swiftsures and Trafalgars.

But how many Astutes would that mean in all? There had been a hope, maybe, of nine. Or at least eight. In fact, as the budget was squeezed and came ever more under strain after 2005, the Navy's fear was that it might only be six, or even fewer, perhaps just four. In that sense, the 2010 SDSR proposal to maintain the commitment to build seven Astutes turned into something of a relief for the Naval Staff.

As with the carriers, there was at least a suspicion that the decision to go ahead with seven Astutes had as much to do with the concerns of the builder, BAE Systems, and the need to sustain industrial capacity, as it had to do with any strategic calculation. It was in that sense an inevitable side-effect of the SDSR decision to delay plans for the replacement of the Trident submarines. Still, it was certainly a fillip for the Navy amid the gloom of all the other SDSR news. But does even seven Astutes represent a viable force? And can it even remotely be described as cost-effective?

Because of their very nature, the operations and capabilities of submarines remain more shrouded in secrecy than those of most other units and weaponry, even with the end of the Cold War. It lends them still an alluring and mysterious air. Nevertheless, the very striking appearance of HMS *Astute* and her sisters probably does betray a very significant leap forward in capability over their predecessors.

These attributes include improved stealthiness and better intelligence-gathering equipment, improved endurance, and a significant increase in weapons-carrying facilities, with a combination of up to thirty-eight Spearfish heavyweight torpedoes or Tomahawk cruise missiles. Sensors include a very advanced active and passive search-and-attack sonar, the Type 2076, as well as huge and sophisticated flank arrays along the submarines' sides. Housed in the fin are a forest of masts for communications and electronic eavesdropping, as well as two advanced 'optronic' masts which replace the traditional periscopes and whose advantages include not needing to penetrate the pressure hull. The class also has an advanced combat management system. And one of the advantages of the submarines' modular construction has been that the entire command deck could be assembled in a separate, cleaner, more controlled environment before being installed as a completed, 178-ton unit, into the pressure hull. It is certainly all a far cry from the early, oily days of submarines. Also strikingly, the PWR2 reactor at the heart of the Astutes is powered by a core, known as Core H, which is meant to last their entire planned twenty-five-year operational life span, completely obviating the need for refuelling.

There is also what is now a *sine qua non* for submarine operations. That is a comprehensive capability to carry and deploy an admittedly still quite limited special forces detachment. And *Astute's* increased size, coupled with great automation and improved equipment sustainability, means a reduced crew size, down from 130 in the Trafalgars to just ninety-eight, thus avoiding that bane of the submariner's life down the ages, 'hot-bunking'.

The world of HMS *Astute* and her sisters is one in which the attributes of the submarine will become more valuable, not less, and technology may allow them to exploit these more effectively. But does that mean that Britain needs to stay in the nuclear-powered submarine business, with boats like *Astute*?

In many ways, submarines remain what they have always been, the ideal instrument for the weaker naval power to frustrate and embarrass more powerful adversaries. Conventionally-powered submarines of modern design have proliferated. Many of them are extremely quiet, making detection very difficult. They are potentially very useful for the A2/AD mission, and will represent a major challenge for navies embarked on expeditionary operations, or even attempting to police threats to sea lanes.

Such submarines have become indispensable building blocks in the development of emerging maritime powers. There may be question marks over the proficiency of some of the submarine forces that are developing. But an additional factor is the 'trickle-down' effect of new technology, and the impact that that is having. The increased ability of modern conventionally-powered attack submarines to host advanced command systems, improved sensors, and above all the latest in torpedoes, anti-ship missiles, and even cruise missiles, has to some extent closed the firepower gap with the SSN, and increased the level of threat that the conventionally-powered boats pose to naval formations generally.

Then there is the proliferation of air-independent propulsion (AIP) systems such as advanced fuel cells, increasing the submerged endurance of modern SSKs. Now, such submarines can remain submerged at low speeds for previously unheard-of durations.

Above all, perhaps, there is the question of the likely battleground of the future. If it is to be, as it has been recently, off coasts and near the shore, in the confined waters of the littorals, some argue that smaller, quieter, more manoeuvrable SSKs are better than lumbering, ultra-expensive SSNs.[5] Indeed, it would be folly – so it is argued – to risk such valuable vessels as SSNs in such shallow waters.

In that sense, could the great ballooning in the size of *Astute* compared to her predecessors, never mind her cost, be a serious handicap? More broadly, have the advances in conventionally-powered submarine capabilities significantly shifted the balance of calculation over whether pursuing a nuclear-powered solution is the right one? Has the Royal Navy, and for that matter the US Navy, made a strategic error in abandoning conventionally-powered submarines altogether?

In terms of operations in the littoral, British SSNs can deploy and have deployed there. And the SSN fraternity certainly disputes some of the alleged advantages of the SSK in confined waters, pointing to the much greater power that an SSN always has available, key to manoeuvrability and, if necessary, escape. And the greatest differentiation in such a challenging environment is almost always going to be the skill with which any submarine is handled.

In addition, conventionally-powered submarines still cannot compete with their nuclear-powered brethren in one crucial area, nor is there the prospect that they will be able to do so in the foreseeable future. It is that ability to deploy at great speed over great distances, if necessary secretly, and to loiter for long periods undetected and quite independent of support, in the most remote and challenging of operational areas.

The SSN can still cover unlimited distances at thirty knots and more underwater, whereas even the most advanced SSKs would be restricted to very slow progress, or would have to resort to transiting on the surface, still more slowly than an SSN, and giving away any real chance of hiding their deployment from any adversary which has even moderate airborne or satellite surveillance cover. For a navy and nation that has aspirations to have real expeditionary warfare and power-projection capabilities, to be a global player, the nuclear-powered submarine retains huge advantages, its endurance still limited only really by that of its crew, and the supplies that they need.

Also, the SSN itself is proliferating, and the number of members of the owners' club has been growing and is likely to grow further. At the same time, that other key member of the club as far as Britain is concerned – indeed its founding member – is also facing challenges in maintaining the size of force that it would like for the future. The US Navy once had nearly a hundred SSNs, but this total has in effect been halved and the United States will struggle to have many more than forty in service by the end of the 2020s. For all these reasons, SSN ownership is likely to be become strategically more rather than less important.

As a result, the Navy will fight hard to retain an SSN capability. But does it have choices other than an all-nuclear force? Would a mixed flotilla of SSNs and SSKs be viable? That would almost certainly mean a further reduction in SSN numbers, which are already considered to be down to a critical level. And how cost-effective would it be to try to recreate a support structure for another submarine type? If there were to be any extra resources available for submarines, the temptation in the Naval Staff would undoubtedly be to push for an extra SSN or two rather than acquiring even a handful of SSKs. However, questions will persist over whether British SSNs need to be as sophisticated as the Astutes. Even some Royal Navy SSN veterans question the size of *Astute* and her sisters, compared to the previous-generation Trafalgars.

As it is, the Royal Navy's force of six or seven SSNs has a demanding set of tasks to cover, to say the least. These include protecting the Trident missile submarine force, supporting task group operations, providing key surveillance capabilities, the land–attack mission (demonstrated again in the Libya crisis in 2011), and independent operations to maintain a strategic presence in key regions. What is more, with the rest of the Fleet shrinking, but with the strategic picture and relationships continuing to evolve in far-flung regions, the temptation to exploit the SSNs' deployability even more will surely mean that they will be even more in demand and increasingly stretched.

The sustainability of the Royal Navy's nuclear-powered submarine force in the long term quickly turns to the linked issues of the industrial base and the future of the country's nuclear deterrent force. In 2005, the then government's Defence Industrial Strategy described the continuing ability to design, build, and support nuclear-powered submarines as 'essential', with the ability to design, build, and maintain the propulsion system itself – the 'Nuclear Steam Raising Plant' – described as a 'strategic capability'.[6] However, it also warned that the whole maritime industry sector had to improve performance and streamline itself.

But the doubts remain. It has been estimated that the cost to the country of maintaining a nuclear-powered submarine capability is over £1 billion a year. Some question whether continuing to bear these costs is viable in the long term for 'an industry that produces one product – costly nuclear-powered submarines – in small quantities for one customer, the Royal Navy'.[7] Not even a likely increase in the international market for nuclear-powered submarines will be of any relief to the United Kingdom. Its treaty obligations to the United States over sharing nuclear technology will continue to preclude any hope of exports to, say, Brazil as a way of defraying costs. Increased co-operation with France may be one possible route, but that will be sensitive enough. Another more obvious avenue might be to explore even closer collaboration with the United States.

One potentially significant variable in the cost equation of nuclear-powered submarine building and operation will be whether there is a sustained revival of the civilian nuclear power industry. Such a development may be a short-term challenge, bringing increased competition over a limited skilled workforce. But it could offer long-term benefits by expanding the skills base. Events in Japan in the aftermath of the March 2011 earthquake and tsunami may change the calculation again. But another part of that equation, in a world of climate change and the growing scarcity –and thus rising cost – of fossil fuels, is how much more of a premium will there be in the future in having a nuclear-powered military capability of great sophistication and considerable flexibility? The question in the long term may not be whether a nuclear-powered submarine capability is sustainable, but whether nuclear power can and needs to be spread more widely throughout a fleet. Will it, for example, be seen at some point during their fifty-year planned life to have been a strategic error to have rejected the option of nuclear power for the new carriers?

Of course, conversely, there could be significant further advances in conventional submarine propulsion systems. So the Astutes and the Trident successors could still turn out to be the last British-built nuclear-powered submarines.

The next challenge for the Navy and British industry on the submarine front is the issue of replacing the current strategic nuclear force of four Vanguard-class Trident missile submarines. Two successive governments now, in 2006 and 2010, have committed themselves to doing just that. And, in its 2006 White Paper, the then Labour Government endorsed the view that the replacement system should be based on a new class of ballistic missile submarines from 2022, when the Vanguards – it was then assumed – would start to go out of service.

The 2010 SDSR essentially endorsed that judgement, but with some qualifications and modifications. Thus, in some ways, it appeared in fact to settle nothing. That was in large part because the Liberal Democrat element of the coalition government held a position that raised doubts on cost grounds about the modernization plan. The party's platform advocated something other than a 'one-for-one' replacement of the existing force, possibly involving submarines equipped with nuclear-armed cruise missiles.

So, while the SDSR heralded the imminent start of detailed design work on the new submarines, it simultaneously slowed the ticking of the replacement clock. It announced that studies had shown that the life of the Vanguards could be safely extended into the late 2020s and early 2030s. Thus, the aim would be to deliver the first new missile submarine in 2028. This crucially achieved two key political objectives for the coalition – reducing costs in the short term, and essentially getting the government off an awkward political hook by postponing the final decision on procurement until 2016, after the last possible date for the next general election.

In a further nod to the disarmament agenda, the SDSR also announced that the number of operational missiles for each submarine would be reduced to eight, with no more than forty operational warheads. However, the submarines themselves may still be built with at least twelve missile tubes – that is the baseline design that the United Kingdom has been working on with the United States for a common missile compartment for each country's new submarines. The other key question that the SDSR left open was whether three or four new submarines would be needed to maintain the continuous at-sea deterrence, to which the government declared that it remained committed.

The plan to delay building the first of the Successor class of submarines, as they are being called, clearly had a significant bearing on the decision to commit to a seventh boat of the Astute class, essentially to help fill a production gap. That was a bonus for the Navy. More broadly, the Trident replacement debate surely presents it with a set of tricky dilemmas.

Sustaining deterrent patrols uninterrupted for more than four decades has clearly been a huge undertaking for the Navy, but also a source of considerable pride and prestige. Operating the country's ultimate nuclear capability has bestowed a special status on the Navy. That status is more ambiguous right now, as the capability clearly has a less central role in the immediate security agenda, whatever the arguments for it might be as an insurance against an uncertain future. That itself has had implications in terms of maintaining morale and motivation in the Trident force. But it would still be a huge step for the Navy to have to give it up.

While the current government has committed itself to replacing Trident, a future one might not. It would be a huge political step to take. On the other hand, rather as with the ownership of aircraft carriers, Britain has always seemed more self-conscious as a nation with its nuclear weapons state status than the other acknowledged nuclear powers. And there may yet be a serious debate to be had.

A decision not to replace Trident at all would have huge consequences for the Navy. The likely context of any such decision would be that the current Vanguard class would also be swiftly decommissioned. Given all the investment in operations and infrastructure down the years, it would be an upheaval for the Navy at least as great and traumatic as the CVA-01 cancellation in the 1960s – probably more so given that it would almost certainly be irreversible. It would also mean a new set of calculations over how and whether to maintain the existing SSN force, and over future submarine construction and operations.

A decision to keep a deterrent, but to base it on something other than a new class of submarines, would only delay those questions. The Vanguard class would presumably still need to be kept in service until the new capability – presumably air- or ground-launched – was ready. But, after that, again, the issue of sustaining the SSN force would also have to be revisited.

Of course, one possible consequence of either decision for the Navy might be to free up funds for more SSNs. For some submariners, that might be a tempting prospect. Likewise, the oft-touted option of a more limited future nuclear capability based on cruise-missile-armed submarines might appear attractive as well. A force of, say, nine SSNs, with some equipped to carry nuclear-tipped cruise missiles, might be both cheaper and more flexible than maintaining separate flotillas of SSNs and dedicated SSBNs, albeit that the ultimate nuclear deterrent capability would be significantly reduced.

As it is, the Navy can look forward to a significant modernization and enhancement of its submarine force, from its current level, into the 2020s, as the Astutes steadily enter service. On current plans, attention will then switch to the Successor SSBNs.

And, for all the talk of the door to a different future still being open on the deterrent front, it is also clear that significant work and investment is already well under way. On 18 May 2011, Liam Fox announced early outline details of the new-generation SSBNs, including a new reactor design, PWR3, that the MoD hopes will be more cost-effective and even longer lasting. And the plan is to carry over as many systems from the Astutes as possible. However, it is also clear that the Successors will be much bigger than the Astutes. For the sake of the coalition, the announcement also included the initiation of a study to be undertaken by the Cabinet Office to review the costs, feasibility, and credibility of alternative systems. But the strong impression was left that the course has been set for the United Kingdom's nuclear force through – according to the plan – until the 2060s. And, according to the government, the cost of the programme remained within the previous estimates from 2006 of £15–20 billion.

A technological breakthrough that suddenly makes the oceans more transparent would, of course, change all the assumptions. But, otherwise, the next goal for the Navy and industry after the Successor SSBNs will be starting to think about what comes after the Astutes, probably from about 2038 onwards.

The need to keep costs down will be a powerful imperative. But will technological advance make a dramatically different design possible? A key avenue of research is bound to be whether it will be possible to reverse the trend in size which led to *Astute* becoming a third bigger again than her predecessor.

For all the talk of *Astute*'s sophistication, there is one area in which she and her sisters appear to be caught in a technology straitjacket. They have significantly more weapons storage than their predecessors. But their launch system still comprises six very traditional torpedo tubes. That inevitably restricts what weapons, or indeed other types of vehicle, they can launch. US Navy equivalents already have more flexible vertical-launch systems.

The Americans have also taken what could prove to be an important step in submarine operations, by converting four former Ohio-class SSBNs into, in effect, underwater 'arsenal ships'. Their ballistic missile compartments have been converted to carry 154 TLAMs, as well as providing accommodation and launching facilities for some sixty special forces operatives. With enhanced communications, these submarines have a very significant multi-purpose capability. Their vastness is too great for any operator other than the US Navy. But they may be an important pointer to the future. It was revealed that one of these submarines, USS *Florida*, took part in the initial missile strikes on Libya in 2011, firing ninety TLAMs[8] – believed to be more than the Royal Navy's entire stock. The Astutes are sure to become more potent 'capital ships' for the Royal Navy as they exploit advances in UUVs, off-board sensors, and underwater communications. As strategic assets, their value in a more sophisticated maritime century will increase. But what of life beyond the Astutes?

The Royal Navy's thinking about the underwater future is encapsulated in a programme entitled Maritime Underwater Future Capability (MUFC). The very acronym is an indicator perhaps of how nebulous the thinking may be. But one strand of that thinking could be that a future manned submarine might be much smaller than the current classes, because it will merely be a command or processing platform for a host of other remote-controlled or autonomous UUVs, from sensors to actual weapons.

Or a future submarine might be a 'mother ship' for such an array of vehicles and sensors. Traditional launching tubes could be replaced by a form of floodable hangar compartment, which could house and deploy a range of UUVs, torpedoes, missiles, or even mini-subs for special forces. Such a mother ship would be a much more flexible platform than today's submarines. Eliminating the need for torpedo tubes could also offer the chance for a radical redesign of the submarine.

However, cost constraints may yet dictate a much more evolutionary process. For example, if the new missile compartment for the Successor class of SSBN is sufficiently adaptable that it could house those future unmanned systems, plus some special forces too, it could become the MUFC solution.

But even if, three decades hence, submarines might still look quite similar to those of today, the way that they will be used and what they will be able to do is likely to be very different. And a sophisticated underwater capability will be even more crucial to the effectiveness of a navy with ambitions to operate globally than it has ever been.

CHAPTER EIGHT

The Tale of the Type 45

The saga of the Royal Navy's experience with destroyers in the missile age has not been an entirely happy one. The Type 45 is, at the moment, at the highest point of what has been a steep learning curve. What the trajectory now is for the design and the concept is far from clear.

The Royal Navy began actively considering missile developments immediately after the Second World War. The first official staff requirement for a ship-to-air guided missile was issued in March 1948.[1] This was what was to become the rather extraordinary contraption that was the Sea Slug missile.

The Navy's initial focus for an ocean-going missile ship was a cruiser, and various designs were studied ranging from about 8,000 tons. Perhaps inevitably, as the studies progressed through the 1950s, the specification grew and grew until, in the end, what was on the drawing board was an 18,000-tonner with a crew of over 1,000.[2]

But the Navy was also having to come to terms with its own reduced circumstances. The shock of the Suez crisis intervened to underline the fact that the world had changed. Almost immediately afterwards, the cruiser project was terminated and attention switched to a more modest destroyer design, work on which had just started.

What emerged was one of the most handsome of modern warship designs, the County class. These ships were themselves, in the end, the size of Second World War light cruisers, but with a dashing, raked appearance about the bows and long, graceful, uncluttered lines.

They were a bit of a hybrid, a transition between worlds, a glance back as well as a focus on a fast-developing modern age and supposedly a glimpse into the future. There were vestiges of imperial twilight and the desire still to cling to a global role in some of their design details – air conditioning sufficient for the tropics, comfortable accommodation and furnishings enough to take an admiral and act as flagships on far-off deployments, as well as keep the crew happy far from home, and even a partial wooden deck to help with those 'showing the flag' port visits to distant parts.

The Counties also had a pair of sturdy twin-4.5-inch gun turrets forward (and would be the last ships in the Navy able to fire a proper broadside). But their purpose lay in their radars and missiles mounted further aft.

The ships' universally-admired appearance at once belied but was also dictated by the clunking, cumbersome main armament that was their *raison d'etre*, the Sea Slug missile. Their long, graceful lines resulted from the fact that the Sea Slug was stored not in a conventional magazine, but what was in effect a long hangar that stretched horizontally through the hull, and which was an automated assembly line which prepared the missiles with their wrap-around boosters before they were fed through elaborate blast doors out onto their launcher at the stern. That itself was a sight to behold, a box-like rectangular skeleton of metalwork and ironmongery that seemed to be a hangover from an earlier industrial era. It all seemed somehow like a rather uniquely British solution to the challenges of the new technological era at sea.

The Sea Slug was a brave effort but not a great design success. Its technology was already being overtaken as the County class entered service. The ships' operational lives were, in the end, relatively short. Two of them, HMSs *Glamorgan* and *Antrim*, were deployed to the Falklands in 1982 and did valuable service. Both were badly damaged, and, while both launched Sea Slugs, neither was able successfully to employ their then venerable weapons system in the manner originally intended.

By then, the successors of both the ships and their chief armament were well established in the Fleet. The follow-on to the Counties was the Type 82 destroyer, slightly larger and more capable, due chiefly to its much more modern Sea Dart main missile system. The Type 82 was specifically designed to escort the planned new aircraft carrier, CVA-01, and her sisters. When the carrier was momentously cancelled in 1966, the Type 82's role disappeared.

But one ship, HMS *Bristol*, was built. She was a fine-looking vessel in a very different way from the Counties, more modern and imposing rather than elegant, with a tower-like bridge structure. But she was an orphan child. A major boiler room fire early on in her career did not help. She did not really fit in to the Fleet, and had no real role except as a trials ship for new weapons, and later as a command platform when many of the Navy's other big ships were being scrapped. Although she was paid off in 1991, she has lived on as a static training ship in Portsmouth.

The upheavals caused by the cancellation of CVA-01 spread throughout the rest of the Fleet, as it prepared to reinvent itself primarily for a more narrowly-focused role in the NATO context in the north-eastern Atlantic. One of the consequences was a whole new range of more compact escorts, designed more specifically for what were the Navy's reduced horizons. These included what was essentially a cut-price air defence destroyer.

That was the Type 42, which seemed in many ways to epitomize the new Navy of the 1970s. The Type 42s were modern-looking, and fielded the latest weapons and equipment, like Sea Dart and gas turbine propulsion. But their stubbiness and lack of presence somehow seemed to underscore a more modest status for the Navy as a whole. Official literature at the time made a virtue of their numerical lack of weaponry compared to earlier generations of warships, implying that that was a sign of just how capable and impressive were the new systems. That was, of course, at best, only part of the story. It may have been just an impression, but suddenly all the Navy's new ships did not quite seem to measure up to the much larger, more heavily-armed equivalents being introduced into the US and Soviet navies. And those fleets were also introducing new classes of warships which had no equivalents in the Royal Navy at all.

The Type 42 turned out to be one of the most controversial of modern Royal Navy designs, due in no small part to the high-profile loss of two, most particularly HMS *Sheffield* but also HMS *Coventry*, in the Falklands War. Of course, it has always been debatable how much these losses were down to the shortcomings of the ships themselves and how much to the other gaps in the task force's defences. It was actually a combination of both.

To keep costs down, the Type 42s were very compact and cramped, with virtually no margins for improvements during their operational lives. Indeed, when the opportunity came, the last four ships were stretched considerably. Having said all that, the tight reins placed on size, capability, and cost of the ships meant that, in the end, fourteen were built in all. No other Western navy except that of the United States could boast a screen of air defence ships even approaching that number or capability.

Even so, by the late 1970s, there were growing doubts about whether these ships on their own could measure up to the scale of the challenge of defending Royal Navy task forces against Soviet missile and air strikes in their likely operating areas. One Naval Staff study in 1976 suggested that the Navy would need up to thirty-four Sea Dart-equipped ships to have a chance of doing the job.

Plans were by then in hand for a follow-on design to the Type 42, and an update to the Sea Dart system, essentially a Mark Two version. The ship design that resulted was huge, and hugely expensive. The Type 43, as it was called, positively bristled with weaponry. It had twice the number of Sea Dart missile launchers and missile director radars as the Type 42, plus *four* multiple Sea Wolf point defence missile launchers, room for a large helicopter, and a powerful new gas turbine propulsion system.

It was vastly too ambitious. The Type 43 and an effort at a cheaper variant, the Type 44, plus the Sea Dart Mark Two programme, all fell victims to the 1981 Nott review.

In one sense, the Type 43 was the precursor to the Type 45. But there was a critical difference as well.

Part of the Royal Navy's difficulty at this time was that it and all other navies were about to be outpaced by a US Navy development that would transform the air defence abilities of its fleet. The Aegis combat system, with multifunction phased-array radars and greatly improved computer processing capability, would massively increase a ship's ability to track and engage multiple air targets. It went to sea operationally for the first time in the cruiser USS *Ticonderoga*, which was commissioned on 22 January 1983.

The Royal Navy, in contrast, seemed stuck with the limitations of its existing systems. The Type 42/Sea Dart combination could engage just two targets at a time. Even the Type 43 would have managed only four with its Sea Darts. The Type 43, if it had been built as planned, would itself have been totally outclassed by what the Americans were then contemplating, and probably also by the scale of the threat that the Royal Navy was facing in terms of Soviet capabilities at the time.

The designers of the Type 43 believed that it would have been quite easy to adapt it to take the Aegis system, and that that would have been both a more sensible and cost-effective approach than the one being contemplated by the Navy's planners.[3] But it never happened. And it would take more than another quarter of a century before the Royal Navy would find itself on the verge of deploying a comparable system.

In the interim, it had to soldier on with its remaining Type 42s and the Sea Dart missile system. Some of this combination's limitations were brutally shown up in the Falklands – the Sea Dart's problems with low-level targets and missiles, plus the Type 42's trouble in tracking targets over land and lack of a last-ditch missile defence. But the missile did score some successes. The fact that the Argentine Navy had two Type 42s of its own, and knew the Sea Dart's capabilities, is also credited with forcing Argentine aircraft to adopt more difficult attack profiles which reduced their effectiveness. In fact, for a good part of its service life, Sea Dart was an effective and creditable system by all but US Navy standards.

The Type 42s and Sea Dart did also receive incremental upgrades. The ships, in particular, were fitted with the Vulcan-Phalanx close-in weapons system (CIWS), a radar-guided Gatling gun to make up for the deficiency against missile attack. The Sea Dart improvements included increasing its range and its ability to cope with multiple targets. In the Persian Gulf in 1991, HMS *Gloucester*, escorting the battleship USS *Missouri*, shot down an Iraqi Silkworm anti-ship missile with a Sea Dart, although the attacking weapon was no longer a threat by the time it was intercepted.

By the 1990s, the Royal Navy's air defence capability was beginning to get left behind by others as well as the Americans. A remedy was needed with increasing urgency. Hence the huge expectations that were placed on the Type 45, which from the outset was meant to provide a quantum leap in capability.

After the cancellation of the Type 43, a collaborative project looked as if it might provide the solution to the Navy's need for a Type 42 successor. Initially, for much of the 1980s, there were the studies for a NATO-wide frigate project, NFR 90, which at one stage looked set to bring together Britain, the United States, France, Germany, Italy, Spain, Canada, and the Netherlands in creating a common new warship. But differing national requirements meant that it struggled from the start, and by the end of the decade it had in effect foundered.

In the aftermath of that, different countries split off to pursue other collaborations. Britain, France, and Italy clubbed together on what was initially called the Common New Generation Frigate (CNGF), but which came more commonly to be known as Project Horizon. An initial agreement between the three was reached in December 1992.

But this grouping proved fractious from an early stage as well. The chiefly Franco-Italian Principal Anti-Air Missile System (PAAMS) was to be the main armament, with the highly-manoeuvrable Aster 15 and 30 short- and medium-range missiles. But a key early difference was over Britain's decision to incorporate a more capable active phased-array radar, its own Sampson system, as its main sensor, rather than the European Multifunction Phased-Array Radar (EMPAR) chosen by the other two.

The Royal Navy's more demanding requirements were based on its bitter experiences in the Falklands War. These led it to draw up a concept for a local area air defence capability, as it was called, to deal with complex multiple attacks by aircraft and missiles, in the open ocean and over land. Its originators probably had no idea at the time that it would take so long to bring this concept to fruition.

There were other differences between the CNGF/Horizon partners over industrial work-share and management structures. Consequently, in April 1999, Britain announced that it was leaving Project Horizon and pursuing its own national solution, the Type 45.

By then, the need for the new ships was getting increasingly urgent. Because of that urgency, and the need to make up for much lost time, the Type 45 would retain many similarities in hull shape and basic design with the Horizon-class vessels that emerged to serve with the French and Italian navies. The British also stuck with the PAAMS system, albeit in their own modified form.

With all the delays and false starts, some critics suggested that the Type 45 would be outmoded before it even arrived. It was a very conventional ship design, they said, when the US Navy was embarking on what appeared to be a radically different destroyer concept, what became the DDG-1000. The problems with the DDG-1000 design, and the US Navy's reversion to a destroyer design dating from the 1970s, undercut some of those complaints at least.

But, if the Navy thought that making use of much of the work that had gone into the CGNF programme would reduce the risks and potential problems in creating the Type 45, it was to be sorely disappointed. There were initial disagreements over how the ships would be assembled. They were built in blocks. The final assembly, launching, and outfitting of the vessels ended up being concentrated at the BAE Systems yards at Govan and Scotstoun in Scotland.

Given the length of time since the United Kingdom had built ships of this nature, the amount of new technology involved in the Type 45 design was also significant, at about 80 per cent of the overall design. So delays and complications inevitably arose. The Type 45 assumed the mantle of a 'problem project'.

Some of those problems arose from the fact that the planned size of the class was cut in half. The original Royal Navy intention was to build twelve, in effect a one-for-one replacement of the remaining Type 42s. Perhaps that was never realistic. But, in any event, the mini-review of 2004 saw the planned number in the class cut by a third to eight, as the overall size of the Navy's destroyer and frigate force was reduced from the target of thirty-two in the 1998 SDR to twenty-five.

And, while orders and work went ahead on the first six ships, the prospects for the seventh and eighth got ever dimmer until, in June 2008, the government confirmed that they too would not be built. With rising costs and delays, political and public dismay with the programme was also growing. Its cost rose to nearly £6.5 billion, an increase of almost £1.5 billion on the original target. With just six ships in the class, that implied a cost to the British taxpayer for each one of more than £1 billion. And the programme was more than two years late.

The cost increases and delays were highlighted in a report on the programme published on 1 June 2009 by the House of Commons Public Accounts Committee. It put these down in large part to the MoD's 'failure to take sufficient account of the technical risks involved in such a complex project'.[4] This also led, the Committee said, to a poor relationship between the MoD and industry.

The Type 45s were beginning to look like very bad value, and they began to be saddled with an unenviable reputation. They were among the projects regularly cited by government critics as a waste of money while the troops on the front lines in Iraq and Afghanistan were going short of vital resources. Why, it was asked, was the MoD wasting money on such extravagant ships which had no relevance to the kind of conflicts in which Britain was actually engaged? Even within the Navy, there were growing doubts about whether these ships represented a good investment.

If even some of the Navy's senior admirals were starting to shuffle uneasily as the criticisms of the Type 45s mounted, everything in terms of mood seemed to change – at least within the Navy – on 18 July 2007. On that day, the first of the class, HMS *Daring*, embarked on her maiden sea trials. After a long period in which the Navy seemed to have been starved of good news and new ships, this was a good day, and the most tangible evidence of a potentially bright future.

The Type 45s weigh in at 7,350 tons full load, with an overall length of 152.4 metres and a beam of 21.2 metres. One of the main justifications for their considerable bulk is the need to mount the six-ton Sampson radar atop a very substantial mast for maximum coverage. Their size means that their most direct ancestors are probably the Counties and the sole Type 82, HMS *Bristol*, rather than the Type 42s.

The Sampson radar, on its prominent perch some thirty-five metres above the sea, is a defining factor in the ships' appearance, and a key element in their capability. It is coupled with the long-range S1850M search radar, and the ships' main weapons system, PAAMS, which has been given a more traditional Royal Navy name, Sea Viper. As for the missiles themselves, the longer-range Aster 30s can reach out to seventy-five miles (120 kilometres), with the shorter-range Aster 15s for more close-in defence up to 18.5 miles (29.5 kilometres). They are housed in a large vertical-launch missile silo forward of the bridge.

This ensemble, but perhaps particularly the presence of the Sampson radar which sets it apart from its Horizon half-sisters with their less capable EMPAR system, has led the Navy to dub the Type 45 'the best air defence ship in the world'. There have been some crowd-pleasing claims for aspects of its capability, like a detection range for Sampson of 250 miles (400 kilometres). The Darings are also said to be able to track at least a thousand air movements an hour. In others words, the ships have the ability, from a position in the port of London, to monitor all the take-offs and landings in and out of Heathrow, Gatwick, and Birmingham airports, as well as Paris' Charles de Gaulle and Amsterdam's Schiphol airports, and a few others besides, and then assess the overall threat level. It is also claimed that the Sea Viper system can intercept a cricket-ball-sized target travelling at three times the speed of sound.

If the Type 45 can really provide the kind of air umbrella claimed, it will go some way to justifying its cost. But, like all other similar systems, it remains untested in real combat. And actual combat usually exposes critical limitations and weaknesses of even the most sophisticated systems. The harsh realities and environment of the Falklands War showed up many of the Navy's then weapons systems to be rather less than fully reliable. In some cases, like the then new Sea Wolf missile, only that operational baptism led to their development into really effective weapons.

But that was three decades ago. Technology has moved on in something of an operational vacuum, at least in terms of high-end combat at sea. As a result, some question the whole concept of area air defence at sea. It is an approach adopted by all major navies, as part of an overall concept of layered defence. But a lot is riding on the Type 45s.

However, to step aboard a Type 45 destroyer is indeed to enter a different world from that previously inhabited by Royal Navy sailors. They are truly imposing vessels to behold. Their scale is masked at a distance by their modern, uncluttered lines, in part in pursuit of a stealthy radar profile. But it is so very obvious when one gets up close.

The view from the bridge is another one that marks them out as unlike anything that has gone before. The old open bridges, like those on the previous generation of Daring-class destroyers from the 1950s, may have long been consigned to history. But the busy, crowded, clattery environments of the enclosed bridges of more recent British warships also do not prepare one for the Type 45 experience. The bridge of a modern merchant ship would be closer to the mark. As well as the new consoles with their computer-generated read-outs, the huge bridge windows offer a panoramic view the like of which no previous Royal Navy destroyer captains will have enjoyed. The height of the bridge above the water and the expanse of the deck stretching out forward to the bow are further reminders that these are much bigger vessels than the rather squat Type 42s that they replace.

The impression of space when aboard is also dramatic, with broader passageways and larger compartments than on either the Type 42s or the mainstay of the frigate fleet, the Type 23. This is also apparent in the accommodation, with even junior ratings enjoying just six-berth cabins, and all officers getting single-berth cabins. Entering the wardroom is also a revelation in terms of the space available for what is, after all, still described as a destroyer. And, of course, these ships have crews of about 190, compared to more than 280 on the much smaller 42s.

Indeed, the ships have the feel of modern incarnations of the colonial cruisers of old. Of course, the fittings and the equipment are more modern. The facilities of a Type 45 are light years away from what the crews would have actually experienced aboard even major Royal Navy warships in the early decades of the twentieth century. But the generosity of scale in the design of the Type 45s has, in some ways, a more direct link back to those times than to the design philosophy behind their 1970s, NATO-orientated immediate forebears. The critics might call that extravagance. But it suits the ships better for what will be their most likely use in the decades ahead, on extended deployments to unpredictable parts of the globe, often on their own. Even as the Navy's numbers have shrunk, its potential horizons have expanded in the uncertainties in the modern world, and its new generation of ships will have to sustain both themselves and their crews accordingly.

Come what may, these ships seem destined to be the major and most prominent units of the Fleet, apart from the new carriers, for decades. Fittingly, therefore, they are equipped – or at least they have the space – to act as flagships. Just off the main operations room, there is a designated compartment – dubbed the Joint Planning Room – for a flag officer and his or her staff. They may not have even the partial wooden decks of those first-generation missile ships, the old County-class destroyers, but their character, and their employment, particularly as task-force leaders on showing-the-flag deployments, may well prove to be very similar.

Another innovation with the Darings is that they have an integrated electric propulsion (IEP) system, based on two Rolls-Royce WR-21 gas turbines and two diesel generators, with electric motors rather than mechanical connectors to transmit to the propeller shafts. In a major aid to flexibility, all electric power for weapons and domestic services is also provided by the same units. While the complexity of the WR-21 means that the Type 45s will probably end up being the only warships ever fitted with it, it helps give the ships great endurance. They have an unrefuelled range of 7,000 nautical miles (12,880 kilometres), so they can make it all the way to the Falklands from Portsmouth. Again, that is a useful attribute for a navy that expects to use its ships more intensively, and probably more often at greater distances from the United Kingdom, than it has done for more than a generation.

Another dramatic leap forward takes place when entering a Type 45's operations room. Instead of a huddled, cluttered, darkened compartment, there is the sweep of a large space with neat rows of almost uniform consoles. The visual impression is less that of a traditional operations room, more of the high-tech call centre of a modern corporation. It seems strangely un-warlike. That might take a bit of getting used to for some of the more experienced officers. But the actual level of capability embodied in those consoles and the combat system is again a dramatic advance over what the Navy had available to it before.

For all that, in many ways *Daring* and her sisters merely represent the Royal Navy catching up with other navies. In some areas, they actually still lag behind. It has not gone unnoticed that, relative to their size and cost, to the original plans for them, and to the capabilities of many equivalent ships in other navies, their multi-role capabilities are very limited, at least initially. The Type 45s are, in their early service, essentially air defence vessels rather than true all-rounders. And they lack some basic self-defence capabilities, for example to counter torpedo attack. To some of the critics, they are woefully under-armed.

Some of the shortcomings will be relatively cheap and easy to rectify. These include, for example, the fitting of Vulcan-Phalanx CIWS guns, and Harpoon anti-ship missiles. Indeed, these are likely to be added whenever the ships go on actual operational deployments.

Others are of a more long-term, challenging nature. Space has been deliberately left for improvements. And the Navy, in the end, accepted an incremental approach to acquiring capabilities for the ships in order to get them into service as the costs rose. But they will still only add to the final bills for the class, and the arguments surrounding them.

Fitting the US Navy's Co-Operative Engagement Capability (CEC) will be a huge boost even to the ships' core air defence role. It will enable them to link into a massively more detailed and extensive tactical picture shared by other CEC-equipped ships, greatly improving the effectiveness of their weapons systems. But it will not be installed before 2014 at the earliest.

Another enhancement that would make a real difference to the overall effectiveness of the ships would be the incorporation of land-attack cruise missiles. But their current missile silos cannot take them. There is space to add some 'strike-length' launchers. But for maximum flexibility in terms of air defence and land-attack weapons, the whole missile silo would have to be upgraded. Again, the space is available to do that, but only at a cost. And all the European ships which stemmed from the original Horizon programme have been criticized for having only limited missile magazines relative to the amount of money that has been spent on them, and to their foreign counterparts. Each has a missile silo for forty-eight weapons. That compares with 96 aboard the most recent versions of the US Navy's Arleigh Burke-class destroyers, while the air defence ships of Japan and South Korea also sport significantly bigger missile magazines – in the case of the South Korean vessels, 128 launch tubes in all.

The Type 45s have become perhaps the modern embodiment of the gold-plating, quantity versus quality debate. In mitigation, the Royal Navy has, on more than one occasion, had the cost of having inadequate air defences, and the vulnerability of ships to air attack, seared onto its modern consciousness, whether it was in the Falklands, or with the sinking of *Prince of Wales* and *Repulse* in the Second World War. In that sense, it is understandable that it should choose to invest in a capability which even the United States seems ready to admire in certain respects. It was claimed in 2006 that the Type 45 would be the only ship in the world able to shoot down the SS-N-27.[5]

But the Type 45s have a lot to prove if they are ever to justify the money and effort spent on them. Early test failures with the SeaViper missile did not help. Nor did some serious teething troubles with HMS *Daring*'s propulsion system.

And yet, there is a sense among the crews who operate these vessels that they have an enormous potential. And there is an impatience also to have the chance to prove it. There will be only six. But each one could, in the end, represent a significant and comprehensive capability, even operating independently. A Type 45, with its air defence capability and its long range, and equipped with cruise and anti-ship missiles, the CEC system, and with the ability to operate a Chinook-size helicopter from its flight deck and accommodate a military detachment of sixty personnel, really will offer a significant range of capabilities. It will be a major, self-contained unit. With the requisite, imposing, impressive presence as well, a single Type 45 on deployment could have a major effect as an instrument of twenty-first-century gunboat diplomacy. Much will depend on how the Navy learns to use the Darings, and whether it ever gets the chance to develop them fully.

One other uncertainty on the horizon for the Type 45s, the Navy, and the British government is the question of ballistic missile defence. It is not a requirement as of 2011. There is no money for it. But developments over the next decade could turn it into a top defence priority. If that were to happen, the Type 45s would be the obvious, and perhaps the only realistic, option for a British national capability. But the implications would be significant.

There are elements of the ships' systems that are more easily adaptable to BMD than others. The radars and tracking capability offer the most immediate potential, as part of a network of sensors in a multinational system. Providing a full capability for interceptions as well would be much more demanding, and expensive. Again, with what in many eyes was typical British short-sightedness, they have the wrong type of missile launchers. More capable ones would have to be fitted to house the weapons needed to take on ballistic missiles directly. None of this will come cheap, on top of an already hefty price tag for the ships.

However, if the proliferation of ballistic missile technology does accelerate and become a significant new strategic risk as some predict, BMD could become a major new task for all major navies. And the Type 45s and their Horizon half-sisters could become a significant foundation for a European BMD capability.

For the Navy, all this could represent a significant new national defence task. Not on a par with deploying the nuclear deterrent perhaps, but a high-profile mission in direct defence of British territory, and that of its allies, as well as potentially a critical capability in defending British and coalition forces in future expeditionary operations. But it would certainly be a double-edged sword. It would require extra funding. And it would stretch the Daring class even further, when many believe there are already too few of them to fulfil all the tasks for which they will be needed.

As the House of Commons Public Accounts Committee pointed out, while the planned number of ships has been cut, the MoD's requirement has remained that five should be 'available for tasking' at any one time.[6] The Type 45s are designed to have much greater operational availability than earlier ships. But the Committee stated that it 'remains deeply concerned' about availability. Adding BMD to the list of missions would only make matters worse.

Could the Royal Navy start buying more Type 45s again, even if it had the money? It may not be a cost-effective idea. Building new versions of the Sea Viper missile system may not be a major obstacle. But trying to construct an extra batch of Type 45 hulls would probably result in the new ships being even more expensive than the first six, even if suppliers could be persuaded to restart production of key components to fulfil new orders.

But additional air defence ships need not duplicate all the capabilities of the Type 45s, which could be reserved for the most demanding tasks. It might be possible to contemplate a simpler air defence ship based on the investment and effort that has gone into the Sea Viper system, but installed in a version of the Navy's next-generation Type 26 frigate.

The overall system need not be as elaborate. A compromise in terms of detection range could be accepted, so the Sampson radar need not be mounted on such a tall mast. The new vessels need not have flagship facilities. This would all allow for a smaller ship. The Navy made the progression in the 1960s and 1970s from the big and ambitious Type 82 to the Type 42, producing a more compact and cheaper ship with a development of the same missile system. There were limitations with the Type 42s, as has been discussed. But the ships in the end were produced in good quantities, and did admirable service. And a combination of Type 45s and air defence variants of the Type 26 could provide the right mix of abilities. The Sea Viper/PAAMS system is surely a better foundation for development than Sea Dart ever was. Indeed, it seems almost extraordinary, having gone to the effort and expense of producing such a capability, that the investment is not being exploited more widely.

The classic example of the potential of such a system has been the US Navy's Aegis experience. The Americans, with the fruits of their initial investment, have continued to exploit and develop the system. As a result, the US Navy now has some eighty vessels equipped with Aegis, deploying a total of some 8,000 vertical-launch missile cells. Overall, it represents an astonishing capability.

As for the Type 45, its story might have developed in other ways. The basic hull was considered on a number of occasions as the Navy almost endlessly waded through the options for its future frigates. The idea might have seemed superficially attractive. But, in the end, it did not get very far, and probably rightly so. There would have had to have been a significant and costly redesign if key frigate capabilities were to have been included.

One other variation did briefly make an appearance. In 2007, BAE Systems unveiled a rather extraordinary-looking concept based on the Type 45 hull, which it called the UXV Combatant and described as the 'next-generation evolution of the surface warship'. It was not a design to meet any particular requirement. It was more a flight of corporate fancy, to illustrate a collection of potentially significant technologies, especially linked to the future of unmanned vehicles of various descriptions. The entire aft half of the ship was dominated by a flight deck. And splayed out rather awkwardly on either side were angled runways, chiefly for the operation of UAVs. Ahead of the flight deck was a self-consciously futuristic block of superstructure, angled for stealth and reminiscent of the US DDG-1000 design. The BAE design would have been able to operate helicopters, with a hangar under the flight deck, there would have been facilities to operate USVs and UUVs, space to stow vehicles, and a ramp to land them. There would also have been an elaborate set of weapons, including a sixty-four-cell vertical-launch missile silo for air defence, anti-ship, and land-attack missiles.

The UXV Combatant was not pretty. But it could have been seen as a modern interpretation of the traditional cruiser for the globalized age. As it is, the Type 45s themselves seem destined to fulfil that role in large part for the Royal Navy, and could yet be fitted with some of the capabilities illustrated in the UXV Combatant – such as, for example, hosting unmanned vehicles. In some ways, the tale of these ships has been prematurely curtailed by rising costs, tightening budgets, and an inhospitable climate. In other ways, the tale of the Type 45s is only just beginning, and they will inevitably play a prominent part in Britain's future navy. There is a good chance that the maritime century and the threats associated with it will unfold in a way that will mean there is much less questioning of the sophisticaion of the Type 45s than there has been.

CHAPTER NINE

Defining a Frigate

The frigate. It has been variously the eyes of the Fleet and the workhorse of the Fleet. The Royal Navy's perennial complaint has been that it has never had enough of them. Rarely will that sentiment have been more acutely felt than now.

In the decades after the end of the Second World War, the frigate became overwhelmingly associated from the Royal Navy's viewpoint – as well as that of many other navies – with the military task of anti-submarine warfare. But it was not exclusively so, and the ability to perform 'general purpose' functions was highly prized.

One does not need to delve too far into the past to find an exceptionally successful line of development in British frigate design. The Type 12, initially a specialist anti-submarine frigate in the early years after the Second World War, would develop in stages into the Leander class, the name ship of which was laid down in 1959.

The Leanders rank as one of the most successful modern warship designs of all. Twenty-six were built for the Royal Navy, the last commissioning in February 1973. Many others, in modified form, were built for other navies. Extraordinarily, a series of descendants of the Leanders, albeit almost unrecognizable, would enter service in the Indian Navy as the Brahmaputra class between 2000 and 2005, more than forty years after the original, and more than half a century after the initial Type 12 design was first conceived.

The Leanders lived up to the adage that 'if it looks right, it is right'. They were compact, balanced, and modern in their appearance. They were seaworthy, reliable, and reasonably comfortable. And they had a good balance of armament. That included a medium-calibre twin-gun turret, a short-range missile system for self-defence, an anti-submarine mortar and basic sonar, and a long-range radar for surveillance. Critically, it also included comprehensive facilities for operating a small naval helicopter. That had a significant impact on the design. But the Navy deserves credit for having taken a far-reaching decision to incorporate the helicopter across the Fleet as widely as possible as a key priority and concept of operations. Its utility has paid untold dividends ever since.

There were more heavily-armed frigates than the Leanders, and designs that were faster. But the Leanders had a good range of abilities. Perhaps most importantly, the Navy was able to afford them in sufficient numbers.

But things started to go wrong soon afterwards, as the Navy began to tamper with the ships, modifying them with more specialized weaponry of increasing complexity at ever-increasing cost. One of the better decisions of the Nott review in 1981 was to bring that practice to a shuddering halt. But the Navy had by then also got itself into difficulties in designing the Leanders' successor.

First, as an interim measure to plug a gap, the Navy resorted to a commercial design, the Type 21 as it became known, developed by Vosper Thorneycroft in conjunction with Yarrow shipbuilders. These were fine-looking vessels, with a rakishness the Leanders lacked and which harked back to the dash of destroyer designs of old. They were the 'greyhounds' of the Fleet. They were a clear advance in terms of propulsion, with gas turbines that were being adopted universally across the Fleet to replace steam. In several other ways, too, their arrangements were more modern.

They were a reasonable stop gap and relatively cheap. But they offered little advance in terms of actual military capability. They had good anti-surface capability, their ASW ability was reasonable, but their self-defence capability was poor. They were popular with crews. But two of the eight members of the class, *Ardent* and *Antelope*, were lost in the Falklands conflict, and they were saddled with a reputation for being fragile.

But the true successors to the Leanders were the Type 22s. And they were already the subject of significant criticism before any of the class had even appeared on the scene. Admittedly it was by now the 1970s, and the dark days of galloping inflation, prolonged economic crisis, and growing unease about the country's position and performance in the modern world. But it was probably in connection with the Type 22s that the term 'gold-plating' first began to be used widely at this time, as their increasing size and cost reignited the perennial argument over quantity versus quality.

Certainly, they were much more ambitious ships than their predecessors. The first of the class would emerge with a full load displacement of some 4,000 tons, compared to 2,900 tons for the last of the Leanders. But how on earth would the Navy be able to afford them in sufficient numbers? The answer was that it could not.

The other focus of criticism with the Type 22s was that they were designed with no main gun armament. The Navy made a virtue of this, describing them as its first 'all-missile' major warships, and thus imbuing them with an image of modernity. But that meant that their only offensive armament was a mere four French-made Exocet anti-ship missiles. Again, this was in large part a function of the Navy's enforced new focus above all as an open-ocean anti-submarine force in the context of NATO. But it led to unflattering comparisons with contemporary designs in other navies.

Ironically, as a result of the lessons learned in the Falklands, the last batch of Type 22s to be built would be dramatically modified, and emerge as perhaps the most capable and most valuable general-purpose warships in the Navy.

They would remain so throughout their careers. They received a main gun, an advanced close-in anti-missile weapons system, the Goalkeeper, and a more powerful battery of US-made Harpoon anti-ship missiles in place of the Exocets. All this was in addition the other weaponry standard on the rest of the Type 22s. But there were only ever four of these very capable vessels.

The Navy would develop them further, with improved command facilities and intelligence-gathering capabilities. They would, in reality, become the cruisers of their age, powerful units in their own right, but able to operate as flagships as well. The Navy would do its best to cling on to them despite their advancing years and heavy running costs. Such were their capabilities that many speculated that the Navy would prefer to hang on to them rather than vessels from the successor class of frigate, the Type 23s. But they were expensive to maintain and operate, and all fell victim to the 2010 SDSR.

Thanks to the fallout from the Falklands, fourteen Type 22s were built in all. But, overall, they were never really considered a success. And, apart from those last four, the Navy quickly dispensed with the others when the Cold War ended.

But what the saga of the Type 22 did prompt was a break in the trend of frigate design. It became clear as the early ships emerged that the Navy could not go on like this. The next generation of frigates had somehow to be more affordable. That was the genesis behind the Type 23.

Some of the early concepts for the Type 23 were truly austere in an effort to reduce costs. The ships would have been little more than garages for a big anti-submarine helicopter and tugs for the then new technology of passive, towed array sonar with its promise of much greater detection ranges against Soviet submarines. The Falklands intervened to change the calculations somewhat. The Type 23 acquired additional capabilities, like a main gun. It also acquired an advanced self-defence missile system and anti-ship missiles.

Still, economies were achieved, and compromises accepted in terms of crew numbers, capabilities, and construction. The ships' endurance and their ability to sustain themselves at long range were also restricted, in order to focus on the specific task at hand, the anti-submarine fight in the north-eastern Atlantic.

Ironically, barely had the first of the class, HMS *Norfolk*, entered service in 1990, than that mission promptly evaporated with the end of the Cold War. That would be a lesson in the risks that are run in focusing a design too precisely on a specific scenario of the moment which might not necessarily endure. It is certainly a lesson worth bearing in mind right now.

As early as 1992, HMS *Norfolk* embarked on one of the Navy's Far East deployments to test the design's suitability for prolonged operations far from home. There were, inevitably, weaknesses. And yet, as the post-Cold-War world has turned into the post-post-Cold-War world, the Navy has come to rely on the Type 23s in more varied circumstances, in more places in the world, and for longer, than it ever envisaged.

To some extent, that is a validation of the original design, which retained enough general characteristics – for example, its ocean-going capabilities – to be adaptable. That was in large part thanks to the additions made in the aftermath of the Falklands War. But some argued at the time that the Type 23s would themselves become too elaborate and expensive, defeating the original intention of producing a cheap escort.

In all, the Navy built sixteen of the ships, which entered service between 1990 and 2002. For some, that was evidence that the Navy was clinging on to Cold War thinking. It should have acknowledged that the Cold War was over, and started planning then for a cheaper design, without the paraphernalia of passive sonar operations, that could have been afforded in greater numbers.[1] Could a different design have been pursued then that would have been better suited to the tasks on which the Type 23s are now routinely engaged? Something, at the very least, better suited to global deployment.

Others took a very different view. The Type 23 was the design that the Navy had at the time. Changing direction might have caused delays in the much-needed modernization of the Fleet. Indeed, Admiral Sir Jonathon Band, in typically pugnacious fashion as he prepared to step down as First Sea Lord in 2009, argued that the Navy should have capitalized even more on an established design: 'it was a disaster to stop the Type 23s, for as each ship was built it took less and less people to build each one, such was the high level of experience. The platforms themselves cost less and less to produce.'[2]

In fact, neither course was adopted. The last Type 23, HMS *St Albans*, was completed in 2001. No Royal Navy frigates have been built since then. Hence the Blackham/Prins critique of the long-term consequences for the Fleet. At the moment, that gap looks set to extend to a full two decades, a remarkable discontinuity by modern historical standards for a navy that purports to be one of the world's major fleets.

And what has actually transpired in the meantime has seemed like another painful object lesson in how not to do things. For whatever reason, the Navy has seemed to end up tying itself in knots over what it wants as its future frigate. It has seemed almost as if the Navy has become paralyzed in a search to create 'the perfect frigate'.

A number of factors have coalesced to produce this state of affairs. There has been more than the usual amount of strategic uncertainty on the international scene, and therefore over the role of the Navy and maritime forces more generally. There have been tightened budgets exacerbated by the urgency of supporting ongoing operations. And there has been the Navy's own focus on other priorities – like the carriers. However, other navies have pressed on with building new designs. Once again, the Royal Navy has been in danger of being left behind. The Type 23s have been looking more and more outmoded.

Of course, there have been significant updates along the way. In terms of fighting capability, the Type 23s have remained formidable ships. But, as the Fleet has dwindled, and as the tempo of operations has if anything increased, they have been wearing out. Their original design life was eighteen years. But it looks as if some will have to remain operational until about 2030, and pretty much all of them look set to serve at least thirty years, if they are not scrapped or sold earlier in further cost–cutting exercises that will reduce overall fleet numbers again.

There have been compensations which have meant that the Type 23s have lasted better than might have been expected. When they were built, it was assumed that they would spend most of their time being pounded in the harsh waters of the GIUK Gap. That has never really happened. Of course, they have been used much more intensely elsewhere, such as in the Gulf and farther afield. And that has raised other problems, like cooling for the equipment (and crew). But the hull stresses have not been anything like those that might have been expected in their original role.

Where those stresses have increased has been in the extra equipment that has been added over the years to keep them effective. And, with all the delays that have been encountered in designing their replacements, something approaching a crisis has arisen in the sense that nothing short of radical remedies will be needed if they are to be kept in service any longer than is now anticipated.

But, as to their long–awaited replacements, the Navy has raised the issue of when is a frigate not a frigate. The answer is, when it is the new Type 26 'global combat ship'. That is what the Royal Navy has almost self-consciously labelled its new design.

In part, that was clearly meant to emphasize its forward-looking flexibility and its relevance in the modern world, and to throw off any Cold War baggage that may now be associated with the word 'frigate'. To the cynical, it was actually just a superficial piece of branding to mask the fact that, after all the years of soul-searching, the Type 26 will in the end be little more than a warmed–over, fattened–up version of the Type 23.

But is the term 'frigate', or more importantly the concept of such a ship, now out–moded? Some navies are clearly breaking out of some of the traditional mindsets when it comes to classes of warship. In the US Navy, the LCS will largely supplant the traditional frigate in its line–up. Likewise, Japan is building 'destroyers' which are really mini aircraft carriers.

But for many navies around the world, with all the current uncertainties, the term actually has a rather useful, non-threatening, not-too-extravagant image attached to it, spiced with a hint of adaptability and ocean-going potential. And, while it seems to cover an ever-wider range of vessels in terms of size, from around 2,000 to 7,000 tons, the frigate concept also seems still to be an attractive one.

And, with some exceptions, the frigate does still seem to occupy a fairly distinct position in the naval hierarchy. As with most warships, there has been a trend towards greater size over the last two decades. But, still, frigates broadly sit between corvettes, which are smaller and lower-capability patrol ships, and destroyers. At the upper end, there may be more overlap in terms of relative size nowadays. Here the definition tends to have at least as much to do with predominant roles. It is different in some navies, but frigates tend to inhabit the more multi-purpose arena, with a further emphasis in some cases on anti-submarine warfare. Destroyers tend still, as in the case of the Type 45, to be the primary high-end air defence ships, protecting not only themselves but others in company. And, whatever it might be called now, the Type 26 is destined to be the Royal Navy's new frigate.

It has certainly been a tortuous process. It began back in 1994 at least, and early studies for what was then dubbed the Future Escort, but which came to be called the Future Surface Combatant (FSC). The thinking then was that the first ships might start entering service from about 2010.

Numerous concepts were explored. They included radical trimaran hulls of up to 10,000 tons, and more conservative developments based on the Type 45. Perhaps even more imaginative than the trimaran designs was the concept of a very large mother ship, perhaps of 15,000 tons or more, that would be home to a contingent of smaller patrol craft of about 1,500 tons. Variations on that particular formula were briefly explored. There was also the concept of a family of different warships of differing capabilities.

It seemed at times as if some of the concepts that were unveiled were deliberately and almost ostentatiously radical, simply to try to send a message that the Navy was not stuck in old thinking and old ways. It was a rollercoaster ride of initiatives that, on several occasions, got close to receiving the go-ahead, only for the project to be stalled and put off.

For a time in 2004 to 2005, the Navy seemed to be indicating it favoured a two-class solution, a medium-sized vessel probably derived from the Type 45 (and called the Medium-Sized Vessel Derivative, or MVD), and a lower-end Versatile Surface Combatant (VSC) that would be a development of an Offshore Patrol Vessel design.[3] That did not seem to last long.

In early 2006, the MoD had another go, starting a twelve-month study into what was now dubbed the Sustained Surface Combatant Capability (S2C2). What the study came up with was a strategy to replace eight different classes of naval vessels, from frigates to survey ships, with three.

There would basically be three variations on the FSC theme. There would be the top-end version, designated C1, which could work with a task force and provide anti-submarine protection and also land-attack capability, probably with cruise missiles. Then there would be the C2, less capable and more orientated towards stabilization operations and maritime security. These two types would essentially be the frigate replacements.

There was a continuing debate about whether the C1s and C2s would actually be based on different hulls or the same design fitted out for different levels of capability. Among the balances to be struck was whether it would cost more to have one hull for both versions, with all the complexity and extra quietening that the Royal Navy believed it needed for first-class ASW work, than to produce two different designs, one of which may have been less complex.

In any event, the planning at the time envisaged ten C1s and eight C2s, to be built at the rate of one a year, and coming into service from about 2021. So it would be the late 2030s by the time all the ships materialized.

But it was the final vessel of the trio – and by far the most modest really in terms of capability – which was in many ways the most significant. That was because it had the potential to shift the goal posts in terms of the surface combatant debate, and arguments over numbers in the Fleet.

The concept of the C3 was for a basic hull that would, in future, replace the Navy's patrol vessels, mine warfare ships, and survey vessels. In response, one company, VT Shipbuilders, even produced images of their proposal to fulfil the requirement that looked remarkably like a basic corvette. The Naval Staff dismissed such a vessel as a 'snatch frigate' when the issue was trading carriers for other capabilities, and possibly replacing full-size frigates. But, as a replacement for minehunters and survey ships, it would seem far more attractive, offering the chance to spread a flexible maritime security capability – patrolling and presence – more widely through the Fleet.

Of course, the key would be to produce a basic, cheap hull form. But if one could be produced at reasonable cost, with key capabilities, like oceangoing potential, adequate speed, and – say – room for basic weapons and a helicopter, it could be quickly adapted as needs demanded. Thus, it opened the door ever so slightly to the possibility that the Navy might finally be able to reverse the long decline in numbers of surface combatants. Of course, the critical concern for the Navy would be to do so without threatening its plans for its more capable frigates. For that reason, perhaps, it quickly became clear that the C3 was being cut adrift from the rest of the FSC programme.

By this time – 2008 – the financial screw was really starting to turn in the MoD, and the dawning realization of the scale of the commitment in Afghanistan was adding to the sense of crisis. Fleet numbers had already been reduced significantly from those set out in the 1998 SDR. The headache that was the soaring cost of the Daring class was public knowledge.

As a result, there was a public acknowledgement that there would have to be a step-change in thinking, particularly on the planned cost of the Navy's new frigates. There could be no repeat of the Type 45 experience. The term was even coined that the future frigates would have to be 'as cheap as chips'.[4]

The Navy itself winced at that particular label. All the same, it went out of its way to try to convince those who needed convincing that it had got the message. There would be no gold-plating. The talk was of utilizing as much existing technology as possible. Whereas the Type 45s had been 80 per cent new technology, and 20 per cent carry-over, the figures for the new frigates should be reversed. That would include a command system similar to the latest version on the Type 23s. Some equipment, like radars for example, might even be removed from existing vessels as they went out of service, and re-used on the new ones.

And yet, the doubts remained. In March 2010, the MoD finally awarded BAE Systems a contract to start serious design work on what had now been revealed would be called the Type 26. At the time, a broad outline existed for a ship with a standard displacement of more than 6,000 tons, a length overall of 149 metres, a beam of 21 metres, and five decks. To many, it still looked big and expensive, and hardly the step-change in ambition that was required. The target cost for each ship was £400–450 million.[5] Maybe the Navy had not 'got it' after all.

As it turned out, that plan did not last very long. The SDSR saw to that. Within weeks of the contract having been announced, there had been a change of government and a sudden realization in the MoD, the Navy, and the shipbuilding industry that money was going to be dramatically tighter even than had previously been thought.

With an expectation that overall frigate numbers were going to be cut further in the looming SDSR, the idea of a two-tier C1 and C2 frigate force started to look untenable. So the two variants were merged. The ships in the class would instead be adaptable to ASW or general-purpose missions depending on circumstances. So, through the summer of 2010 – as the SDSR went through its tortuous and tortured processes in and around Whitehall – a different Type 26 started to take shape.

Perhaps accepting the inevitable, senior members of the Naval Staff began to suggest that they had been growing increasingly unhappy anyway that the Type 26 design had been getting too large, ambitious, and expensive. Six thousand tons had seemed to be edging towards 7,000 tons and the size of a Type 45. The aim switched now to a ship below 6,000 tons, with a lower price. Inevitably, some hoped-for capabilities would have to be sacrificed.

That is still a lot larger than a Type 23. The designers argue that that is inevitable, as standards in terms of such things as accommodation have moved on significantly. Even just trying to replicate the Type 23 to twenty-first century standards would mean a bigger ship. Others were less convinced. Clearly, size mattered, and the Navy was hugely sensitive to it. However, again, the designers argued that making the ship smaller was exactly the wrong thing to do if increased flexibility and adaptability were the aims.

For some, though, the question was, why a frigate at all? Why not a basic merchant ship hull, modified to carry helicopters and maybe some containerized anti-ship missiles? Would that not be even more effective in terms of ASW, given that the helicopter is the key component in that battle? That is especially so if the focus is to be hunting ultra-quiet conventionally-powered submarines in the murky, shallow waters of the littoral, where even a sophisticated frigate would be more of a sitting duck than an asset. And would not the converted merchant ship also be perfectly acceptable for a whole range of other basic maritime patrol tasks? Is the Navy not wedded still to an outdated vision of war at sea? Indeed, is the ASW fixation another hangover from Cold War thinking, and more Royal Navy cultural baggage from a time when it was the NATO leader in the business of hunting submarines? Will it not be the case that these ships will need to be good pirate chasers for most of their operational lives, and very quiet submarine chasers for only a small part of the time?

The Navy's defence is that, in the end, its ultimate task is to be ready to fight in full-scale combat, and for that only a fast, well-built ship, able to fight and to defend itself, will do. That was a bitter lesson of the Falklands War, and it still influences the Navy profoundly. And, in the evolving global environment, conflict at sea between states – which will have submarines – may not be as remote as it might now appear.

And while frigates can perform those maritime tasks at the lower end of the spectrum that the public mostly sees, like the civilian evacuations, disaster relief, and anti-piracy or anti-drugs patrols, the same is not true in reverse of a converted merchant ship in full-scale combat if necessary.

Yes, small patrol craft can carry as many anti-ship missiles as the current Type 23s or the future Type 26, or even more. But they cannot do all the other things as well, like open-ocean patrolling and task force operations, as well as the soft power tasks of disaster relief, and be able to deploy away from home for ninety days at a time, say, at a range of 7,000 miles. Those are the kinds of requirements that Royal Navy warships must meet. Simple helicopter-carrying platforms can do some of these things. But they cannot fight and take damage. At the same time, if they are to be substitutes for frigates, they cannot be kept out of harm's way all the time either – especially in this complex world in which it is impossible to tell where the front line is any more.

But maybe the requirement is wrong. Perhaps the Royal Navy should not be required to have such a focus on high-end war-fighting. And perhaps some of the much-vaunted and expensive survivability that it builds into its warships is not necessary, and may not make as much difference in terms of protection that the Navy and its shipbuilders claim. The Royal Danish Navy works to different requirements, and has produced the much-admired Absalon class of flexible warships. They are not particularly robust, but they can carry a reasonable number of weapons, and have space and flexibility to carry out a number of different missions. They look very useful for missions like counter-piracy and maritime security. Even within the Royal Navy, there are many who would like to see such a ship in service.

In the end, a large part of the difference will be down to different political direction, priorities, and missions. But, for the critics, there may also be a large slice of Royal Navy prejudice – at least at senior levels – against vessels like the Absalons, and an attachment to something that is in a different league.

But are there other alternatives? There is certainly a case, for example, for trying to get more of the hugely-capable Merlin helicopters to sea, and in more than just single flights aboard frigates. The Merlin is another one of those Rolls-Royce-style capabilities, in which huge resources have been invested, but which are not being exploited to their full potential because the money is not there. British defence procurement is littered with such cases. The Merlin, in particular, has been dubbed 'a flying frigate' such is its ASW capability. But there may be other vessels that could carry more of them, without sacrificing frigates in the process.

As it is, and as with the earlier Type 26 concept, the new, post-SDSR 'Mark Two' version will have a hangar big enough to take a Merlin helicopter or two Lynxes, and a flight deck big enough for a Chinook. Such is the perceived utility of the Chinook in the current climate, for everything from troop-carrying to humanitarian relief, that it has become the benchmark in terms of flight deck dimensions for warship designers. Anything less is perceived as dramatically less flexible and useful. There will also be the ability to operate UAVs in various forms.

The Type 26 Mark Two will also have a medium-calibre gun. There will be a missile silo for the successor to the Sea Wolf self-defence missile, the naval version of the proposed Common Anti-air Modular Missile (CAMM). There will be provision for Harpoon anti-ship missiles, and strike-length cells for land-attack cruise missiles. But capabilities have been taken out of the revised version, like provision for a close-in weapons system. For some, that looks like a good decision, showing that the Navy is willing to accept some 'good enough' capabilities rather than perfect solutions in order to keep the Type 26 affordable. For others, it is a worrying sign that the Navy has forgotten some critical lessons in actual war-fighting, like how costly the absence of capabilities like CIWS systems was in the Falklands.

A key feature of the Type 26 will still be the mission bay in the stern, accessed via a stern ramp, and able to accommodate a range of equipment, from fast raiding craft for special forces to sonar modules, and in particular to make it dramatically easier to deploy and recover them in a wide range of situations. Such a facility has almost become the must-have 'fashion statement' of frigate design, perhaps in the way that the helicopter hangar and flight deck did in the latter part of the twentieth century. To maximize flexibility, the Type 26's mission bay is being designed to accept equipment that can fit into the Airbus A400M military transport aircraft. It may also have advanced features such as a rather *Star-Wars*-like automated docking capability, to speed up the launch and recovery of the craft that it is carrying.

The other most critical factor affecting the Type 26's design has been the desire to attract international partners and customers. This was underlined in a speech in London in late 2010 by Defence Secretary Liam Fox. He said that he wanted the Type 26 to be the equivalent of the Joint Strike Fighter programme[5]. That may have been an unfortunate parallel, given the troubles and setbacks that that particular project has suffered. But it was easy to see what he meant in terms of the international partnering process, and the prospects for sales around the world. From the outset, key partners that the British were targeting for the Type 26 programme included Brazil, Canada, Australia, and Turkey.

For the Royal Navy, that offers the mouth-watering prospect of reduced unit costs, and therefore – perhaps – more Type 26s for the Fleet. But it has also meant an acceptance of compromise of a type that it has been deeply resistant to in the past. The aim is to produce a platform that is as common as possible across different navies, with modularity and adaptability built in. It means being able to offer different versions – for general purpose, ASW, and air defence, with room for different choices of weapons and equipment.

The Royal Navy has an ambitious target to reduce core crew numbers to about 130, with room for an extra thirty-six personnel for specific tasks. In comparison, the Type 23s – lean-man ships themselves in their day – have crews of 185. The much lower aim for the Type 26 implies much more automation. But that will be too ambitious a goal for many navies for such a ship. So there will have to be flexibility. Crew space will also have to be reduced compared to the Type 45s, to save money. But the Navy will still need to keep its skilled personnel interested in staying. So the living conditions aboard will still have to be 'retention-positive' in the jargon.

The Navy's demand for a quiet ship of sufficient speed to carry out ASW missions is still likely to dictate a combined propulsion system of a gas turbine and diesels. But for most potential customers, diesels will probably be good enough. Accommodating both options will be a key determinant of success.

Britain and British industry have a lot of ground to make up in terms of re-establishing a position in the international market for major warships. And while the Royal Navy was anguishing for years over its new frigate design, and desperately searching for the money for it, others have been forging ahead. In April 2011, the first of the French Navy's versions of the joint Franco-Italian multi-mission frigate programme (*fregate multi-mission*, FREMM), *Aquitaine*, put to sea on trials. In the market-place, the FREMMs are surely to be the Type 26's arch rivals. So, on current plans, they have a decade's head start.

For the Royal Navy, the SDSR pared down its destroyer and frigate force to just nineteen ships. With the six Type 45s all in service or on the way, the implication is that – at most – there will be a need for thirteen Type 26s. That could be the Navy's entire frigate force for the next three decades and more. As recently as the 1970s, that number would have represented just two out of maybe half a dozen frigate squadrons. However, experience strongly suggests that the plan will never materialize exactly like that anyway, especially given that – on current assumptions – the last ship in the class is not due to appear until the mid-2030s. The historical trend suggests that frigate numbers will be cut further long before that. The Navy's dearest hope, of course, is that a swing back towards a more maritime outlook, coupled perhaps with a successful effort to control project costs (perhaps aided by some foreign orders), might offer the glimmer of a chance finally of bucking that trend. In that respect, the key would not only be to keep costs down but to produce a ship with a final price tag that actually corresponds to its forecast cost.

But, for the moment, the jury will have to remain out on the Type 26, and may have to be for some years. The first one is still not due to raise the White Ensign for the first time until 2020 or 2021 at the earliest. The message has been that the Navy and industry have learned their lesson at last. And yet, the Type 26 still looks a worryingly large and complex vessel. It may still be too rich a confection for many foreign navies to contemplate. So the Royal Navy may struggle ever to get the numbers that it believes it needs. That will have an impact not only on its operations, but also on its character and role. The Type 26 is a crucial programme. Because of its timing and what it represents, getting it right will be vital to the Navy's case and its credibility in arguing for a revitalized future.

CHAPTER TEN

The Balance of the Fleet

S tanding magnificently tall and imposing among the assembly of international warships in the port of Bahrain at the beginning of 2011, the RFA *Lyme Bay* rested at her moorings. Directly across the berth, four Royal Navy minehunters – two Hunt-class and two Sandown-class – were also tied up. Between them, these rather unglamorous and unsung naval vessels were fulfilling what had become a crucial commitment for the Royal Navy, and were maintaining a key presence in what remains a vital strategic waterway.

The significance of this presence was underlined within just a few weeks. Bahrain became one of the states convulsed by the popular upheavals of the Arab Spring. It was a reminder of the potential volatilities of the region, the impact of which could bear directly and profoundly on British interests.

The Labour government's announcement of a withdrawal from East of Suez in 1968 presaged the closure of Britain's permanent bases in and around the Gulf by the end of 1971. But, in truth, the Royal Navy hardly left at all. British naval vessels were back visiting the Gulf within a few years. In October 1980, with the outbreak of the Iran–Iraq War, the Navy established the long-running Armilla Patrol, initially with a destroyer and two frigates detached from one of its, by then, regular Far East deployments.

In early 2011, the British naval presence in and around the Gulf stood at about a dozen vessels of different descriptions on different tasks, all overseen by a commodore based in Bahrain. As well as *Lyme Bay* and the minehunters, they included a clutch of frigates, a survey ship, support vessels, and an SSN.

But that scene in the port of Bahrain signified change as well as continuity. Critics of the Navy and the Naval Staff have long expressed exasperation that, no matter how the world has altered, the prescribed formula for British maritime power has seemed unchanging – a balanced fleet has meant more or less the same make-up of some aircraft carriers, submarines, an escort force of destroyers and frigates, and a supporting cast of amphibious ships, mine countermeasures vessels, patrol vessels, and auxiliaries.

But the centre of gravity in that balance has certainly been undergoing change. And the presence in Bahrain of *Lyme Bay* and the minehunters reflected that. Some of the shift had been forced on the Fleet, as it had shrunk.

Equally, it is possible to argue that the change had not gone far enough. But, at the same time, ships like these, how they are used and regarded and, perhaps even more importantly, how their role is developed, could be one path to reshaping and even reviving British naval capabilities in at least the near future.

Lyme Bay is not a warship, but an auxiliary. For some, rather than an imposing presence, she might look like a big, tempting, and vulnerable target, in waters which – while relatively calm at the time – have been for a significant period, and remain, troubled and treacherous. Still, as she sat there in Bahrain, the presence of two newly-installed Vulcan-Phalanx CIWS gun systems on each beam at the forward end of her flight deck underlined the fact that the distinction between warship and auxiliary has become increasingly blurred.

As for the minehunters, they were, by the beginning of 2011, part of an established force. But it was one which had started as an experiment just five years earlier. Under the pro-active direction of the rather larger-than-life character of the then Commander in Chief, Fleet, Admiral Sir James Burnell-Nugent, the Royal Navy had 'forward-deployed' first two, and then four, minehunters. In a break with the common practice, the ships were to be maintained in the region for a prolonged period, rather than being sailed back and forth from the United Kingdom. The crews, however, have been rotated every six months or so.

Burnell-Nugent found resistance and scepticism at first. But, in many ways, it was perhaps the only option for the Royal Navy to maintain that kind of presence. It quickly attained the status of a success story as far as the Navy was concerned, and may – by necessity if nothing else – become a blueprint for the future. The ships' deployment certainly fitted into the sentiments of many in the Navy at the time, including Burnell-Nugent, that something had to change in order to alter the course of the Navy's fortunes. It was part of a broader initiative at the time from the top at Fleet headquarters for the Navy to be more deployed. An SSN and a survey ship would also be sent to the Indian Ocean to beef up both presence and real naval capability.

RFA *Lyme Bay* was also part of a rejuvenated flotilla of amphibious forces. And this group of large but rather ungainly vessels now forms both a larger proportion of the Fleet and a more significant element of it than it has done at any point since the end of the Second World War. Even so, many in the amphibious community clearly still feel that they remain undervalued, partly because they are indeed unglamorous, and that that has cost the Navy dear.

The Fleet's amphibious forces were probably at their Cold War peak in the late 1960s and early 1970s. Then they consisted of two converted light aircraft carriers, the 27,000-ton sister ships *Albion* and *Bulwark*, then dubbed 'Commando carriers' and equipped to accommodate twenty Westland Wessex troop-carrying helicopters, four landing craft on davits, and some 750 Royal Marines. They were the result of an experiment which was tested and judged to have been one of the practical successes of the otherwise ill-fated Suez intervention in 1956.

Also as part of the amphibious flotilla at the time there were two purpose-built 12,000-ton amphibious assault ships, *Fearless* and *Intrepid*. And there were six Sir Lancelot-class landing ships, originally built for the British Army but transferred to the RFA in 1970.

But this collection of vessels still seemed somewhat on the periphery of the Fleet's main business, certainly as it focused more on its NATO mission. There was a whiff of colonial embers about their role. They, and the Royal Marines that they supported, did find a new lease of life, as a key element of NATO's plans to reinforce its northern flank in the event of an East–West confrontation. The Royal Marines became Arctic warriors. But still there was a sense that they were expendable, and sure enough they proved vulnerable as a succession of defence cuts bit.

Albion paid off in 1973, but was replaced by another converted aircraft carrier, *Hermes*. But *Hermes* was then further converted into primarily an anti-submarine carrier. *Bulwark* paid off in March 1981. And *Fearless* and *Intrepid* faced the axe as a result of the Nott review, although they were reprieved just before the Falklands War. There they had a crucial role, as did the landing ships, two of which, *Sir Galahad* and *Sir Tristram*, were devastated with heavy loss of life in a disastrous Argentine air attack at Bluff Cove.

In spite of that, the amphibious force still withered. The Navy's efforts to get a new generation of amphibious ships were repeatedly delayed. It was not until 1993 that an order was placed for what was, in effect, a new Commando carrier, but this time designed for the purpose from the outset.

This was HMS *Ocean*, which was finally commissioned in September 1998. There should have been two such vessels, but the second never materialized. It was certainly part of the Navy's concept that there should have been two new Commando carriers. But, as part of the 'peace dividend' Options For Change review in 1990, it was reluctantly accepted that, instead of a second purpose-built ship, the Navy could fall back on the ability of the Invincibles to perform as assault carriers in a secondary role, or that the auxiliary aviation training ship RFA *Argus*, a converted container vessel purchased after the Falklands War, could be used in that role. Ironically, it was soon after this that *Argus*' shortcomings as a base for large numbers of troops were underlined when she was pressed into that role in the Adriatic/Balkans operations.

Although *Ocean*'s basic underwater hull design was modelled on that of the Invincibles, she was built to modified, largely merchant ship standards in order to keep costs down. Indeed, she was even built in a commercial shipyard before being sailed to Barrow-in-Furness for fitting out with her military equipment. The target price for the ship was approximately £150 million, not much more than the cost of a new frigate at that time, even though she weighed in at more than 20,000 tons. That inevitably meant compromises in systems and capabilities.

For some, the cost-cutting went too far, and the Navy has paid the price subsequently. The propulsion system was far from ideal. The ship's company, of not many more than 280 compared to about 700 for an Invincible, sometimes struggles to keep her going. But the Navy got a custom-built helicopter carrier. She had tailor-made wide passageways to ease the movement of fully-equipped Royal Marines. It was a formula which – for many others – has not been repeated often enough since. The break in escalating costs which her design and construction represented is what marked her out as a vessel of real significance in the eyes of some of the Naval Staff's sternest critics. And what was produced from this hard-fought battle and acceptance of compromise was a vessel which has come to play a central part in the Navy's modern line-up.

The next phase in the amphibious modernization was the again long-delayed replacement of *Fearless* and *Intrepid* with two much bigger assault ships, the new *Albion* and *Bulwark*. They were ordered in July 1996, and commissioned respectively in June 2003 and July 2004.

But of much greater note has been the introduction of the Bay-class ships like RFA *Lyme Bay*. They were conceived as replacements for the Sir Lancelot-class landing ships. But what emerged was a class of hugely more capable vessels, displacing 16,000 tons to their predecessors' maximum of 6,700 tons.

The four vessels were ordered in November 2001, and they were commissioned in 2006 and 2007. Their construction was not a happy experience, with costs overruns and delays. But, perversely, the result has been perhaps the most cost-effective class of major vessels in naval service.

The ships are based on the Dutch Enforcer design, similar to the Royal Netherlands Navy's amphibious assault ship HNLMS *Rotterdam*. They have a floodable well deck for landing craft, a large flight deck, and huge amounts of space to carry equipment and stores. They lack a helicopter hangar, but that could be added. Some critics say they are critically short on power. They are not pretty, but they are certainly imposing, due largely to an astonishing tower-block of superstructure.

And their utility has also been demonstrated in the way that they have been deployed. In part, that has been because the Navy has been forced to be imaginative, due to shortages of other ships. As well as fulfilling its primary role of amphibious support in exercises and Royal Navy deployments, RFA *Largs Bay* acted as West Indies guard ship in 2007, South Atlantic patrol ship in 2008, and deployed to Haiti in February 2010 to provide humanitarian assistance after the earthquake there.

In early 2008, RFA *Cardigan Bay* deployed to the northern Gulf for more than two years, to support coalition naval forces protecting Iraq's offshore oil installations and carrying out the mission to train the new Iraqi navy. And then there was *Lyme Bay*, acting as mother ship to the four Royal Navy minehunters in the Gulf, and providing support for other navies there as well.

Of course, the revival of interest in amphibious ships, and their increased prominence in the Fleet, was the inevitable result of the switch in focus following the end of the Cold War, with a shift away from blue-water navy tasks and towards power projection and expeditionary capabilities. This has produced a renewed interest in and acquisition of such ships – the power projectors – across many navies, including some in Europe which had not previously had any experience of such capabilities.

In view of all this, it came as some surprise that one of the cuts announced in the SDSR was the decommissioning of one of the Bay class, *Largs Bay*. They had, after all, seemed to have established themselves as amongst the most versatile and useful of naval vessels. What was not a surprise was the level of interest quickly shown by other navies in acquiring the surplus ship.

The other surprise was the decision to keep only one of the amphibious assault ships operational, the other one being put into extended readiness. Having only just acquired these vessels after a long fight, and with littoral manoeuvre at the heart of its doctrine, it seemed odd that the Navy should be accepting these moves. But in a context in which, given the scale of overall MoD cuts being demanded for the SDSR, an option included the abandonment of the entire amphibious capability, maybe this fell into the category of 'it could have been worse'. At least the decision with the assault ships means that the second can be reactivated in reasonable time, although a key concern will be whether the Navy will retain the scale of manpower to be able to do that if needed.

The Royal Navy is still in a better position than many fleets, and better placed than it has been itself in the past, in terms of this capability. And yet, the suspicion remains that institutional resistance has meant that more could have been done to exploit this capability as a more integral and important part of the Fleet. In the context of many of the scenarios in which maritime forces will continue to operate in the near future, maybe these vessels are the ones that should really be regarded as the workhorses or backbone of the Fleet, rather than the frigates.

And, having taken the lead in the acquisition of such ships, maybe the Navy has been left behind by others as it has focused its efforts elsewhere in the interim. The designs and concepts for such ships continue to evolve as the demand for expeditionary and littoral manoeuvre capabilities also continues to evolve. From the early 2000s, the US Navy began to pursue the concept of 'seabasing', to increase further its ability to mount and sustain independent operations in far-flung trouble-spots, including its ability to land forces with the minimum reliance on shore support. In a limited but pragmatic way, the Royal Navy has been exploring this concept for some time. Other navies have been pursuing the idea in more modest form.

Such vessels as these, simply because of their size and capacity, are potentially useful tools in a variety of contexts. They can be platforms to support a range of maritime security operations, not least because of their ability to operate helicopters or even UAVs and, if necessary, embarked forces to operate as boarding parties. And they can act as command ships and mother ships for other vessels. With the right facilities, particularly medical, they can act in a 'soft power projection' role, much as the US Navy has been using its specialist hospital ships, USNSs *Comfort* and *Mercy*, across the Pacific, and in South America and Africa, to try to win friends and influence people. They have proven to be very useful tools for humanitarian relief operations, a task that is increasingly being built into the mainstream thinking of armed forces across the globe. As part of that, such vessels can host a range of activities on behalf of a range of different agencies, official and non-official.

And such vessels can also perform the naval presence role, up to a point. They will not have the full war-fighting potential which a fully-fledged frigate would have to deal with certain situations if they arise. They tend to be very slow. And they do not have the same visual impact as a fine-lined destroyer with its weaponry and combat systems. But they can have an impact of their own which, in the modern world, may be just as effective in 'showing the flag' in certain situations. Their generous flight decks for helicopter operations are again a bonus here. For this reason, some of the public anguish that was expressed when it was revealed in January 2011 that a warship would be permanently replaced by an RFA in the Caribbean guard-ship role may have been misplaced.

A number of other European navies have been developing designs with a multi-purpose role in mind. Chief among these is, again, the Royal Netherlands Navy, with its Joint Support Ship (JSS), of up to 28,000 tons, combining the features of a replenishment vessel and a logistics support ship, able to carry helicopters, vehicles, and other equipment, and able to carry out force projection, humanitarian, and soft power missions if necessary. The Canadians are interested in something similar.

The Italian Navy has long had a clutch of small helicopter-carrying ships, built in the 1980s and early 1990s, the San Giorgio class of around 8,000 tons, and able to fulfil a number of support roles. It would like to replace them with much bigger and more ambitious amphibious helicopter carriers of around 18–20,000 tons, if money allows.

And, at that level, many Royal Navy officers must look enviably at the position of their French counterparts. Their amphibious forces may not be as diverse as the Royal Navy's. But the French Navy has acquired three modern and smart amphibious helicopter carriers, the Mistral class of about 21,000 tons. They may not have all the capabilities of HMS *Ocean* in certain respects, but they are a big step ahead in one way – they have a floodable stern dock which *Ocean* does not possess. Moreover, this uniform fleet of three multi-purpose vessels begins to make the Royal Navy's assorted collection of ships look a little ragged.

But, until the Queen Elizabeth-class carriers finally appear, perhaps the most remarkable warship to emerge from a European shipyard in the recent years (at least since the French Navy's carrier *Charles de Gaulle*) has been the Spanish Navy's new flagship, the *Juan Carlos I*. This 'strategic projection ship', at 27,000 tons, is the biggest warship ever built for the Spanish fleet. And, with her tall, slab-sided design, she has a considerable presence. The design has a carrier-style flight deck and island with a ski-jump ramp at the forward end, to operate STOVL aircraft and helicopters. It has space to carry 900 troops and military equipment. And it has a floodable well deck with a stern ramp. It is designed to undertake four different primary missions – as an aviation ship with a capacity of up to twenty Harriers, as a military transport, as an amphibious assault ship, or as a non-combat vessel for humanitarian missions.

The *Juan Carlos I* is perhaps the closest that any other navy has come to duplicating the US Navy's huge amphibious aviation ships, the Tarawa-class LHAs and Wasp-class LHDs. These are the centrepieces of its Expeditionary Strike Groups, and are – in their own ways – vessels almost as impressive as the US Navy's full-size carriers. The Australian Navy was sufficiently impressed by the design of the *Juan Carlos I* to order two very similar vessels.

For some time, the Royal Navy has appeared to have its eye on very similar or even larger vessels to replace HMSs *Ocean*, *Albion*, and *Bulwark*. But whether that will now be realistic, or even if it is, when it might come to pass, is open to serious doubt in the light of the SDSR. So much will depend on what eventually happens to *Queen Elizabeth* and *Prince of Wales*, and whether one might be turned into a giant helicopter carrier for amphibious operations.

So much may also depend on the prospects for the whole concept of power projection and expeditionary warfare, amphibious operations, and littoral manoeuvre, both for Britain specifically and more generally. If the focus for maritime operations switches again, back to high-end inter-state gunboat diplomacy if not actual war-fighting at sea, or defending sea lanes and protecting energy security for example, many of the ships now being built and operated could become the legacy equipment of the future, as Cold War escorts did when that confrontation ended.

Whatever the prospects for conflict at sea, the chances are that amphibious forces will become even more important, not less. But they are another area in which Britain is taking a step down in capability, at least for the time being.

The Royal Navy has continued to aim high, for the genuine military capability of littoral manoeuvre with integrated combat forces in the shape of the Royal Marines, rather than simply amphibious transport. For many navies, in contrast, the quest has simply been for more effective logistics to deploy forces at long range into relatively benign environments.

Of course, the Royal Navy is the last major maritime force to have carried out a major landing, with the assault in San Carlos Water in 1982. It was not an opposed landing in the classic sense, against a fortified beach, although it became opposed when the Argentine air force arrived on the scene. But it was an enterprise of great skill, based on both the deep understanding that still existed within the Fleet and among the Royal Marines of how these things needed to be done, and also on rigorous training. But it also still depended on a considerable amount of luck. Even then, against a less than first-class opposition, whose air force itself was operating at the extremes of its range, it still required a very considerable effort of shipping and resources. All these factors combined to act as a reminder of what a huge challenge such operations entail.

More recently, the feint of a possible amphibious landing by US-led forces played a significant part in easing the path to retaking Kuwait in the 1991 Gulf War. In the 2003 invasion of Iraq, there was no full-scale amphibious assault, but the decks of both HMS *Ark Royal* and HMS *Ocean* were used to launch Chinook helicopters to spearhead part of the initial attack with specialist elements of 40 Commando and then to keep the assault forces supplied in the early stages of the invasion.[1]

But even the mighty US Marine Corps is having to search its soul about its future and that of amphibious warfare. US Defence Secretary Robert Gates once more interposed his views to put some serious writing on the wall – or rather on the beach – when he declared, 'we have to take a hard look at where it would be necessary or sensible to launch another major amphibious landing again – especially as advances in anti-ship systems keep pushing the potential launch point further from shore'.[2]

Despite this questioning of the future for classic storming of the beaches, the ability to carry out genuine littoral manoeuvre – to deploy forces rapidly at and from the sea, to out-flank an opposition, and to put troops ashore 'where the enemy isn't' – seems certain to have increased attraction in a post-Afghanistan world in which limited footprints ashore, for limited periods, but with the hope of creating maximum effect, will be the political order of the day. In Britain, the SDSR cut into the Navy's amphibious forces and also lowered the target for the scale of landing force to which the country would aspire. From aiming to be able to land the equivalent of a brigade of troops – say 5,000 troops or more – the target was reduced to a Commando Group of 1,800 personnel.

In part, that was an acknowledgement of reality. In existing circumstances, in the shadow of Afghanistan, Britain would be hard-pressed to do any more. At the same time, in the view of the critics, the move seemed to fly in the face of the professed power-projection ambitions of the SDSR, and the thrust of thinking from the previous SDR onwards. As much as the carrier question, and more so than the loss of actual amphibious shipping in the SDSR, the step down in ambition over the scale of landing force that Britain would aspire to deploy was one of the most dramatic impacts of the review. But, unlike the carrier decision, it went almost unnoticed publicly. It seemed to raise serious questions about the long-term prospects for the overall force, 3 Commando Brigade, as a brigade-level formation, and therefore of the overall amphibious force as a capability of real strategic significance. But, as with the carrier question, restoring this capability could – and, for many, should – be a long-term strategic aim. Clearly, the Royal Marines' case is that theirs is the capability that fits the bills of flexibility and impact, of influence from the sea to the land, including in what will be an increasing number of places where there will be no welcome mat or host facilities of any kind, with the minimum of political and practical ties and encumbrances on land, and agile enough and trained to switch from fighting to supporting a range of other objectives.

In May 2011, the Commandant General of the Royal Marines, Major General Buster Howes, suggested that ten years of bitter experience in Iraq and Afghanistan should surely have provided the impulse 'to find a different way'.[3] His argument was that there is choice and the need for choice, and alternatives to 'the inescapable logic of mass and the mantra of minimum force densities' that have underpinned much of the evolving doctrines behind these interventions. If there are to be interventions in the future, but political imperatives dictate that they should if at all possible be of a different character, the Royal Marines could fashion an enhanced future for themselves. For a maritime-based strategy, the Royal Marines should be one of the essential lynchpins between flexible deterrence and when deterrence fails and action is needed, and – to give credibility to the concept of limited-liability intervention – to be a key link in terms of engaging with and bolstering those local forces and other actors who will provide the lasting presence and effect.

In terms of the Fleet and its future, a comprehensive approach to the prospects for the Navy's amphibious forces, its auxiliaries and support ships, and its minor warships, could also produce further significant dividends. It could go a long way to squaring the eternal circle of power versus presence, and spreading more maritime capability around the Fleet.

For the next few years, the Navy should have HMS *Ocean*, either *Albion* or *Bulwark* as the operational amphibious assault ship, and the three remaining Bay-class RFAs. But the RFA also has an 'odd couple' of specialist support ships whose replacement in the years ahead might offer the opportunity to be imaginative. These include what is now referred to as the 'primary casualty receiving ship', RFA *Argus*. The other is the heavy repair ship RFA *Diligence*, which has in many ways become a prototype for the US seabasing concept, acting as a support ship for the Royal Navy's presence in the Gulf, the North Arabian Sea, and on the counter-piracy mission in the Gulf of Aden and the Somali basin.

In addition, there is the RFA's long-running, on-off, stop-start plan to modernize its support fleet under the Military Afloat Reach and Sustainability (MARS) programme. The most urgent need is for new support tankers. But included in MARS has been a requirement for up to three Joint Sea-Based Logistics (JSBL) vessels, to support power projection and amphibious operations.

A simple common hull might provide the basis for a class of ships to fulfil all these requirements – to replace *Argus* and *Diligence* and act as JSBLs. It would be built to merchant-ship standards. It would need to have a large – maybe even full-length – flight deck and a sizeable hangar or garage space. There would need to be ample ramp access to and from these spaces for the transfer of equipment and for loading and off-loading of supplies. A large, heavy-lift deck crane would probably be another capability to be included in the basic design. And there would need to be lots of spare accommodation and support facilities for extra specialist personnel or passengers over and above what would, ideally, be a small core crew.

These ships might be similar to the escort carriers built in the Second World War on merchant ship hulls, or the light fleet carriers that were built with mercantile hulls and main machinery designed for destroyers. Perhaps they might be called Fleet Support Ships, or FSSs.

Crucially, the Royal Navy would also need to invest in modularized or containerized equipment for the different specialist missions that would need to be undertaken. As with the US LCS concept, the idea would be to have a number of hulls, plus a stock of modules, to be used and interchanged as requirements dictated. But the Fleet would, thus, have a class of basic ships which, at different times, could perform a wide variety of support missions, such as:

- A support ASW ship with Merlin helicopters and containerized aviation facilities.
- A support LPH, with containerized aviation facilities to operate troop-carrying helicopters.
- A maritime security vessel (e.g. an anti-piracy flagship), with limited containerized command, surveillance, and intelligence facilities, some helicopters and perhaps UAVs, and an embarked force of troops for boarding parties.
- An aviation training ship, without military command and control, but with containerized aviation support facilities.
- A casualty evacuation/hospital ship, with some helicopter support to sustain that mission, but mainly a major containerized/modularized medical facility.
- A heavy repair/forward support ship, chiefly with containerized engineering workshops for the hangar/garage spaces. The former light fleet carrier HMS *Triumph* performed the heavy repair ship role in the 1960s and early 1970s.
- A mother ship, to support other Royal Navy units on long-term deployments, and to provide storage for other modularized equipment for their use, such as in the mine warfare role.
- A limited power-projection capability, with containerized multiple-launch rocket systems or even containerized cruise missiles.

It would be important that the equipment modules and containers would also be compatible with the Navy's existing amphibious shipping. They would, for example, greatly enhance the flexibility of the Bay-class ships in many of the roles which they are already undertaking beyond amphibious support.

Even with the cost-cutting opportunities of using commercial designs and off-the-shelf equipment, affordability would obviously be a major issue. Another key issue for the Royal Navy with any concept of a family of multi-purpose vessels of this type would be how to crew them.

Some of the functions that might be combined in the future are currently performed by fully-fledged Royal Navy warships, and some by the civilian-manned RFA. But the picture is already changing significantly, as RFAs are being called upon increasingly to perform tasks previously undertaken by warships. This is already having an impact in terms of the training needed for, and mindset required of, RFA personnel. The RFA itself has a challenge for the future. Its numbers too have dwindled as the force that it supports has shrunk. The ways of supporting the Fleet in the future are evolving, with more support from the civilian sector in maintaining warships over the whole course of their operational lives. And yet the implications of a Navy vision of the future, of even more global deployment, and working what ships that it has even harder, suggest a continued and even greater need for the kinds of services that the RFA has long supplied.

For the foreseeable future, the Bay class are likely to remain star performers in the Fleet, and will continue to be much in demand. The Navy will be hoping that the prevailing climate will be such that, in the not-too-distant future, it will be able to reinstate the second operational amphibious assault ship. HMS Ocean's prospects beyond the arrival of HMS Queen Elizabeth are uncertain, and may be rather limited. On present plans, those prospects may not stretch much beyond 2018. Even more uncertain are the chances of the Navy being allowed to buy new, purpose-built amphibious ships in the longer term to take over from the current generation. Queen Elizabeth may indeed become Ocean's de facto, but far-from-ideal, replacement. The Navy still cherishes the dream of perhaps two large, specialized ships along the lines of the Spanish Juan Carlos I, or the US Navy's next-generation LHD. If the Navy still holds to that hope, it will probably need to hold on to Ocean as long as it can, to continue to demonstrate the need for such a purpose-built ship.

There is another opportunity for rebalancing, and perhaps rejuvenating, the Fleet, which has already been discussed briefly in the previous chapter. The C3 concept for the Future Surface Combatant has ended up under the umbrella of another programme, the Future Mine Countermeasures/Hydrographic/Patrol Capability (FMHPC). The redefinition may be to protect the Navy's future frigate plans. But the potential for a single, simple warship hull design to replace a range of the Navy's current minor vessels is still significant.

Technology, in the shape of modularity and the increased use of remote, unmanned vehicles, especially for mine countermeasures, has helped again. With a remote stand-off capability, taking the ship and the crew out of the minefield, the need for a specialized MCM hull design can be discarded. So producing something that could also be more suitable as a generic patrol vessel suddenly becomes a real possibility. And, if the same basic hull could also serve in the survey fleet of the future, so much the better. On top of that, the Royal Australian Navy also happens to be looking to rationalize its own fleet of patrol craft, MCM vessels, and survey ships. So the tempting possibility beckons of collaboration. As it is, the Royal Navy has already begun collaborating with France on an MCM equipment module for whatever the new vessels turn out to be.

It was certainly striking just how much like a corvette the early C3 design proposal put forward by VT Shipbuilding looked. It was for a vessel of about 2,000 tons, 101 metres in length, with a top speed of 24 knots. Indeed, the company itself stated that it was a development of, among other things, one of its other corvette designs. In comparison, the 1950s-era second-rate Royal Navy frigates of the Blackwood class displaced 1,450 tons at full load, measured 94.5 metres in length, and could manage twenty-six knots.

The design outline included a twenty-six-metre 'mission deck' at the stern, open to the elements, but with a stern ramp and sixteen-ton capacity crane. It would be here where the focus of the missions of different ships would mainly be switched, from mine countermeasures to surveying to ocean patrolling, with UUV modules, survey launches, or raiding craft for a boarding team. There was also a flight deck and basic hangar for a Lynx helicopter. And there was a medium-calibre gun.

Getting such a vessel past the Treasury mandarins as a replacement for the current crop of minehunters, let alone a survey ship, would certainly be a daunting challenge for the Navy. Before that, getting it through the rest of the MoD would be tough enough. And yet …

Once again, the key would be to produce a simple hull with good basic characteristics – good seakeeping and a reasonable turn of speed. A mission deck, a helicopter deck and ideally a hangar, plus space and the structural sturdiness for a decent gun and other weapons would be all that was required. Something in the 1,000–1,500-ton class might fit the bill.

And, in 2011, the total number of hulls in the MCM, patrol vessel, and survey fleets stood at twenty-two. A pool of even twenty C3s would certainly have great potential. Even if most of them were only lightly armed for most of the time, they may hold the answer to the Royal Navy's ability to sustain many of those basic maritime missions, whether it is patrolling home waters, minehunting in the Gulf, chasing pirates, or establishing British interests in some future offshore dispute over access to resources, a modern incarnation perhaps of the old Cod Wars off Iceland.

Once again, the Royal Netherlands Navy may have offered a glimpse of the possible way ahead. Its new Holland–class patrol vessels could provide a model of how something C3-ish might develop. The four ships are 108 metres long, displace 3,750 tons, and have an admittedly rather modest top speed of 21.5 knots. They may actually be too large, certainly for an MCM vessel. And they may not have all the adaptability that would be needed to fulfil the Royal Navy's original C3 vision. But they carry a 76mm gun and a helicopter, have a crew of fifty and room for about forty supplementary specialist personnel. They are certainly handsome ships, well able to perform the naval presence role. And the contract price for the four vessels of the class was less than the target price for one Type 26.

At the moment, it seems, there is no money at all available for the C3/FMHPC in the Navy's plans before 2023. Might that change? There may be some spare capacity in the shipbuilding industry following the peak of the carrier programme before the Type 26 project gets fully under way. Might industry itself take the initiative, and build a demonstrator hull, or even a clutch of prototypes, to get the concept going? The concern for the Navy will be that nothing should be done which might be a threat to the timetable for the Type 26, which has become a desperate requirement. BAE Systems could take a leaf out of the French book. DCNS has built an ocean patrol vessel with its own funds, and is lending it to the French Navy for three years. Perhaps, just to get things moving, BAE Systems should press ahead with a couple of C3 prototypes, with a 'you don't have to pay for three years' sticker on them.

But how might the C3s fit in to a future Navy vision? In the mid-to late-2020s, the equivalent of that flotilla in Bahrain might look rather different, and have considerably greater, and more flexible, capabilities. At its centre, there may still be one of the Bay-class RFAs, or perhaps one of the new, multi-purpose support ships suggested earlier, configured as a mother ship. Either way, the vessel would be more capable than the current Bay class. It could have enhanced helicopter support facilities, mainly containerized. It might have more containerized weaponry of its own, including for self-defence. More importantly, it could provide storage for a variety of different mission modules for an accompanying flotilla of perhaps three or four C3s. These could include UUV modules for minehunting, or fast raiding craft for maritime security.

Such a formation would be able to undertake a wide variety of roles, and its components would have much more scope to carry out a range of tasks, be genuine patrol ships to counter pirates or terrorists, and even perform the mine warfare role, than the collection of minehunters tied up in Bahrain in early 2011. Such a grouping of vessels might become a standard formation for the Navy, in the same way as larger task forces, but available for prolonged deployment to key regions like the Gulf or the Horn of Africa. Maybe they could be called Global Support Groups or Maritime Support Groups.

Clearly, there would be limits to how much these vessels could be put in harm's way. Obviously, the risks involved in using less robust vessels do not change. But it goes to that balance between being able to do what the Navy is most being called on to do, and being ready and able also for those most demanding but less regular tasks for which only a complex warship will do. As has been said, in the longer term, the balance may change. Conducting piracy operations off inhospitable coasts may not be the Navy's chief task for the coming decades. State competition at sea may become a much more pressing problem. But the approach of expanding the capabilities of the Navy's minor vessels and auxiliaries, rather than compromising the capabilities of its task-force ships, may be the only course open that will increase useable numbers, maintain presence, and be cost-effective in terms of the overall flexibility and usability of the Fleet.

CHAPTER ELEVEN

A British Maritime Case

When he addressed the Navy's senior officers at HMS *Collingwood* in the aftermath of the SDSR, the then Defence Secretary Liam Fox seemed to betray that sympathy for the maritime case of which he was suspected. Of course, he was a politician. It was a naval audience. Still, he declared a support for the Royal Navy 'not based on historical legacy or sentiment, but on a hard-headed assessment of the future needs of national security'.[1] As well as making the case for sea power in the future, he said, the Royal Navy should be in the forefront of redefining deterrence for the twenty-first century. There was even a suggestion that perhaps the long years of shrinkage of the Fleet might yet be reversed: 'the size of the fleet has shrunk considerably and the outcome of the SDSR will not reverse this quickly – though in my view it will in time.'

A large part of the Navy's problem in modern times has been that its supporters have seen the case for a strong maritime capability as based on self-evident truths. But, as has been said, for large parts of the society that the Navy serves, they are not self-evident, or at least not any more. The particular circumstances of the time may have made the 2010 review a lost cause in terms of turning the tide as far as a shrinking fleet is concerned. But can the Navy still do so, if and when the opportunity presents itself? It will remain a major challenge.

In some ways, the SDSR trumpeted an even greater level of global ambition than before. And yet the cuts in capability were very real and significant. Libya quickly exposed some of them to a harsh spotlight. The plan for a process of painful restructuring implicitly assumed, if not an intervention pause, at least a respite to regroup. The government acknowledged risk, but asserted that it was calculated and acceptable. But there is what seems like an almost organic relationship between such declarations and the unfolding of subsequent events to the embarrassment of planners and politicians.

What is more, the criticism that was most widely levelled against the SDSR, at least initially, was that it had turned into simply a cuts exercise. And yet, on that score too, it seemed not to have succeeded. It quickly became clear that the force cuts outlined would not deliver all the savings promised. Nor would they completely fill the funding black hole. And, on top even of that, the heralded return to better health of the armed forces, in Future Force 2020, will only be possible at all if there is also a return to sustained real increases in defence spending after 2014. Indeed, in presenting the SDSR to Parliament, the Prime Minister, David Cameron, declared that it was his own view that there would have to be such a real increase. But, while that was an expressed hope, it was not a policy commitment. In July 2011 the government did announce a one percent increase per annum in the equipment budget after 2015. But that is unlikely to be enough to make the figures add up. In view of all this, the Navy – and indeed the other services – may have enough on its plate defending what it has left at the moment, let alone advocating any rebuilding or rebalancing in its favour.

Events may play a part. They may be a necessary but probably not a sufficient condition for maritime matters to recapture the political and public attention that the Navy's supporters believe that they deserve. For the Navy, that will mean more assertiveness in making its case. Work and manoeuvring for the next review, in 2015 or thereabouts, is already well under way. For the Navy's supporters, the question is how might it position itself for the fray once again?

In the age of jointness, the Navy has been more than dutiful to the collegiate culture. It has certainly put great effort into making the case for 'the maritime contribution to future British defence and security'. Such a formulation has echoes of the Cold War. Then, the United Kingdom made a 'contribution' to NATO maritime capabilities. However, as the Navy found out, the word could be interpreted very broadly when it came to force levels. But what about making more explicit what is implicit in much of the argument contained in the Navy's case, that there is a maritime future to the country's defence and security? Another term deployed has been 'maritime-enabled' expeditionary capability. Again, the alternative might simply be to say that what the country needs is 'a maritime strategy' in its broadest sense.

Half a century ago, the Navy took a bold step to seize the strategic initiative. It was feeling embattled then, too. So, in May 1961, it made a pitch to ministers and the other services for the adoption of a 'world wide maritime strategy'. It was the start of a decade of uncertainty. Economic woes were crowding in. How could the country retain the ability to project military power East of Suez when the future of its foreign bases was in doubt? The Navy's solution was a 'joint service seaborne force'. All the services would co-operate and play a part. RAF planes, for example, could fly from the Navy's aircraft carriers. The carriers themselves would be 'national assets', to be viewed as 'mobile self-contained airfields'.[2]

The vision was rejected at the time, and may have fuelled the intense inter-service rivalry between the Royal Navy and the RAF that became a hallmark of the decade. Maybe it was before its time. Some of the concepts that it outlined have subsequently been adopted. The conundrum it sought to resolve is now expressed in globalized rather than post-colonial terms. But it is fundamentally the same as it was then. It has just become more acute.

The Navy deployed similar arguments to greater effect in the 1998 SDR. Enacting the vision then became the big hurdle. Indeed, it has taken so long that the vision itself has again been challenged.

With a very similar perspective to that of the Royal Navy, and facing similar challenges (albeit on a much grander scale), the United States' sea services have been emphatic in their view of the utility of maritime forces. This is how the US Navy, the Marine Corps, and the Coast Guard see their place in national security:

> In an increasingly complex world, naval forces provide the Nation with the global presence and the freedom of manoeuvre needed to influence world events. Persistently postured forward, naval forces are continuously engaged with global partners in co-operative security activities aimed at reducing instability and providing another arm of national diplomacy. Their expeditionary capabilities enable and support the joint force effort to combat both conventional and irregular challenges ...
>
> We believe that naval forces uniquely contribute to overcoming diplomatic, military, and geographic impediments to access, while respecting the sovereignty of nations. Even as security, stability, and the global economy become more interdependent, resistance to a large US military 'footprint' abroad will continue to increase. Naval forces provide the ideal means in such a security environment to accomplish a wide variety of missions conducted independently or in concert with joint, interagency, international, and non-governmental partners that share the United States' interest in promoting a safe and prosperous world.[3]

Nothing in that prospectus differs substantively from the Royal Navy's view of itself and its role. And yet the tone of it conveys a centrality to the role of the naval forces in the national security effort which the phrase 'maritime contribution' somehow lacks. But could such an approach work for the Royal Navy? As the early 1960s showed, it clearly has its risks of exacerbating inter-service frictions.

And defence as a whole is under a cloud. It held a position in which it was viewed as one of the few organs of government worthy of admiration, and was one of the few areas of collective activity in which Britain still had a world-class competence. Individual service personnel still elicit admiration. But the MoD has descended into the ranks of 'barely fit for purpose', the British confidence in the armed forces' prowess has been punctured, and the services as institutions have come to be viewed as wasteful. The spectacle of inter-service squabbling brought on by increasing overstretch has not helped. And a decade of conflict has raised doubts about the ultimate usefulness of military power. Defence, collectively, still has a case to make, and it would clearly be better for the services to be able to present a united front.

Maybe the country really is changing. Perhaps there is not the political will after all to play the global role any more in a military sense. Public ambivalence to the Libya intervention may simply have been war-weariness. Or it may have been more profound.

Beyond political will, there is the conviction of the political leadership. The official rhetoric may still be that of an activist nation, of security being the first duty of government. But does the new generation of leadership really believe it, or have a genuine attachment to it? Or is it, instead, political and rhetorical inertia, and a fear that to suggest anything else, a genuine change of course, would be too much of a political gamble? Is there a new body of opinion behind the scenes that would be happier to forego the option of hard-power intervention, sees it as a dangerous temptation, and would prefer to head down the soft-power route? And, without political conviction about the place and purpose of the nation and its armed forces, and a real sense of their utility, and indeed how they should properly be utilized, no amount of capability will bestow either real security or real influence.

Just a few months after Prime Minister David Cameron was declaring that his government would be more selective on its use of the armed forces, he was leading the initiative to establish a no-fly zone over Libya. Both the real impulse behind that decision, and the political significance of it, remain unclear. And Libya served only to highlight the country's constrained and diminished (or diminishing) capacity post-SDSR. A key participant, the frigate HMS *Cumberland*, was on her final voyage home for disposal when she was diverted to the crisis. The RAF's final Nimrods had to have their retirement delayed.

As things stand, all the services face crises of different descriptions. The Navy will struggle to cling on to its SDSR settlement, unbalanced as it was, with further cost increases in the carrier programme looming. The RAF faces the prospect that the number of its combat aircraft squadrons could fall to six by the early 2020s, a very small force indeed, and there is the long-term issue out there of how it responds to the march of the drones, and what that will do for its core structures.

The Army may face the biggest challenge of all. In the aftermath of Afghanistan, it will have to take on a huge reorganization and recuperation. Its consuming focus on counter-insurgency has left it ill-prepared for other contingencies, and that will only be rectified with great effort. What will happen to its patchwork legacy of equipment bought urgently for Afghanistan, but with an uncertain role beyond, and its long-term equipment programme, which has been in long-term disarray?

And what will be the rationale for its future? It has learned the lessons of counter-insurgency at great cost. But the appetite to repeat that experience will be slim indeed. It may be that it is the Army, more than the other services, which needs to reassess its level of ambition for the future. It is certainly possible to question how it can be a logical way forward for the defence posture of a country like Britain, with its globally tiny population, to gear up for further manpower-intensive, messy campaigns that all Western societies will find ever harder to prosecute and justify. Long-term demographics argue against it. Trends in public attitudes to casualties – whether friendly, civilian, or even enemy – will raise ever higher the barriers to the successful use of force in this way. The incessant exposure of prolonged military commitments to the media spotlight will only increase. It all plays to every Western weakness, and every likely adversary's strengths. What is more, the jury may still be out on just how successful the doctrine of counter-insurgency, thrashed out over years of bitter experience, really is.

The tyranny of relentless land campaigns and their operational demands has meant that, by 2015, British land forces will make up 64 per cent of the country's overall military establishment. That is a higher proportion than is currently the case in key allies like the United States and France (55 per cent), Canada (53 per cent), or Australia (50 per cent).[4]

The implications of the SDSR are that that will change, and that there will be a rebalancing. The Army is in for some significant and painful personnel reductions after 2015. In July 2011 the government confirmed a cut from 102,000 personnel to perhaps only 82,000 by 2020. There will be a compensating increase in the role of better trained and equipped reservists. The government declared that that will still produce an overall force of nearly 120,000 personnel, split 70/30 between regular and reserve personnel. Even so, the Army will also have to fight to carve out a new strategic rationale for itself in a post-Afghanistan world.

It is a reasonable assumption that the United Kingdom does, indeed, remain an outward, engaged nation. But the calculus of what the public will accept in terms of the real (as opposed to the financial) cost of that engagement in military terms may be changing. That is the Wootton Bassett effect. Defence will need to adjust to take account of that.

Everyone may also have to adjust to what could be a hinge-point in recent history. The 'Arab Spring', the Libya intervention, the killing of the al Qaeda leader, Osama Bin Laden, the apparent light at the end of the Afghanistan tunnel, and Europe's sobering realization of the stirring of Asia and the shift of the balance of power eastwards promise to change the strategic landscape dramatically. Of course, there may be another shock, a devastating new terrorist attack for example, that will force a further reassessment. But even that is unlikely to provoke the same response as last time. The pendulum is clearly swinging, even if it may not be certain just how far or how fast.

Another change in the calculus is that the death of Bin Laden could hasten the military departure from Afghanistan. The military advice may caution against it. But the political and public dynamic in favour in the United States, and therefore in Britain and among the other coalition partners in Afghanistan, may be irresistible.

So this may, indeed, be the opportunity for the Navy to reassert the value of mobile expeditionary forces delivered and supported chiefly from the sea. But, in the post-SDSR ferment, the first service to put its head above the parapet and pitch for more resources when they become available was the RAF, perhaps hoping to benefit from the limelight of Libya.[5]

Arguably, the most strategic thing about the SDSR was the financial context in which it took place, and the government's absolute determination to tackle the public deficit. Will it, or a successor, be prepared to consider additional funding overall for defence in the future or not? If not, any hope the Navy – or any of the services – has of securing extra resources will be at someone else's expense. Will it be possible, in that context, to secure a consensus on a maritime strategy as the most stable framework for defence for the future? If not, are there other alliances to be forged? With the RAF? With the Army? With other agencies?

It was a grand bargain with the RAF that initially helped secure the carrier commitment in the first place. But it turned out to be a fragile affair. If the Army is likely to be the one most casting around for a new strategic rationale after Afghanistan, might it be a more natural partner? The Navy can claim the maritime environment as its own, but offer the Corbettian link between the sea and the land as the most secure path to the future for both services – for the Navy and its littoral manoeuvre forces including the Royal Marines, and for the Army with its new multi-role brigades in a revitalized expeditionary concept. And that could shore-up once again the partnership with the RAF on carrier strike as the best way of maximizing the utility of air power in the long run.

Generals down the decades may have been haunted by the remark of the former British foreign secretary, Sir Edward Grey, that the Army was a projectile to be fired by the Navy. But in a world in which the garrison role, at home or away, is not going to be in high demand, and manoeuvre warfare in divisions may be hard to justify as well, this may not be a bad relationship for either service to embrace again.

Of course, that is all just the tactics of Whitehall. But it is precisely here where the Navy's supporters believe it has lost its most key battles down the recent decades. However, the Army has its own ideas on its profitable path of advance, and certainly on how it thinks the world will shape up. It is here where there is still a gap to fill. And, of course, the RAF will be weighing its own options. After all, it was when the Army finally came down on the RAF's side in late 1965 – and saw land-based air power as its key supporter in covering the long road home from empire – that the Navy finally lost the argument over CVA-01.

But then there is the strategic perspective. Here the case is that Britain's long-term interests remain maritime, and will become more so. If the strategic aim is to safeguard those interests in the most cost-effective way with minimum entanglement, to project power in those areas of particular interest, and to influence friends and potential adversaries most effectively, then it will be in and from the maritime environment.

The need to counter terrorism, and the threats posed to and by failed or failing states, will endure. But the emphasis will switch back to more mobile, expeditionary forces, deployed very often by sea. Nobody, not even the United States, will have the appetite to do Afghanistan again and again. Maritime forces will offer the best method of sustaining a presence to deter and stabilize, of engaging in a region, and of responding to different contingencies. As has been said, the key will be developing a doctrine that means that this limited liability can still produce lasting effects. That will mean integrating even more with soft power, other agencies, other international actors who can bring other capabilities, and local players. But the classic maritime advantages of being able to poise and apply influence, pressure, or force as required, where and when, and if necessary to exit in short order, will have even greater attraction.

But, while the country will continue to have a global outlook, it will have to choose where to focus its concerns. The direct military threat at home is likely to remain limited and remote. The most likely looming issue here will be ballistic missile defence. Otherwise, the domestic defence effort will remain in support of others.

From London, the broad bands of strategic and security interests start with Europe. In terms of risks, the chief concerns are around the edges, or on what in Cold War days were called 'the flanks'. Both to the north, and into the Arctic, and in the south, they have a significant maritime dimension. The Mediterranean, in particular, is likely to become a choppier strategic waterway, with tensions potentially all along its northern and southern shores.

How long will the Arab Spring last? It may falter and fade. But it is likely to have a lasting impact, and has complicated the task for the West of managing its interests in what remains a vital region of the Middle East, the next broad geographical swathe of interest. There are likely to be years of turmoil ahead. That will be true particularly in the Gulf, where the Arab states on one side and Iran on the other have much to digest, and possibly face painful political upheaval against the backdrop of continuing uncertainty over Iranian ambitions. It could become an even more pivotal stretch of water.

And how much, in future, will that affect access to and the ability to influence developments in the Indian Ocean area? Here is where maritime power projection is likely to be most tellingly employed in the years ahead, at least as far as the United Kingdom is concerned. But what, also, about an increased focus on another area of similar distance from the United Kingdom, but of equal potential interest, the developing strategic picture in the South Atlantic, and along the maritime trade routes of the southern hemisphere? The most difficult calculation will be how far Britain wants to engage even farther afield, in the dynamics of East Asia, which may quickly come to appear far less remote than they have hitherto.

Washington's gaze, politically and militarily, is increasingly settling there. Expect the path to advancement for the senior US military to pass with greater regularity through a succession of Pacific rather than European appointments.

With that in mind, what weight will be given in Washington to a greater willingness to fly the White Ensign in these waters, not just on passing deployments, but more permanently and with a higher profile? And how much will that matter in London? Again, the naval way may be the only way of having a sustained ability to exert influence through the military at this distance.

But the maritime domain itself will become more congested and contested, less benign, and less permissive. Room for manoeuvre at sea will itself be increasingly challenged. It will no longer be possible to take it for granted. Nations like Britain will increasingly need to protect their interests at sea and their ability to influence from the sea. They will increasingly have to contend with adversaries attempting to apply 'keep-out zones'.[6] That will threaten the global network more generally, but also risk cutting the United Kingdom off from key allies, crucial regions, and new partners.

Britain's most crucial ally, the United States, appears to be rediscovering its identity as a maritime nation, in part driven by a dawning realization of its increasing vulnerabilities at sea as well. Almost universally, the emergent nations are placing a considerable premium on being strong at sea. Thus, maritime capabilities could be increasingly valuable both in sustaining established relationships and developing critical new ones, and being able to stake a claim to influence in new strategic arenas that may be increasingly remote geographically from the United Kingdom. Such are the Royal Navy's comparative advantages still in key areas of naval operations – including extended deployments, command and control, and high-end capabilities – that it represents a significant opportunity for Britain to demonstrate leadership and influence. Against such a background, maritime capabilities offer the best opportunity to shape rather than simply react to the geo-political re-mapping that is under way.

The United States will be recalibrating its alliances and relationships. The era of the subsidized security ride under the American umbrella is certainly coming to an end. Washington will expect its friends to shoulder more of the burden, and to take care of more of their own regional problems. That may turn out to be one of the most significant lessons of Libya. It will certainly also look for more support for its own new security priorities, and will judge its relationships – 'special' or otherwise – on that basis.

It is likely to be a world of looser alliances, more ad hoc arrangements, and à la carte relationships. Maritime forces, particularly those of significant strategic value, like aircraft carriers, littoral manoeuvre forces, and SSNs, have a significant amount to offer across that range of potential involvements. Chiefly, they provide the best chance of operating independently at a distance in the decades ahead.

Such capabilities will also be of great importance should Europe, or a collection of European countries, wish to mount an intervention on any scale without the Americans. Only France really has equivalent capabilities, and a similar outlook. Between them, Britain and France could form the core for whatever European coalitions might come together in the future. Again, as Libya has determined, being able to predict which European countries might join which particular contingencies in the future will not be easy, so relying on ad hoc European coalitions to fill critical capability gaps will be a chancy business.

Equally, capabilities like carrier air power will also count in the counsels in Washington, and among the key emerging players, over the coming decades, in terms of being able to bring strategic effect to bear. A carrier-based navy will, potentially, be a major asset for creating a new special relationship with India. The Americans will certainly be making the most of theirs in that respect, and no doubt the French too. Britain may already have missed a great strategic window of opportunity to win friends and influence people in Delhi and Mumbai by opting out of the carrier business for the next decade, just when the Indian Navy is striving to get a more formidable carrier capability up and running. It will no doubt be in the market for helping hands.

So, a global navy, based around carriers and capable of independent operations, is a dual-use item both for providing options without the Americans, and equally for bringing significant cards to the playing table to stand with and exert influence on the Americans. It will also be a dual-use instrument in the sense that it offers a significant tool for a world of increased global competition, but can also be a valuable asset with which to foster global co-operation. It is a very high-powered form of defence diplomacy.

The Royal Navy has already been playing a leading role in the collaborative efforts to counter piracy in the Gulf of Aden and the Somali Basin, providing command and headquarters facilities. Its own centre of gravity is already shifting in that direction. For the first time, a British SSN, HMS *Tireless*, operated in support of the French *Charles de Gaulle* carrier group in the North Arabian Sea in late 2010 and early 2011. The submarine also supported other counter-terrorism and counter-piracy operations. HMS *Tireless'* patrol on that occasion, of more than ten months, was one of the longest in more than a decade, and a sign of things to come. The horizons that are beckoning for the Navy are, once again, increasingly East of Suez.

But could all this be the country and the Navy foolishly aspiring to be a pocket-superpower to try to recapture old glories, as many contend? The country's continuing level of ambition is a critical issue. But the label pocket-superpower may be both loaded and a legacy of old thinking itself. There will be only one superpower for the next two to three decades at least. But there will be more contenders in the ranks of significant medium powers. And, in a world of multi-polarity or non-polarity, with what will likely be a significant reshaping of alliances, blocs, and relationships, this is potentially a very significant grouping, and one in which the United Kingdom could comfortably contend.

Britain remains the world's fifth, or sixth, largest economy. It still has comparative advantages in terms of military skills and the ability to project power. But it will also require the political will, conviction, and confidence to exercise those capabilities if it is still to be a global player. There will be no point in retaining the capabilities without them.

Of course, other medium-sized powers choose not to do so, or at least not to the same extent, and exert their influence in other ways. And Britain has huge comparative advantages in many areas of soft-power influence, which governments will be certain to try to exploit further in the future. These are diplomatic and cultural, in education, commerce, and science, and many other areas besides.

But military capability has also been one of those levers. And the Royal Navy has been widely perceived as a strategic instrument by the rest of the world. So when others see a Royal Navy whose capability is deliberately being contracted, and whose standing at home seems diminished, they may draw conclusions about the country's real level of commitment as a global player. And that will also affect how those other instruments of power – soft or hard – are perceived, and what they can purchase. For Germany, it may be different. How strong or otherwise its navy is may not affect its international standing. For Britain, reducing the Navy to just nineteen destroyers and frigates may get noticed more overseas than at home.

This, then, is the maritime case. Or, at least, it is *a* maritime case. But making it, and making a difference to the trajectory of Britain's naval future, let alone its future Navy, is probably going to get even harder not easier. And what will the impact be of the reforms proposed to the running of the MoD itself in the Levene report?[7] Aimed at streamlining the organization and increasing the effectiveness of central decision-making, it removed the service chiefs from the strategic decision-making forum of the Defence Board. It also advocated giving them more control of their own services. How far that will really happen in practice is another matter. The Levene report, like so much surrounding the MoD in its crisis, was motivated by the desire to get to grips with the programme management. The need to streamline and slim down the top-heavy bureaucracy was almost universally accepted. Whether these changes will really improve central direction in terms of real strategic outlook may be open to question.

And a full-blown maritime strategy never comes cheap. Britain has anguished over whether it could really afford it before. In the 1960s, it decided that it could not, and essentially abandoned the idea. In so doing, it chose to give up a significant element of its ability to act independently. But then the strategic certainties were greater, and the maritime scene more stable, with a reliable naval custodian on which to fall back.

The political reaction to remarks in June 2011 by the First Sea Lord, Admiral Sir Mark Stanhope, on the challenges that the armed forces faced in sustaining the Libya mission, ignited new questions about the relationship between ministers and the military. The Prime Minister publicly slapped down the head of the Navy following media reports of his remarks.[8] The words may have been ill-timed. But the response of the Prime Minister seemed to be more a reflection of the political sensitivities surrounding the trajectory of the Libya mission than it was about the substance of what the First Sea Lord actually said.

Libya may have been almost an accidental intervention. It appeared to be an effort at least to try to do such things differently. But the strains that it revealed – political, military, and diplomatic – also underlined that this was still a doctrine in the making at best. And that is an issue for the Navy and the maritime case, since turning what Professor Lindley-French has described as a 'punish, strike, and support short-term defence strategic concept'[9] into a workable and robust blueprint for future intervention seems to be at the heart of that case. And it may also be at the heart of that redefinition of deterrence for which Liam Fox made a plea.

The SDSR has placed all the services in a rather precarious holding pattern. And while there is a declared direction to follow, no one is quite sure how or whether they can, or what the final destination might be. In terms that have become popular among security academics and observers, the ends may be fairly clear if questionable, but the ways and means of getting there seem to be much more open to debate and doubt.

CHAPTER TWELVE

In Line Ahead

When HMS *Daring* made her debut at sea in July 2007, it did seem to shine a light on the future in a way that had not happened for a long time. It was certainly a boost to morale. Likewise HMS *Astute*'s roll-out a month earlier, even if her introduction into service turned out to be an unhappy affair.

But a most evocative glimpse into the future came at the beginning of April 2010. For years, the Royal Navy and its supporters had to content themselves with admiring endless computer-generated images of the new aircraft carriers. But at last, emerging into public view for the first time, came a real, recognizable piece of that future. The great bulbous bow section of the first carrier, HMS *Queen Elizabeth*, edged its way on a pontoon out of Babcock Marine's Appledore shipyard in North Devon and on its way to the Rosyth dockyard in Scotland for the vessel's final assembly. To add to the visual impact, the bow was suitably adorned with the ship's crest.

And, in great chunks around half a dozen shipyards, HMS *Queen Elizabeth* was increasingly taking on massive shape. On 28 May 2011, the first official steel cutting took place for the second carrier.

In earlier, simpler days, more would no doubt have been made of this as a great national industrial enterprise. As it is, the anticipation in the Navy is bound to grow as *Queen Elizabeth* begins to take shape. There will be countless and key moments to mark the progress as what really will be a huge part of Britain's future navy finally and literally comes together. There will be the 'launch', completion, the start of trials, and finally what surely will be a momentous day, *Queen Elizabeth*'s acceptance into service. That first arrival into Portsmouth, as the carrier becomes the biggest ship ever to squeeze through the narrow harbour entrance to her berth, will certainly be a historic occasion.

And, given the chance, the Navy will certainly make much of it. But will it really be ready for it? The controversy over the costs and the ambition will not go away. Will the Navy be ready to exploit what will be – despite the scepticism – potentially a transformative change? How much will anyone beyond the Navy and its circle of admirers (and detractors) notice or care? Will the Navy have really made the case for what HMS *Queen Elizabeth* and her sister ship will be able to deliver, how the rest of the Navy has also changed, and what potential that offers? Above all, will it be able to capture the public's and the politicians' imaginations again, to change perceptions about the Navy, and within the Navy? The answers to these questions will bear significantly on what the overall shape and standing of Britain's future navy – at home and internationally – will be.

A large part of what the Navy will look like, for several decades to come, is entirely predictable. That is because the vessels now entering service, or about to, will be with the Fleet into the 2030s and beyond. The very first of the new generation of warships, the aforementioned HMS *Daring*, the lead ship of the Type 45s, will – on present plans – remain in service until at least 2035. If the programme for the Type 26 frigates unfolds in the way that the SDSR implies, the last of that class will just have joined the Royal Navy when *Daring* decommissions, and will be serving until the 2060s. Between them, these two types of ship will almost certainly provide the backbone of the Royal Navy for the majority of the twenty-first century. It will require a significant change of heart, a massive technological upheaval, or some as-yet unknown calamity (an 'unknown unknown') for that to change.

And yet there is also plenty that can and almost certainly will change that could affect the character and identity of the Navy, and its role. It is these potential changes of course that could define the Royal Navy for the first half of the century.

As it is, the SDSR mapped out several years of carrier-free operations for the Navy. The Fleet's amphibious ships will inevitably be more centre stage, as perhaps the core capability around which the rest of the Navy will be focused. It will be a different, lesser navy, certainly for a while, more limited in its abilities and the range of operations it will be able to perform. It will be a challenge for the Navy's leadership to demonstrate that it retains some coherence, if not complete balance, and that it has capability to offer as an overall force.

It will not have the same ability to operate independently at long range against any opponent with significant air power at its disposal. But then that has to a large extent been the case since the Sea Harrier was withdrawn. The argument over whether the Navy could mount a Falklands–style operation again may be a stale one. Anyway, the answer from most of those who did it is 'no'. It will be able to muster a task force to carry out littoral manoeuvre, or variations on that theme, like a major civilian evacuation. But it will have to fall back on its new Type 45s for air defence, or an air umbrella from the RAF or an ally, if they are available.

Will the Navy in that time have the appearance of a real, cohesive fleet at all, or just a collection of ships? What chance will there be to operate in task groups, to practise those skills of commanding and deploying such formations that has been part of the Navy's self-image and sense of purpose? What price, in these years, the opportunity to come together, to deploy as a real, serious task force with, say, HMS *Ocean* and an amphibious flotilla at its heart, with perhaps a couple of Type 45 destroyers, frigates, and maybe an SSN, to demonstrate that the Navy can still assemble a fleet of some significance? And to trumpet and parade that fact? Will that be possible, with all the other tasks that the Navy must fulfil? If not, will there be a danger that the Navy will come to be seen only as an assortment of individual ships, on lonely patrols, performing limited tasks?

It has been a central part of the Navy's operations to form such task groups regularly, to deploy and exercise. In 2011, the Navy did deploy its new, reworked post-SDSR task group into the Mediterranean and beyond. The Response Force Task Group (RFTG) basically took what was left of the Carrier Strike Group and combined it with the Amphibious Task Group. It was labelled as a main contingency capability. The RFTG brings together virtually all the Navy's amphibious ships. But, for most of the time, the Navy could muster just one frigate as an escort during the deployment.

Come 2016 or thereabouts, the appearance of HMS *Queen Elizabeth* will inevitably overshadow all other developments – even, probably, the prospect that the first of the new class of successors to the Vanguard-class SSBNs could be ordered around then. For the Navy, the chance to get to grips with the new ship will be a massive challenge and opportunity.

But, under the SDSR vision, she will be able to operate helicopters only, unless an obliging ally is able to lend the Navy some Harriers with which to practise on occasion (or Britain itself might still have a clutch of F-35B STOVL variants left over from the JSF development programme). So the Navy's sense of excitement will be tempered somewhat. And her future, beyond the arrival of her sister ship, is clouded in uncertainty.

So, what of the Navy of the early 2020s, after the scheduled arrival of the second carrier? With luck, there should also be a few new jets – ideally, the first of the F-35Cs – with which the Navy and its RAF partner can begin to rebuild the United Kingdom's carrier air power. But it may be only a handful of planes. And it risks being a long, slow climb – possibly spanning the whole decade and more – before a full carrier capability can be rebuilt, if it ever is.

By the early 2020s, the Type 45s should be well-established in service. The first of the new Type 26 frigates should also have made an appearance. Let us speculate and call them the Leander class, since the Navy would dearly love them to emulate the success of the previous Leanders of the 1960s. A growing number of Astute-class SSNs should be making their presence felt. Work should be under way on the next generation of SSBNs. And the Naval Staff should have turned its thoughts to the new class of vessels to replace the Navy's minehunters and other vessels.

This all could amount to the rebirth of the Royal Navy as a force with real strategic reach and clout. But is that how it will really seem? What are the dangers? One is that the SDSR envisages, at best, a fleet of just twenty-one or twenty-two operational major warships, and eleven submarines. But in no decade in living memory has a British defence programme remained intact.

In the 2020s, a Royal Navy task force of just a handful of ships, centred on a Queen Elizabeth-class carrier with at least a reasonable complement of F-35s, will have significantly more firepower than the much bigger Falklands task force. But the threats will be more potent too. In a serious fight, even the best navy will lose ships. But there is no provision for that even in the current planning. And, by the beginning of the next decade, the number of destroyers and frigates could have fallen further still, down to say fifteen, or fewer, if the British economy remains in the doldrums and political and public attention have strayed elsewhere.

Will that be a coherent force? Will the Navy be able to mount an effective task force with such numbers, let alone maintain a useful presence at sea? Or will it be a navy that is too small to use, neither robust enough for serious war-fighting, nor sufficiently numerous for presence and patrolling? And will the money and effort put into construction of two 65,000-ton carriers, and everything that the Navy has foregone in terms of the rest of the Fleet, have been worth it if the result will actually in the end be that just a dozen aircraft at most are likely ever to go to sea on a regular basis?

The forthcoming locust years for defence spending could yet prompt a further dramatic change of direction. Among the possible scenarios is that the nation will indeed lose the political will to carry through on the carrier programme and sustain the level of strategic ambition that it implies. The ships could still be built, but will never – or only briefly – fly the White Ensign. Instead, bids would be invited from around the world for the purchase of both ships.

The Navy that would be left would be very different from the one currently envisaged. The interim, post-SDSR years would become the permanent future. It might still be a navy with global reach, but with a much reduced capacity for independent action on any scale. It would chiefly be a 'global support navy', able to contribute to the task forces and operations of others, with assets like the Type 45s and SSNs, but with less ability actually to lead them or mount them by itself. This would be a change of course for the Navy equivalent to that imposed in the late 1960s, the last time the Navy's big-carrier plans bit the dust. It would be a force similar in character to that being planned by Australia, able in particular to dovetail with the Americans rather than replicate their capabilities across the board – the Australians would have the advantage in amphibious ships by then, but the Royal Navy would still have its SSNs.

More drastically still, the former First Sea Lord, Admiral Band, once raised the spectre of Belgium. The Belgian Navy has fewer than 1,600 personnel, just two frigates, and a collection of fast attack craft and minehunters. That may be too extreme. But a constabulary navy, or 'global blue-light navy', might in the end have more ships at its disposal. However, they would be limited to the more basic tasks, like counter-piracy, maritime surveillance, soft-power projection, and peacekeeping. The Type 45s might be retained as command ships, but with no more money spent on enhancing their capabilities. The Type 26 would be abandoned in favour of a simpler design, like perhaps the Danish Absalon class. Otherwise, the Fleet would be made up of amphibious support ships like the Bay class for humanitarian assistance and perhaps to support peacekeeping operations, and patrol vessels for homeland defence. But the high-end, war-fighting task would be largely abandoned.

Such a change of direction might seem drastic, but perhaps not implausible in the ages of both uncertainty and austerity, and with a nation perhaps recoiled from Afghanistan. Both the support and constabulary options would offer some safeguards and protection for British interests, including the large population of British citizens abroad, but little in the way of strategic influence. It would not be the Royal Navy as it has been.

When the Navy had to come to terms with the loss of its hoped-for new carriers in the 1960s, it carried out a thorough remodelling of the Fleet. It was based on the ASW task group, with three new classes of ship – the new ASW carrier, a new destroyer (the Type 42), and a new frigate design (that became the Type 22).

Such a moment this time might offer the chance to contemplate something more radical. Perhaps dispense with all the elements of the balanced fleet. A Royal Navy of a dozen HMS *Ocean*-style helicopter carriers, a dozen corvettes, and a dozen SSNs. Such a fleet would offer a lot of capacity to support stabilization and peacekeeping missions, carry out maritime security patrols, and provide a major capability with the SSNs to contribute to other people's task forces – like the Indians or the Americans – for major operations.

This discussion of options may seem to be putting the equipment cart before the policy and strategy horses – a repetition, perhaps, of past mistakes. But they at least illustrate some options, and what they mean in terms of Britain's ability to exercise maritime power in the future. Of course, a lack of continuing strategic debate may mean that the country and the Navy may end up with one or other of these options more by accident than design. But then, it really will be too late to change course.

The academic debate over what kind of country Britain really wants to be will go on. So will that over the NSS and SDSR. Are the visions of the NSS complementary or contradictory, of protection at home and projection beyond? How much will the spectre of new security threats like cyber attack take on more solid form, and how will that shift the balance of investment? Will the country's ability to exert influence rest more on trade, technical innovation, and soft-power levers like cultural creativity? If it is to have a strong military dimension, the Navy would seem to have a strong argument – particularly in the world as it seems to be shaping up, with the players who are increasingly taking the stage – that the maritime dimension offers the country the greatest opportunity to make a cost-effective and strategically significant impact.

And is there a chance, as Dr Fox suggested on that dark evening in December 2010, to reverse the shrinkage in the Fleet? A turning of the tide might be possible. A significant naval expansion seems much more remote. It would probably take a maritime-orientated strategic shock on the scale of the Falklands to prompt that. And, even then, the Navy would have to be ready and able to demonstrate its worth. And there are those who doubt that it is or could be. But it might be possible to produce a strategic navy that would satisfy the two main camps, of power projectors and maritime patrollers.

A case exists for a return to a more maritime strategy for Britain. But the existing plans for the forces already imply a post-Afghanistan rebalancing away from the land and back towards air and sea power, even to produce the Future Force 2020 Fleet. Anything more would be an achievement indeed for the Naval Staff. The Navy will be lucky enough if it can keep the politicians to the SDSR promises on the future Fleet. A real bonus would be a verdict in the end to keep both new aircraft carriers, and to use them both as proper carriers. And maybe also to get that second amphibious assault ship out of mothballs and operating again. Whatever the form of words may have been in the SDSR that the military advice had been that the country's requirements could be met by just one carrier, the First Sea Lord made it clear that, from his point of view, 'if you want a capability that's available to this nation continuously, then you can't do that with one carrier... you need both carriers'.[1]

The room for manoeuvre will certainly be limited. The prospects for future defence funding are hardly bright. The academic arguments that the country has reached a moment of unavoidable strategic choice will become more insistent. But arguments, and the British instinct, in favour of maintaining essentially a balance of capabilities will remain strong.

Part of the problem for the Navy has been that the political leadership in Britain has got out of the habit of asking for the Navy when crises loom, and certainly of asking for it first. It has long been the proud boast of the US Navy that, whenever a crisis erupts, the first question that a US president always asks is, 'where is the nearest carrier?' If the Royal Navy is to prove its contention that it remains one of the nation's strategic instruments par excellence, it may have to take a strategic decision to impose itself more firmly on the political and public consciousness. That may involve political and tactical risk, to be both more activist and assertive, to return to some of its leadership roots of action, initiative and, hopefully, anticipation, to be ready to demonstrate usefulness, to remind those that need reminding that those task force exercises mean that there are real resources available for use. They have been in the past. But sometimes, perhaps, more urgent and pressing initiatives might have made a difference to how the Navy has actually been used. One or two more 'Henry Leach moments' might have meant that the anxiety over sea blindness would not be quite such an issue.

Of course, it will not be easy with so few assets now. Indeed, it will be doubly hard when it will be denied the opportunity for up to a decade to demonstrate one of the pillars of its own future vision, the value of carrier air power. The academic debates over the utility of carriers for the Libya scenario will remain just that, academic. Timing is everything. Had Libya happened a few months earlier, the *Ark Royal* anguish and the carrier 'holiday' may have been easily deflected.

Fisher took radical action to redeploy the Fleet to meet a new set of strategic circumstances. He brought the squadrons home. Fleet headquarters in the modern era may need to be more determined to do exactly the opposite. That may include looking anew at the directed deployments that the Navy currently undertakes. It is a risky approach, as it is one of the few specific sets of criteria on which the Navy has been able to base a case for the required size of the Fleet. And yet it still has not protected the Navy from cuts in numbers below those that the Naval Staff has deemed that it needs. There is nothing wrong as such with having an RFA fulfilling a patrol function previously assigned to a warship, but it should probably be because the operating environment suggests it, and as part of a strategy, rather than as a response to cuts.

By the mid–2020s, the new maritime players will be genuinely beginning to make their presence felt. This will raise the bar for the traditional stagers like the United Kingdom and France. Just how much skill the new navies will be able to demonstrate is another matter. That could still be an area of comparative advantage for the Royal Navy and the French navy. But there will also be an increased premium on those exceptional capabilities that will still set those navies apart, like SSNs.

The new players will include Turkey in the Mediterranean, and Brazil and South Africa in the southern oceans. South Korea will genuinely have joined the established maritime powers which will have also set a course on renewing themselves, like Japan and Australia. The game-changers will be China and India.

New patterns of maritime activity will be beginning to assert themselves. How open or contested the 'high seas' will be is uncertain. But deliberate policy and action will be needed to ensure that they remain as far as possible a global common. The United States will remain the key player. It will be up to others to decide their level of engagement, from indifference to tokenism to real partnership. Volatility at sea will increase. But it will also persist on land. And it could be most significant at the interface between the two. Secure footholds on land will be even more at a premium than now. But free use of the sea will not be automatic either. Sea control will be more of a live issue than it has been in the entire post-Cold-War era up to now.

To be both relevant and responsive, the Navy will have to be even more deployed than it has been hitherto, in what might be called the Burnell-Nugent way. And to make a point that it is there. Perhaps the operational amphibious assault ship could be based at Gibraltar, not in Devonport, with perhaps a frigate for company. That way, they would be quickly available for operations in the Atlantic and the Mediterranean, in the manner of the dashing Force H of Vice Admiral Sir James Somerville in the Second World War.

What about a Bay class, suitably equipped, and a frigate, permanently on station in the Indian Ocean? And a Type 45, and possibly an SSN, attached to the US Navy in the western Pacific? Unlike the Force H example, this would not be a repeat of the ill-fated Force Z experience of December 1941, when HMSs *Prince of Wales* and *Repulse* fell victims to the Japanese and British overreaching. This would not be a British show of force. It would be a significant contribution to the global partnership that the US Navy seeks, a visible presence in what will be an increasingly important arena, and crucially one that will more and more be the centre of gravity and focus of attention of the Royal Navy's most significant ally. These deployments would also provide the opportunities for establishing and re-establishing relationships with other key players, like India, Japan, and Australia. The Indian relationship may be the most crucial of all, and the Royal Navy one of the most obvious vehicles for fostering it. Again, a regular Royal Navy contribution to Indian Navy exercises – if it were welcome – would surely be a strategic priority.

Another critical factor will be the Navy's embrace of the new technology opportunities. Here, the carriers may be the key. They could, and should, be used as exceptional platforms for the exploitation of technical changes over the decades that they will be in service. That could alter political and public attitudes to both them and the Navy itself. Initially, that surely means UCAVs, if they can be proven in the carrier context, and making the most of other airborne platforms for persistent surveillance and intelligence-gathering, command, and if necessary strike. It could mean the carriers, with their huge electrical power output, becoming the platforms for the Navy's first directed energy weapons. It could mean a steady reinvention of carriers as the hub of a maritime capability, as the 'eyes of the fleet' as well as its striking power, in an age in which information and intelligence will dominate, and in which reach, flexibility, and adaptability will be even more vital than hitherto. It is an area where the Navy, with the particular carriers that it has chosen, could once again be at the leading edge.

But is there more? Is there a further realignment that could begin to rebuild the Navy, reverse the long decline in the size of the Fleet, and fill the gaps that have been left by the pursuit of those flagship capabilities like carriers? A Future Force 2020 Plus? That actually leaves little time to make much difference. More likely it would be a Force 2025 or 2030 and beyond. Will there be the strategic impetus for that? Of course, a strategic shock could mean that the arguments will suddenly switch from whether the Navy should have one carrier or none, to why not three? More likely it would be the country lifting its gaze from the deserts, valleys, and mountains of Afghanistan and the Afghan–Pakistan border, and seeing a maritime era starting to unfold. And then a positive and determined decision in favour of reinvesting in a thoroughgoing maritime strategy could have a dramatic effect in shaking up the rest of the world's view of whether and how the country counts on the international stage. Australia achieved such an effect with its bold new maritime defence strategy. There may be doubts about whether it will ever come to pass in full form. But, suddenly, Australia is a feature on the strategic map of its region in a way that it had not been before. And that effect has even spread farther.

What might constitute a new Royal Navy, credibly able to exert influence, project power, and equally to attend to the everyday chores of patrolling and presence? First, a decision definitely to operate two real carriers, with real capabilities, would be a significant statement of commitment.

Secondly, if the new Type 26 can prove itself able to meet real targets of affordability, it might be possible through the course of the 2020s to rebuild a force of a minimum of twenty-five destroyers and frigates. Some of the extra Type 26s might also be an air defence variant, to supplement the Type 45s. That capability is likely to become more of a premium, as potent A2/AD capabilities proliferate, and a requirement for BMD may become a priority. Such a force should be enough to furnish the escorts for two serious task groups, one centred on a carrier, and one on the Navy's amphibious shipping.

From the perspective of 2011, of course, that looks an impossibly ambitious dream for the Navy. But twenty-five destroyers and frigates are barely more than the pre-SDSR level. Twenty-five was the figure set in 2004, in that mini-review, and which provoked howls of naval protest. It is still more than 20 per cent below the target set in the 1998 SDR.

It would still be a very difficult target to achieve just from an industrial point of view. Warship building is now so tightly constrained at such a critical level – essentially to be able to produce one complex warship a year. Any change of plan, to produce anything more, would require significant new investment. Given the toxicity in the public mind surrounding much of the defence industry, any arguments over premiums to be paid for building extra warships could turn out to be a significant political headache. Unless, of course, a decision was to be made that some of the new ships would be built abroad. What if, for example, Turkey was to agree to buy an air defence variant of the Type 26 for its navy, which would be assembled locally, but also to build the hulls for one or two such ships for the Royal Navy?

Similar flexibility should apply to what should be another priority, the purchase of a dedicated new helicopter carrier – or preferably two – both to replace HMS *Ocean* but also to form part of a rejuvenated amphibious force. Second-hand US Navy LHDs might be the answer, if the Americans have any to sell, or buying off the shelf from the Spanish.

One other area of high-end capability could be addressed. This one is even more dependent on the capacity of industry. The most potent platform for real combat at sea that the Navy possesses is the SSN. If the decision could be made soon enough, it might be possible to squeeze one more Astute-class submarine into the building programme before the new SSBNs are needed, if the building tempo could be accelerated. It might also be possible to alternate SSBN and SSN building, at least at the start of the Successor programme, to produce another Astute. Nine Astutes instead of seven would be a very significant addition.

But the biggest difference in terms of the balance of the fleet, and its potential to cover the full range of maritime tasks, would come with the replacements for the support force and the Navy's collection of minor warships. A combination of something like the Fleet Support Ship postulated in Chapter Ten and a flotilla of C3s, 1,500-tonners perhaps with an oceangoing capability, would allow the Navy to spread its net both more widely and more convincingly. The C3s could be like those Blackwood-class small utility frigates of the 1950s, simple to build and lightly armed, but with the space to bolt on more firepower if necessary. The Blackwoods were designed as basic ASW ships, but spent much of their time on fishery protection duty.

The new C3s could do the patrolling in Home Waters. Equally, clusters of an FSS and two or three C3s could be based in, say, Simonstown, for the South Atlantic, and to help build a new partnership with South Africa, in Diego Garcia for the Indian Ocean, and perhaps also still in Bahrain for the Gulf. How they would be employed would depend on events, but the roles could be switched as those events unfold. It could be that, by the late 2020s and beyond, as climate change and the oceanic environment both evolve, it will be the oceanographic modules and hydrographic launches that the C3s will be able to host that will be of the most regular value.

The Naval Staff has veered away from this 'high-low' mix of capabilities up to now. The fear has been that it would threaten the core war-fighting capabilities of the Fleet. With the Navy the size that it has become, it would be a formula that would risk producing an inefficient force with insufficient numbers of any type of vessel. But if the concept is to raise the game of the supporting cast, rather than compromise the capabilities of the star performers of first-rate destroyers and frigates, it should be possible to produce a more capable and flexible, and crucially more ubiquitous, fleet overall, with the right mix of advanced platforms and basic hulls in the water. But it will need more money in the long term. Not vastly more relative to overall spending, or even to the scale of some individual programmes now. But it would certainly require a greater allocation than, at present, the Navy can anticipate. And it would crucially require an ability to deliver capabilities at a price that neither the MoD nor the defence industry have been able to demonstrate in recent times.

It will also be dependent on people, and whether the Navy can attract enough of them to make a reality of such a vision. Here, numbers have also become desperately small. As a result, even small changes of direction will impose huge strains. If the Navy were suddenly asked to crew two carriers instead of one, could it cope? Will it be able to recruit the right number of people, of the right type, able to understand and operate the new technology that will be available, and willing to endure even longer absences from home that a greater globalized footprint will imply? Or will the Navy have to go even further in terms of reorganizing its people, with more rotational crews taking temporary stewardship of vessels which will themselves remain on station for years at a time. Will the relationship between the service and industry become more of a two-way street, with individuals swapping back and forth between career paths at different times in their lives? How will the support relationship with industry develop? There will be increased reliance on private support from the home base. But what about such a relationship on remote deployments as well, with support hubs in, for example, Diego Garcia, or Mumbai, or Mombasa? Clearly, an operational concept for the Fleet that offers tasks that are both relevant and rewarding will be critical to attracting and sustaining both general public interest, but also a sufficient recruitment base.

A Royal Navy based on a couple of operational carriers, with an amphibious force centred on an LHD-type vessel or two of some description, plus twenty-five or more destroyers and frigates, and nine SSNs, with the maritime security missions assigned to a bolstered force of more capable RFAs and C3 patrol vessels, would place it firmly back at the top of the pile of medium-sized navies by the end of the 2020s – a strategic navy able to cover a range of tasks and provide a significant contribution to coalition operations. But for this to become even a remote possibility, something needs to start happening soon for the Navy. Otherwise, its ability to change course will be dramatically reduced.

The ships, the task forces, and the way they are operated will evolve. In the decades ahead the carriers could end up as platforms entirely for unmanned vehicles, supporting also a fleet of ocean surveillance airships monitoring vast tracts of water, and land, where the key concern might be mass migration due to climate change and drought, and whether an amphibious task force needs to be deployed to forestall a sudden flare-up of mass violence. The carriers and their escorting destroyers would be equipped with directed energy weapons for defence, with ever more intricate network links to other ships and forces. The links would allow ships to operate as integrated units across entire oceans, with UCAVs from the carrier providing constant cover for a flotilla operating off a coast a thousand miles away, all the units feeding off a net of floating sensors forming extensive surveillance lanes in the water.

The nature of warships is that they serve for long periods, often through great change, and have to be adaptable to that. The lesson has tended to be that the bigger they are, the more adaptable they prove to be, and the longer they last. The career of the USS *Enterprise* is a testament to that – entering service in the world of the Cuban Missile Crisis, and leaving it in the post-Osama-Bin-Laden era. The fourth HMS *Ark Royal* was designed in the age of the Swordfish torpedo plane. She served through the introduction of the steam catapult and the angled deck, and the advent of the missile age. As she left service, she was operating supersonic Phantoms and Buccaneers able to drop nuclear weapons. The final verdict on the design and utility of HMS *Queen Elizabeth* may well have to wait until 2068.

CHAPTER THIRTEEN

Conclusions

The levers of sea power often act slowly. The role of navies seems unlikely to change fundamentally. They seem likely to get busier, as technology extends even farther their reach and their ability to see and act across oceans and onto the land, and a maritime agenda asserts itself again, not least because the coming nations of the next decades have decidedly maritime outlooks. The leading navies will be able to apply these technologies to their advantage, to gain the information edge and to defeat that spreading array of A2/AD capabilities that could inhibit their effectiveness and ability to range the oceans. But as those information and other technologies proliferate, they too could challenge the operations of even strong navies, and eventually could call into question the viability of some of the established instruments of sea power – like, for example, aircraft carriers. But not just yet.

Where does this leave the Royal Navy? Strong navies tend to be the property of ambitious and confident nations. The consensus of the political class is that the ambition is still there. But the confidence and the sense of identity are more in doubt. And the consensus is not there yet on whether a maritime century inevitably beckons, or how best to exercise influence and express the ambition.

Is the Royal Navy at a crossroads, or a tipping point? The Center of Naval Analyses' report on the prospects for the US Navy underscores that a tipping point is not attached to a particular number of ships. It is a matter of circumstance. And it may be that only a crisis will reveal whether a crossroads has been reached or passed, and by then it will probably be too late.

Such talk may seem extraordinary when the Navy is about to get its hands on the largest warships that it has ever operated, second only in potential capability to the US Navy's super-carriers, arguably the most strategically-influential weapons systems of the past half-century. But the most uneasy of the Navy's supporters fear that it is getting or has been caught in a trap. It will end up with a little of everything, but not enough of anything to be a credible force. With the carriers, the Navy may not have enough other ships for a truly balanced fleet. Without them, it would be missing those elements of balance that bestow real independence of action.

And even that carrier project is still in doubt. Even as the ships take ever more recognizable shape, and the programme gains more technical and material balance and ballast, the political support for the programme at the highest level is probably at its most tenuous since its inception.

The Navy has endured many ups and downs, and been in a parlous state before. It could be going through another one of those phases. But, for many, it does not feel like that, but rather more terminal. It is in the late stages of a long, long decline that will result in a navy that is of a very different nature. It will be just another relatively ordinary, small-to-medium-sized navy, albeit with extraordinary traditions and professional standards.

But there is that prospect, on the other hand, of a rebirth. It is a course that the Navy has been set on really since the 1998 SDR. But it has been buffeted and blown off course in the intervening years. The Navy's conviction still is that all that has been a deviation, and that the prevailing winds of a globalized world and long-term interests will reassert themselves, hopefully before it hits the rocks.

What would be the impact of a fully-equipped British aircraft carrier task force, part of a three-carrier fleet perhaps, led by the Americans, and assembled for a showdown with, for example, Iran? It would be a contribution to a coalition of a type and scale that Britain has not been able to deploy for decades. Real influence, and the maximum room for strategic manoeuvre. That remains the vision, if that is what the country still wants.

What the Navy probably cannot afford to do is simply wait for that vision to materialize, even if it still has the confidence that it will, eventually, and particularly that others will come to recognize it and embrace it − that the scales of sea blindness with fall from people's eyes. The Navy will have to continue to urge and press its case, to stir up its plans, find opportunities where it can to innovate and demonstrate its worth, and show that it is responsive. Otherwise, another kind of future could entrench itself, and one that the Navy and its supporters would not welcome.

Notes

Troubled Waters

1. 1957 Defence Review, HMSO London.
2. Strategic Defence Review, Cmnd3999, July 1998 HMSO, London.
3. 'The Royal Navy At The Brink', Jeremy Blackham and Gwyn Prins, Royal United Services Institute Journal, April 2007.
4. 'The Royal Navy: Whither Goes Thou?', by Commodore Manohar K. Banger, Indian Navy (Rtd), US Naval Institute Proceedings, March 2008.
5. Letter by Professor Eric Grove, in the US Naval Institute Proceedings, December 2007.
6. 'Britain Re-arms Itself For A Vanished Age', Philip Stephens, Financial Times, 18 May 2009.
7. Speech by US Defence Secretary Robert Gates, Heritage Foundation, Colorado Springs, 13 May 2008
8. 'Why Things Don't Happen: Silent Principles Of National Security', by Jeremy Blackham and Gwyn Prins, RUSI Journal, August 2010.
9. 'Britain's global aspirations carry a price', Philip Stephens, Financial Times, 3 August 2010.
10. Hansard, House of Lords, 19 October 2010, column 784.

Britain, the Navy, and the World

1. The National Security Strategy, foreword by Prime Minister David Cameron and Deputy Prime Minister Nick Clegg, 18 October 2010.
2. Speech by Prime Minister Tony Blair aboard HMS *Albion*, Devonport, 11 January 2007.
3. The National Security Strategy, 18 October 2010.
4. The Strategic Defence and Security Review, 19 October 2010.
5. Interview with the author, London, 9 February 2011.
6. Speech by US Defence Secretary Robert Gates, United States Military Academy, West Point, 25 February 2011.
7. 'Britain and France: A Dialogue Of Decline?', by Julian Lindley-French, Chatham House, September 2010.
8. *The Official History of the Falklands Campaign*, Sir Lawrence Freedman, Routledge, 2005.

9. 'Sea-Blindness: It's Not Just a PR Issue', Dr Duncan Redford, The Naval Review, August 2010.
10. 'The Future Is Bright, The Future Is Dark Blue?' *Cincinnatus*, the Naval Review, November 2008.
11. 'New World, New Britain, New Navy', the Hudson Lecture, by Professor Julian Lindley-French, University of Oxford, 18 November 2010.
12. Speech by the Defence Secretary, Liam Fox, HMS *Collingwood*, 1 December 2010.

What are Navies for?
1. 'Inside The War Cabinet', John Nott, in the Royal United Services Institute Journal, April 2007.
2. 'A Co-Operative Strategy for 21st Century Seapower', US Department of the Navy, October 2007.
3. Statement by International Chamber of Shipping Chairman, Spyros Polemis, 15 February 2011.
4. 'The Navy At A Tipping Point: Maritime Dominance At Stake?', The Center for Naval Analyses, March 2010.
5. *Seapower in the 21st Century*, Professor Geoffrey Till, Frank Cass Publishers, London, 2004.

A Maritime Century?
1. 'The Rise and Fall of Navies', Paul Kennedy, in the New York Times, 5 April 2007.
2. Figures from the British Chamber of Shipping.
3. 'The Future Maritime Operational Concept 2007', Development, Concepts, and Doctrine Centre, MoD, 13 November 2007.
4. Press launch of the IISS Military Balance 2011, 8 March 2011.
5. 'The Geography of Chinese Power', by Robert D Kaplan, in Foreign Affairs, May/June 2010.
6. Jane's Defence Weekly, 4 May 2011.
7. China reveals aircraft carrier plans, Financial Times, 17 December 2010.
8. 'India's Engagement with the African Indian Ocean Rim States', Chatham House paper, April 2008.
9. *The Military Balance 2011*, International Institute for Strategic Studies.
10. Defense News, 28 February 2011.
11. Speech by US Defence Secretary Robert Gates to the US Navy League Air-Sea-Space Exposition, Maryland, 3 May 2010.

New Ship Shapes and Technology Horizons
1. Are Big Warships Doomed? Newsweek special report, 17 May 1982.
2. Quoted in the obituary of Vice Admiral Arthur Cebrowski in the Washington Post, 15 November 2010.
3. 'Design To Fight', Commander Simon Reay Atkinson, The Naval Review, May 2008.

4. US Chief of Naval Operations, Admiral Gary Roughead, at the Brookings Institution, Washington DC, 13 May 2011.
5. Ibid.

The Carrier Question
1. Flight international, 19–25 March 1997.
2. Joint letter by Chief of the Naval Staff and Chief of the Air Staff, 19 January 1998.
3. Naval Staff/Air Staff paper 'Joint Force 2000', Ministry of Defence, 19 January 1998.
4. National Audit Office Major Defence Projects Reports, 2009 and 2010.
5. Letter to The Times, 10 November 2010.
6. 'Navy Ford (CVN78) Class Aircraft Carrier Program: Background and Issues for Congress', Ronald O'Rourke, Congressional Research Service, 13 April 2010.
7. Letter to the Prime Minister, David Cameron, from Admiral Lord West, 12 November 2010.
8. Oral evidence, Chiefs of Staff, House of Commons Defence Select Committee, 11 May 2011.
9. 'Strategic Defence and Security Review', Cm7948, October 2010.
10. Ibid.
11. 'Aircraft carrier costs rise by £1bn', Financial Times, 28 April 2011.
12. 'UK Super Hornets at sea by 2015?' Commodore Steven Jermy, Warships International Fleet Review, December 2010.
13. Oral evidence, op cit.
14. Ibid.
15. 'Long-Range Conventional Strike', Robert P. Haffa and Michael W. Isherwood, Joint Forces Quarterly, 1st quarter 2011.

The Nuclear Equation
1. Report in The Times, 27 November 2007.
2. 'Beyond Artful', RUSI Whitehall Paper, Gavin Ireland, 2007.
3. Ministry of Defence Major Projects Report, National Audit Office, 15 October 2010.
4. Ibid.
5. 'The Right Submarine for Lurking in the Littorals', Milan Vego, US Naval Institute Proceedings, June 2010.
6. 'Defence Industrial Strategy White Paper', Cm 6697, Ministry of Defence, December 2005.
7. 'The Economics of the Defence Review', Keith Hartley, in the Royal United Services Institute Journal, December 2010.
8. Warships International Fleet Review, June 2011.

The Tale of the Type 45
1. *A Century Of Naval Construction*, David K. Brown, Conway Maritime Press, 1983.
2. *Rebuilding the Royal Navy: Warship Design since 1945*, David K. Brown and George Moore, Chatham Publishing, 2003.
3. Ibid.
4. Public Accounts Committee Report, Type 45 Destroyer, 1 June 2009.
5. 'UK Navy Chief Stresses Need for Eight Type 45s', Jane's Defence Weekly, 8 February 2006.
6. Public Accounts Committee, op cit.

Defining a Frigate
1. 'Wasted Warships', Lewis Page, in Prospect, 22 January 2004.
2. Interview in Warships. International Fleet Review, September 2009.
3. Reported on the website navy-matters.beedall.com
4. 'The Politics of the Future Frigate', Julian Lewis MP, in the Royal United Services Institute Defence Systems, February 2009.
5. Speech at a defence industry conference organized by The Spectator magazine, The QE2 Centre, London, 9 November 2010.

The Balance of the Fleet
1. *Strike From The Sea*, Iain Ballantyne, Pen & Sword, 2004.
2. Robert Gates, op cit.
3. Talk at Royal United Services Institute, 12 May 2011.

A British Maritime Case
1. Fox, op cit.
2. ADM205/192, National Archives, Kew.
3. 'Naval Operations Concept 2010', US Department of the Navy.
4. 'Keeping Our Powder Dry?', Malcolm Chalmers, in the Royal United Services Institute Journal, February/March 2011.
5. Interview with the Chief of the Air Staff, Air Chief Marshal Sir Stephen Dalton, The Guardian, 4 April 2011.
6. 'From Protectorates to Partnerships', Jim Thomas, The American Interest magazine, May-June 2011.
7. 'Defence Reform', an independent report, Lord Levene, the UK Stationery Office, June 2011.
8. Royal Navy chief warns on Libya operation, the Financial Times, 13 June 2011.
9. House of Commons Defence Committee, oral evidence, 8 June 2011.

In Line Ahead
1. House of Commons Defence Committee, oral evidence, 11 May 2011.

Bibliography

Ballantyne, Iain, *Strike From The Sea* (Pen & Sword Maritime, Barnsley, 2004).

Brown, D. K., *A Century of Naval Construction* (Conway Maritime Press Ltd, London, 1983).

Brown, D. K. and Moore, George, *Rebuilding the Royal Navy: Warship Design since 1945* (Chatham Publishing, London, 2003).

Cable, James, *Britain's Naval Future* (The MacMillan Press Ltd, London, 1983).

Codner, Michael and Clarke, Michael (eds.), *A Question of Security: The British Defence Review in an Age of Austerity* (I. B. Taurus & Co. Ltd/RUSI, London, 2011).

Grove, Eric and Hore, Peter (eds.), *Dimensions of Sea Power: Strategic Choice in the Modern World* (University of Hull Press, Hull, 1998).

Hill, Rear Admiral J. R., *Maritime Strategy for Medium Powers* (Croom Helm, London, 1986).

Marriott, Leo, *Royal Navy Aircraft Carriers 1945–1990* (Ian Allan Ltd, London, 1985).

Roberts, John, *Safeguarding The Nation: The Story of the Modern Royal Navy* (Seaforth Publishing, Barnsley, 2009).

Till, Geoffrey, *Seapower: A Guide for the Twenty-First Century* (Routledge, Oxford, 2009).

Waters, Conrad (ed.), *World Naval Reviews 2010 and 2011* (Seaforth Publishing, Barnsley, 2009 and 2010).

Index